IF GERMANY ATTACKS

IF GERMANY ATTACKS

The Battle in Depth
in the West

by

CAPTAIN G. C. WYNNE
King's Own Yorkshire Light Infantry (Retired)

The Naval & Military Press Ltd

Published by

The Naval & Military Press Ltd
Unit 5 Riverside, Brambleside
Bellbrook Industrial Estate
Uckfield, East Sussex
TN22 1QQ England

Tel: +44 (0)1825 749494

www.naval-military-press.com
www.nmarchive.com

INTRODUCTION

There is a saying that in a military sense a new war begins where the last one left off; the human imagination is so unreliable that actual experience is needed before changes can be made to an established doctrine. To understand the clash of battle-doctrines which appears to be imminent, unless the political and economic tangle of Europe can be unravelled in the immediate future, it is probably best to examine those of the opposing armies on the Western Front at the end of the last European War of 1914 to 1918. These chapters are an attempt to state them, and to trace their development during that period.

The outstanding feature of those war-years in this respect was the development of the German defensive battle, which produced the battle in depth. The development of the defence in depth is, for that reason, the keynote of these chapters; and, from the autumn of 1915 onwards, it was mainly the work of one master-mind. War between civilized peoples is probably the crudest and most crass of all their occupations, and yet it has a science, and the application of that science to a battlefield ranks high among the arts. But artists in war are rare, and the man who is the chief character of this book appears to be one of the few, if not the only personality worthy of that name who rose to a responsible position in any of the belligerent armies during 1914–18. His achievement is the main interest of this book.

5

It follows that these chapters do not pretend to be a history of the last war, although many of the battles have had to be described in some detail to show the influence which gave direction to the development of the German defence. The formidable array of battle names which are the chapter headings are merely the landmarks selected as a guide along a not too easy trail through a vast jungle of evidence.

The development of the German defence was dependent on the British and French methods of attack. For that reason their several offensives are considered from the German angle of view and any criticisms, such as those of British methods, are intended solely to emphasize their influence, whether by success or failure, on the various stages of the German development; the criticisms are made regardless of any other considerations. For example, the stress laid on the failure of British G.H.Q. to exploit the great weakness of the Wotan and Flandern Positions in 1917 is primarily to indicate a possible further stage in the battle-in-depth if that weakness had been taken into account. From such a standpoint the German experience outlined in these chapters may be regarded not only as an unfinished work but as merely the beginning of a much greater development which is likely to be evolved from that foundation of 1917 if wars are to continue under modern conditions.

The culminating phase of the German defensive battle in 1917, the Flandern Position, has an especial interest for the British army; for the present British defence doctrine is intended to be modelled upon it.

These chapters have appeared in substance in the *Army Quarterly*[1], and, with the kind permission of the Editor,

---

[1] The articles appeared in the *Army Quarterly* as follows: October 1936, 'Battle of Vimy Ridge'; April 1937, 'The Development of the German Defensive Battle and its Influence on British Defence Tactics', Part I; July 1937, Part II of the same title; October 1937, Part III of the same title; January 1938, 'Monchy le Preux and a Com-

they are reprinted here; though the publication last June (1939) by General von Lossberg of an account of his activities has enabled me to give them a more intimate interest.

The principal references for these chapters have been the British, French, and German *Official Histories*; Kronprinz Rupprecht von Bayern, *Mein Kriegstagebuch* (Mittler, Berlin, 1929, 3 vols.); General Fritz von Lossberg, *Meine Tätigkeit im Weltkriege 1914-1918* (Mittler, Berlin, 1939). All other references are mentioned in the text. The photographs are reproduced from the German official monograph, *Flandern 1917* (Stalling, Berlin, 1928). The sketches are only intended as a very rough outline to show the development of the framework of the German defensive battle. My thanks are due to Mr. L. C. Barber for typing a difficult manuscript and making valuable corrections; and also to the staff of the Historical Section for their unfailing assistance.

G.C.W.

Victoria Embankment
London, E.C.4
14th November 1939

mentary'; April 1938, 'The Chain of Command'; July 1938, 'Aubers Ridge'; October 1938, 'Neuve Chapelle'; January 1939, 'The Hindenburg Line'; April 1939, 'The Battle of Arras'; July 1939, 'The Wotan Position'; October 1939, 'The Legacy'.

CONTENTS

9

CONTENTS

MAPS

MAPS

Part I

THE RIGID DEFENCE OF A LINE

Outline of Part I

During August 1914 the French offensive into German territory failed. During September the German effort to win a 'lightning victory' over the French and British armies also failed, and by the end of November the race by both sides to envelope the open northern flank of each along the Channel had ended in a deadlock, and the beginning of position warfare. At that time General Falkenhayn was chief of the German Supreme Command (O.H.L.), and he was faced by the dilemma whether to continue the attempt to smash the British and French armies at once or to transfer all available strength to the Russian Front and neutralize the Russian armies first. Early in January he decided on the latter course, and to hold the Western Front defensively until his eastern plans had been carried out.[1]

This decision entailed the formulation of a doctrine for the defensive battle in position warfare, a situation which had not been taken into account in the pre-war German training manuals. The outline of this new doctrine was given in two memoranda issued by General Falkenhayn to the armies on the Western Front on the 7th and 25th January 1915. They stated that the existing line was to be

[1] References for this Introduction are *German Official History*, vol. VII (Mittler, Berlin, 1931); General Erich von Falkenhayn, *Die Oberste Heeresleitung 1914-16* (Mittler, Berlin, 1920); Kronprinz Rupprecht von Bayern, *Mein Kriegstagebuch* (Mittler, Berlin, 1939).

fortified and organized in such a manner that for a long time, if necessary, it would be capable of resisting attack with a small force against superior numbers. Such an arrangement was necessary to enable the maximum strength to be transferred from the Western to the Russian Front. The construction of a strong foremost line was of the first importance, as it was to be the main line of resistance, to be held at all costs; should any sector of it be captured it was to be at once retaken. Behind it, however, defences were to be built such as could hold up an attack, in the event of the foremost line being overrun, prior to the delivery of the counter-attack by supports. In addition, close behind the foremost trench or breastwork another was to be constructed in which the garrison could shelter in safety during a bombardment of the front line. The memorandum of the 7th January added that as the enemy's artillery would attempt to check the arrival of supports for a counter-attack by a barrage of shells (*Geschoss-schleier*) behind the front defences it would also be necessary to have good and, if possible, covered communication trenches leading from the position of the supports up to the front line. The memorandum of the 25th January went further, and stated that although the foremost line was to be held at all costs, the possibility of a break-through must be taken into account, and that rearward lines out of effective range of the enemy's field batteries must therefore be constructed as an insurance. They were only to be occupied locally opposite the sector broken into; if counter-attacks failed to regain the foremost line, the flanks of this rearward position could be at once joined up with those of the foremost line still in possession. In this manner an attack could at best result only in a bend (*Ausbeulung*) in the line and not in a break-through.

To construct a position of this nature on the entire Western Front was a colossal task, and as no labour had as yet been organized it was left to the front divisions to carry out as time permitted, so that it was not until the autumn that General Falkenhayn's programme was more or less completed. There were also other hindrances. Some of the senior German commanders, including the Crown Prince Rupprecht of Bavaria, who commanded the German Sixth Army opposite the British Expeditionary Force, did not approve the construction of a rearward line of any kind, as they considered that the foremost line would be defended less stubbornly if there was known to be another behind. Experience was to demolish this belief, but it was partly responsible for the absence of a second line at Neuve Chapelle on the 15th March, where the only back defence was a line of machine-gun nests or strong-points each about 1,000 yards apart.

As the front line was to be the main line of resistance 'to be held at all costs', the front divisions concentrated their labour during the first half of 1915 in making that line as strong as possible and in providing shell-proof living accommodation for the garrison. It was not until the 6th May that General Falkenhayn issued instructions ordering that a second or reserve line was to be built 2,000 to 3,000 yards behind the front line on the entire Western Front.

The British and French offensives of 1915 consequently encountered a German defence in progressive stages of construction to meet the demands of General Falkenhayn's programme. The course of the British offensives at Neuve Chapelle in March, at Aubers Ridge and Festubert in May, and at Loos in September are characteristic examples of the practical operation of this method of defence in its various stages.

Chapter I

NEUVE CHAPELLE: 10th–12th March 1915

The intention of German O.H.L.[1] to attempt to force a decision on the Russian Front in the spring of 1915, before making another offensive in the west, resulted in every available man, gun, and shell being transferred to the Russian Front early in 1915. The Western Front was left extremely weakly held, at least in man-power, especially against the sector of the line occupied by the British Expeditionary Force, of whose capacity to deliver an effective offensive General Falkenhayn had a poor opinion. Accordingly, there began a series of offensives by the French and British armies to break through this apparently feeble resistance, and at the same time to relieve the pressure about to be employed against their ally, Russia.

I

The first British offensive was delivered in the Neuve Chapelle area on the 10th March 1915. In this flat, low-lying district the water-level was only a couple of feet below the surface, so that breastworks had to be built up four feet high to supplement the shallow front trench. The village of Neuve Chapelle, a long straggling collection of ruined cottages, lay immediately in front of the main British assault sector. Beyond the village was a thousand

[1] O.H.L. means *Oberste Heeres-Leitung* (Supreme Command) and corresponds to British General Headquarters (G.H.Q.).

19

yards of open grassland, intersected by water-logged ditches lined with occasional pollard willows, which, being still leafless, did not materially affect the field of fire. Then came the Bois du Bièz, a shell-torn wood about a thousand yards long and five hundred yards broad, which was the principle feature of the middle distance. Behind it the ground sloped gently upwards on to the low ridge that took its name from the near-by village of Aubers.

The British First Army, under General Sir Douglas Haig, was to break through in a sector where the German breastwork formed a salient around the village, between Port Arthur and the Moated Grange (see Sketch 1), a frontage of 2,000 yards. For this purpose the First Army massed facing it, and on the immediate flanks, the four divisions of the Indian and IV Corps. A Special Order of the Day issued on the eve of the battle stated that forty-eight British battalions (about 30,000 men) were about to attack three German battalions (about 2,000 men). Further, the Intelligence Section of British G.H.Q. calculated that, allowing for the arrival of the additional German reinforcements from reserve on both flanks, not more than 4,000 additional rifles need be expected within twelve hours, though a further 16,000 might arrive from the Sixth Army reserve near Lille within twenty-four to thirty-six hours. There was little of the fog of war.

If man-power was the only consideration it is small wonder that First Army headquarters regarded success as a foregone conclusion. The front line was a sandbag breastwork, only about five feet thick, through which a direct hit by a shell could smash a hole; and in front of it was a barbed-wire entanglement on a double row of 'knife-rests'. This breastwork and entanglement were to be shelled to pieces by 240 field-guns and thirty-six 4.5-inch howitzers.[1] Then, while sixty-four siege and heavy artillery silenced the comparatively few German batteries, the forty-eight battalions of infantry were, in the words of the First Army

[1] See *British Official History: 1915*, vol. 1, map 3.

instructions, 'to carry the Germans off their legs' and push forward at once across the mile of water-meadows, and then up the slope on to the Aubers Ridge, their objective.

The 8th and Meerut Divisions were to form the centre or spear-head of the battering-ram. After crossing the 80–150 yards of no-man's-land, they were to overrun the front breastwork of the Neuve Chapelle salient held by six German companies (about 900 rifles at most), and then to fan.outwards behind it to right and left. This was to be the signal for the advance of the Lahore and 7th Divisions astride the Estaires–La Bassée and Chapigny–Piétre roads respectively; and the divisions and corps on either flank were to be ready to 'assume a vigorous offensive' in order to achieve a general break-up of the German front.[1]

The actual objective for the infantry was a line Herlies–Illies, six miles distant, on the Aubers Ridge; but so few and scattered were the enemy that, from the angle of view of First Army instructions, there appeared to be no limit to the possible achievements of a battering-ram of forty-eight battalions once loosed behind the German lines. The two Cavalry Corps, almost all the British cavalry available, were to ride through the gap on to the Aubers Ridge, and there make a right wheel behind the German line between Neuve Chapelle and La Bassée; in this manner of a past century they were to clear the southern part of the Ridge of any enemy, while the forty-eight infantry battalions consolidated their position along it.

2

Although the German defence seemed weak at first sight, it was weak only in man-power. By force of its numerical weakness the garrison was distributed deeper

---

[1] The Estaires–La Bassée road is marked immediately south of Port Arthur in Sketch 1 facing the next page.

Chapigny is 800 yards north of Mauquissart, and the dotted line in the sketch shows approximately the line of the Chapigny–Piétre road, which was eventually held as a flanking position by the Germans.

and wider spaced than had ever been customary (see Sketch 1). The front companies holding the breastwork averaged about one man to every three yards; the support companies were 2,000 to 3,000 yards away, to be out of effective range of the mass of the enemy's field batteries; and the reserve companies were in rest billets, 3,000 to 4,000 yards behind again.

In fire-power, however, the defence was strong, and skilfully organized. The backbone of it was the construction early in February, a few weeks before the battle, of a line of concrete machine-gun nests or support points (*Stützpunkte*) about 1,000 yards behind the front breast-work; they were sited about 800 yards apart, so as to cover by fire most of the flat intervening ground. Three of these strong-points were to play an important part in the battle; one in a cottage-garden at the road-junction in Piétre (West), another in a ruined cottage in the Bois du Bièz, a third at the Les Brulots road-junction.[1] These strong-points were normally unoccupied, but in the event of an attack they were to be garrisoned by machine-guns of the support company and to act as centres of resistance (*An-klammerungs-punkte*). Their existence was known to British G.H.Q., but their importance was not sufficiently appreciated.

The general idea of the defence was for the support companies either to reinforce the front line or to block at once the flanks of a break-in, according to circumstances. In the event of a break-in through the breastwork this flank defence was to pivot on any of the machine-gun nests (*Stützpunkte*) conveniently available, and so form a rallying

[1] In the sketch opposite this page the defence construction marked near La Russie, north of the Bois du Bièz, represents an advanced battery (four guns) of field artillery, two guns of which were destroyed during the opening British bombardment. The guns covered the eastern exits from Neuve Chapelle village and the bridges over the Layes brook. The history of the 53rd Regiment which handed over the Neuve Chapelle sector to the 16th Regiment on the 3rd March states (p. 34) that the machine-gun strong-points were completed by the 3rd March.

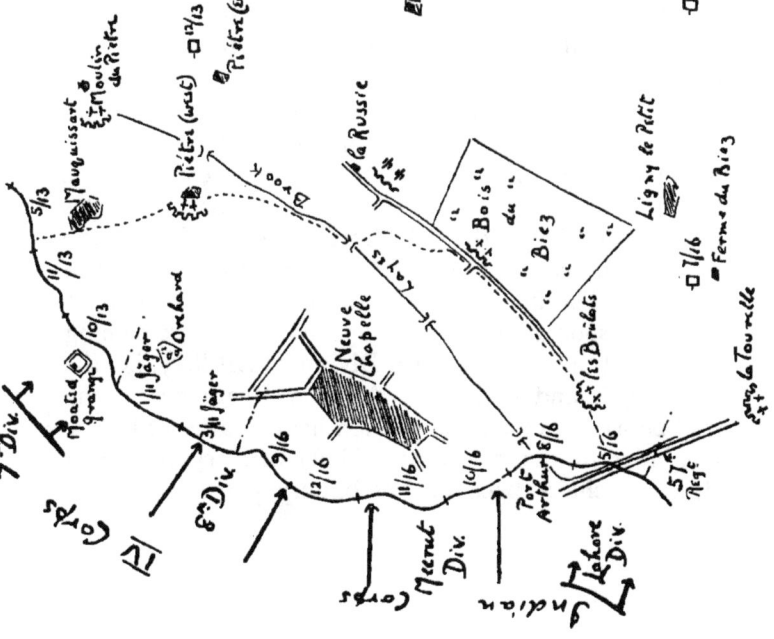

Sketch I.

NEUVE CHAPELLE
10 March 1915

— German front before attack at nightfall
---

0 yards 500 1000

IV Corps

7ᵗʰ Div.

8ᵗʰ Div.

Indian Corps

Meerut Div.

Lahore Div.

Moulin du Pietre
Mauquissart
11/13
10/13
Orchard
Moated Grange
11/14 Jäger
3/14 Jäger
9/16
12/16
11/16
10/16
Neuve Chapelle
Port Arthur
8/16
5/16
57ᵗʰ Regt
gare la Tourelle
Ferme du Biez
les Brulés
Bois du Biez
7/16
Ligny le Petit
La Russie
Pietre (west)
Pietre (east)
5/13
4000 y
Layes

Aubers
Bas Pommereau
Haute Pommereau
3/14 Jäger
4/14 Jäger
Hatbegarbe
6/16
à la Quinque
9/13
7.G.Gr/11 Jäger
Cyclist Coy/11 Jäger
Ligny le Grand
4/16
4/16
1/16
2/16

Corps Reserve
from Fournes (Aubers E et Herlies)
1/13
2/13
3/13
4/13

Herlies

45/ 14ᵗʰ Div Reserve
45/ from Le Marais (3 mls E of Illies)

Illies

line, both to the flanks and rear, for the survivors from the front breastwork. Some of the regimental commanders asked permission at this time to construct a continuous cover-trench (*Deckungsgraben*) to connect the machine-gun nests and make a more definite rallying line, but this request was refused by the Corps commander in accordance with the belief, later found to be a mistaken one, of the Crown Prince Rupprecht, the Sixth Army commander, that the front line would be held less stubbornly if there was known to be another one behind. It was considered that the machine-gun nests could hold a break-in long enough to enable such a rallying line to be formed, and further that the fire-power of such a rallying line would suffice to check the assault until the arrival of the local reserves. These reserves were at once to deliver an immediate counter-attack, before the invaders had had time to consolidate a new line of defence, and, with the help of the support companies from the flanks, recapture the original position. The Germans were confident that the superiority of their infantry in open warfare would enable them to do this; but if not strong enough for the purpose, the Sixth Army reserve from Lille might be expected on the battlefield within twenty-four hours to give further assistance.

The artillery support consisted of six four-gun batteries of the 7th Field Artillery Regiment, of which one was in a forward position hidden near cottages between La Russie and the Bois du Bièz, and the others along a line Bas Pommereau–Ferme du Bièz–Lorgies at the foot of the ridge, at an average range of 2,500 yards from the British front line. The fire of these field batteries could be reinforced as soon as the battle opened by the remaining batteries of the 13th and 14th Divisional Artillery, i.e. the 22nd, 43rd, and 58th Field Artillery Regiments in the neighbouring sectors, and the ten heavy batteries by the remainder of the two heavy (foot) artillery regiments within reach. A back line of battery positions for the artillery was in course of construction on the Aubers Ridge on a general line north and south of La Cliqueterie farm, about 2,500 yards behind the occupied battery positions.[1]

So few aeroplanes were available on either side that they did not affect the course of the battle.

3

The morning of March 10th was damp and misty. The Germans were expecting an offensive. A week earlier, on the 3rd, fifteen Indians had deserted to the 16th Regiment, holding Neuve Chapelle village, and told them that preparations were being made for an offensive 'within a few days' (*in den nächsten Tagen*). Tactically, however, surprise was obtained, as witness the following extract from the history of the German 58th Field Artillery (p. 83). 'On the morning of the 10th the battery commanders were going their usual rounds expecting a day of peaceful routine. The meadows were covered with a shroud of dense white mist. Suddenly a great burst of artillery fire came from the direction of Neuve Chapelle. It was the first real drum-fire (*Trommelfeuer*) yet heard.' To have assembled the British assault divisions unknown to the Germans, who from their observation points on the Aubers Ridge overlooked the entire British position for several miles back, was a notable achievement.

On the stroke of 7 a.m. the bombardment began, accurate and well-planned, except on the left wing. The three thousand shells fired in the next thirty-five minutes broke passages through the wire entanglement and shattered the narrow sandbag breastwork. At 8.5 a.m. eight battalions of the 8th and Meerut Divisions, forming the head of the battering-ram, advanced across no-man's-land as fast as

---

[1] The histories of the German 7th, 22nd, 43rd, 58th Field Artillery Regiments, all published since the *British Official History* was written, make a valuable addition to the history of the battle for any student requiring fuller details.

the mud allowed. The German garrison on the greater part of the assault frontage had been stunned by the sudden intensity of the bombardment, and were unable to man the shattered remnants of the breastwork in time to check the assault. Within twenty minutes a great breach, 1,600 yards wide, had been made in the German line. On both wings, for 200 to 300 yards, the assault had failed for reasons to be mentioned later, but elsewhere the mass of the assaulting battalions were able to press on into the German position. The Corps plan of attack ordered the assault-battalions to halt along a line 200 yards beyond the breastwork, and to wait there for fifteen minutes. The intention was to allow the village to be given a further shelling before the infantry entered it, but on the other hand it took away the whole of the advantage that had been gained by surprise. If the enemy was to be 'carried off his legs', in the words of the First Army instruction, he must be followed close at heel. By this delay, however, time was given for the few Germans who had escaped from the front breastwork to rally near the Bois du Bièz, and time was given for the German support companies to block the flanks of a break-in, and make the necessary defensive arrangements.

The mist was clearing when the centre of the attack, reinforced by two more battalions, pressed on through the village ruins, meeting little opposition. By 9 a.m. British troops were in the open meadows beyond its eastern edge, and had reached an old water-logged trench along which the Corps plan of attack ordered them to wait. From this point the Lahore Division, the right of the Indian Corps, and the 7th Division, the left of the IV Corps, were to join in the battle, and after a further bombardment of the known strong-points at Piétre (West), Bois de Bièz, and Les Brulots, the order for the resumption of the offensive would be given by Corps headquarters.

No enemy could, however, be seen except for a few groups of Germans retiring, many without rifles, and messages to this effect were sent back to brigade headquarters.[1] In the circumstances, the centre battalion commander (2nd Rifle Brigade) asked if the advance should be continued on the heels of the enemy. That request was refused, and from then onwards a paralysis crept over the whole movement.

About this same time (9.30 a.m.) the lines of the left-centre leading battalion (1st Irish Rifles) advancing through the cottage gardens in the road triangle north of the village were suddenly enfiladed by machine-gun fire from their left flank and suffered heavy losses. This opposition came from the two machine-guns in the *Stützpunkt* at Piétre (West), which had taken up position there as a precautionary measure during the bombardment, and which now gave warning of the fate awaiting any further advance towards the Bois du Bièz. But the British battering-ram had already been halted, as much by its own unwieldiness as by German bullets.

It is possible that any further advance would have been checked by fire from two of the strong-points which by then had been occupied, at Piétre (West) and Les Brulots.

But the point is that Sir Douglas Haig's plan of 'carrying the Germans off their legs' could only be accomplished by giving full powers to subordinate leaders on the spot as to whether to stop or to go on, whereas the Corps plan ordered the successive stages of the battle beforehand regardless of anything the enemy might do, a system more suited to attacks with very limited objectives.

4

For about 300 yards on both flanks the assault, as al-

---

[1] The diary of the German advanced battery at La Russie says that its guns did not fire at first, as they were not sure whether the troops coming out of the village, about 1,000 yards away, were friend or foe. They seemed to be wearing German helmets and were waving white flags, and it was not till the smoke of the bombardment had cleared away that the situation was appreciated and the battery opened fire.

ready mentioned, had failed. On the extreme left the bombardment had been inaccurate; neither the breastwork nor the garrison had been seriously affected, and two German machine guns (11th Jäger Battalion) in the front breastwork had sufficed to annihilate almost to a man, as if mown by a scythe, the three leading lines of the 1st Middlesex and 2nd Scottish Rifles; further attempts to advance continued to be checked by machine-gun and rifle fire from this sector of breastwork. On the extreme right a mistake in direction had led to confusion about Port Arthur, and here also no progress had been made. The Corps plan had therefore failed, and under the existing chain system of command that plan, once set in motion, was, like an Aldershot Tattoo, most difficult to alter. The Corps had become a great battle-unit in which battalion commanders had little more responsibility in the scheme of things than non-commissioned officers. Such an organization, rigid under the Corps commander, might work smoothly so long as no opposition was met, but if anything went amiss the situation had to be reported back through battalion, brigade, and divisional to Corps headquarters. The Corps commander in some room five miles or more from the battle had to make a decision on the flimsiest and often false information, and the necessary orders had then to travel back along the same chain, be considered and written out in greater detail at each stage, till finally they reached the front-line companies, who had to carry them out. This most cumbersome system of transmission took some hours under battle conditions, and meanwhile, from soon after 9 a.m. onwards, the leading battalions of the battering-ram had to wait until the flanks could get forward according to plan, and so caused a great block in the battalions moving up in rear.

The brigade commanders facing the uncaptured sectors of breastwork on the flanks each sent forward another battalion into the great breach, with orders to attack outwards and roll up the offending garrison. In addition to

28

these two, a third battalion was ordered forward by the commander of the 8th Division with orders to close the gap of 500 yards he saw must exist between the left of the leading battalions beyond the village and the right of the battalions checked in no-man's-land. It was an unneccessary order, for a single machine gun could have effectively covered this gap of flat open ground against any attempt by the few enemy present to enter it in broad daylight. Neither of these three battalions achieved its purpose and they soon became hopelessly enmeshed in the crowd.

At about 10 a.m., with these three battalions squeezing forward into the breach, there were eleven battalions, roughly nine thousand men, in that narrow space between Neuve Chapelle village and the original British breastwork. They lay, sat, or stood uselessly in the mud, packed like salmon in the bridge-pool at Galway, waiting patiently to go forward. The strength of the battering-ram at this moment was limited to the fire-power of its leading companies, and the remainder of the forty-eight battalions had no offensive value until they could fan out behind the German position, if such an operation was at any time possible. Had it not been for the fact of surprise, and that many of the German batteries had therefore only a small store of ammunition ready for immediate use, the casualties from shell-fire must have been considerably heavier.[1]

At 11.30 a.m., after another heavy shelling, the offending garrison of the northern sector of breastwork, one officer and sixty-three men of the 11th Jäger Battalion, came out from it and, walking across the dead, estimated at about 1,000, lying literally in rows, whom they had slain that morning, surrendered.[2] The IV Corps commander, on hearing of this, ordered a strip of orchard close behind, believed to contain a German strong-point, to be

[1] See *Das Infanterie Regiment 13* p. 77.
[2] German references are: Groos, *Das Infanterie Regiment 13* (Berlin 1927); Balderstein, *Das Infanterie Regiment 16* (Berlin 1927); Otto, *Kriegstagebuch des Jaegerbataillons 11* (Schmalkalden, 1931), and histories of the 7th, 22nd, 43rd, and 58th Field Artillery Regiments.

captured before the general advance of his corps was resumed. There happened to be no strong-point nor any Germans there, and it was occupied almost at once, but this information did not reach the Corps commander at Lestrem till an hour after the event. In fact, it was not till 2 p.m. that he, five miles from the battlefield, was able to obtain some clear outline of the situation and considered his tangled column sufficiently reorganized to justify the resumption of the general advance and fan-out towards the Aubers Ridge. Owing to this waste of time in the transmission of information and orders, the 7th Division, on the left, had been kept inactive.

Meanwhile the sector of German breastwork holding up the right of the battering-ram had been delayed in rather similar manner, and the Indian Corps commander told the IV Corps commander that his troops would not be ready by 2 p.m. The movement was therefore postponed, as it was considered that 'the advance of the two corps to be effective should be simultaneous'.

It is not surprising that Sir Douglas Haig, at Merville, eight miles away, was by now getting impatient. At 2.45 p.m. he telephoned to the IV Corps commander, who said he was waiting for the Indian Corps, but by that time the Indian Corps commander realized that the situation was not so unfavourable as he had imagined. It was thereupon agreed, at 2.50 p.m., that the two corps should continue the advance at 3.30 p.m., and orders were issued accordingly. Seven hours had thus elapsed since their leading battalions had forced the great breach, killed or taken prisoner almost the entire German front-line garrison, and looked ahead confidently towards the Aubers Ridge, that Promised Land to be reached by a mile walk with only a few scattered German companies to oppose them.

The Corps commanders, it will be noticed, only allowed forty minutes for their orders for this attack to reach the front battalions, but nearly three hours elapsed between the writing of them and the time when the companies in the front line received them and could start to carry them out. It was between 5.30 and 6 p.m., and nearly dark, when the advance began, and by that time the new German line of defence was, as British G.H.Q. Intelligence had forecast, more strongly held, in rifle and machine-gun power per yard, than had been the front breastwork in the morning. In addition there was no surprise and no adequate artillery preparation: the new German line had not yet been definitely located. The gathering strength of the opposition had been known to the front battalion commanders all the afternoon: at every move their companies had been swept by machine-gun and rifle fire, with heavy losses. But so little were the facts of the situation appreciated at First Army headquarters that Sir Douglas Haig ordered forward a cavalry division, at 4 p.m., to be ready behind the attack to ride through on to the Aubers Ridge. The attack failed, and that ride of the cavalry was of the stuff of dreams.

4

Cross now to the German side of the battlefield. Four of the German companies (three of the 16th Regiment and one of the 11th Jäger Battalion) had been overrun in the first rush, and only a few escaped back.

Meanwhile, before the bombardment had been completed, the support company (12th) of the 13th Regiment at Piétre (East) had occupied with two machine guns the strong-point at Piétre (West), and at the same time, on the southern flank, a support company (7th) of the 16th Regiment from the Ferme du Bièz garrisoned the strong-point at Les Brulots. If the British assaulting battalions had pressed on at once through Neuve Chapelle a gap of over 2,000 yards lay open in front of them, between the strong-points at Piétre (West) and Les Brulots, with only two guns of an advanced field battery (1st of the 7th F.A. Regiment) at La Russie, and a few stragglers from the front breastwork to defend it.[1] The intervening ground was, however, to a great extent covered by those two strong-points, which could have made very costly to the dense British attack-formations an advance on the Bois du Bièz.

By 9 a.m., when the British assault-battalions were emerging from the ruins of Neuve Chapelle village, the support company (12/13) at Piétre (West) had also occupied for defence a disused trench that lay between the strong-point and the front breastwork on the Piétre–Chapigny road. From this it would be able to enfilade and block effectively any further British advance eastwards or northwards from Neuve Chapelle. So, too, on the southern flank another support company (6th) of the 16th Regiment had been sent forward from Halpegarbe to La Tourelle, where it, together with the 7th Company at Ferme du Bièz and Les Brulots, could block by fire any further British advance eastwards or southwards. Already a bottle-neck had been formed into which any further British progress could be confined, with a gap still open at its eastern end. The history of the 11th Jäger Battalion tells how this gap was gradually filled.

From messages received by runners (all telephone cables had been broken) within half an hour of the end of the bombardment, the Jäger Battalion commander at Halpegarbe gathered that the British assault had broken through the front of his two Jäger companies and of the 16th Regiment south of them, but that the left of the 13th Regiment held firm at the Moated Grange, though the extent of the break-through to the south, in the 16th

---

[1] Two of the four guns of this advanced battery, in position between La Russie and the Bois du Bièz, were knocked out during the opening bombardment. The diary of this battery describes how 'soon after 8 a.m. men of the 11th Jäger Battalion began to fall back, first singly, then in groups from Neuve Chapelle village. The battery officers stopped many of them and assembled them along the Bois du Bièz track, behind cottage ruins, hedges and tree-stumps, and between the gun positions, to form a firing line. The two remaining guns fired direct with shrapnel bursting at 1,000 yards on the British advance.'

Regiment sector, was not known. His first intention, on this information, shows his appreciation of the value of fire-power. The cyclist company and the remainder of his machine-gun company, that is, about a hundred riflemen and four machine-guns, were to advance to the Bois du Bièz; and there this most insultingly small force was to hold the British offensive in front, while his two remaining Jäger companies were to move round to Piétre (West) to assist in blocking the northern flank of the break-in and take in enfilade any further advance. Here again, the first care of a German commander was to block the flanks and only to fill up the centre as reinforcements became available. The brigade commander,[1] however, feared that the break-through might have extended to south of the Bois du Bièz, and he therefore ordered the whole Jäger detachment to meet the attack frontally.

Accordingly, the cyclist company and two machine guns were ordered to the south-eastern corner of the Bois du Bièz, from where they were to command the roads leading back from the front of the 16th Regiment. The two Jäger companies and the other two machine guns were to meet the attack at the northern end of the Bois du Bièz, protect the advanced field battery there at all costs, and work forward if possible to the road triangle north of Neuve Chapelle village. These two companies advanced widely extended, under heavy shell fire, down the slope of the Aubers Ridge to challenge Britain's battering-ram of forty-eight battalions; but, in fact, they had no idea that such a mighty British phalanx lay waiting below. The two

---

[1] The German Order of Battle is different from the British. Taking this case as an example, the division concerned was the 14th, which included infantry, artillery, engineers, and divisional troops. The three infantry regiments of the division (the 16th, 56th, and 57th with the 11th Jäger Battalion attached) were brigaded as the 76th Brigade under a separate brigade commander. A German infantry regiment had three battalions each of four companies, numbered from 1 to 12 in the regiment. The Jäger (light infantry) were organized in separate battalions and not in regiments.

companies passed through the northern end of the Bois du Bièz and reached the road that borders its western edge. There they halted in full view of the leading British battalions 700 yards ahead across the flat water-meadows, the two machine guns taking up position in the strong-point in the Bois du Bièz, covering the bridge over the Layes brook.

From 9.30 a.m. onwards this small force, with the few stragglers from the morning attack, was the only opposition on a frontage of 2,000 yards which faced and awaited the British onslaught; but the flanks of the offensive were blocked, and the strong-points at Piétre (West) and Les Brulots covered the front. The morning hours passed and the British assault remained stationary in front of Neuve Chapelle village, but about midday further German reinforcements began to arrive. On the northern flank another support company (9th) of the 13th Regiment from L'Aventure strengthened the line of the 12th Company at Piétre (West), while, of the two reserve companies at Herlies, the 3rd still further strengthened this flank at Mauquissart and the 6th moved to the wood near Haut Pommereau in close support, behind the right centre. On the southern flank two of the reserve companies (1st and 2nd) of the 16th Regiment marched up from Illies by way of Halpegarbe–Ferme du Bièz–Les Brulots and reinforced the 10th Company in the front line facing Port Arthur, while the other two reserve companies moved to Halpegarbe. At about midday these two companies were ordered to reinforce the two Jäger companies and, at 2 p.m., came up on their right at the northern end of the Bois du Bièz. Encouraged by this support all four companies advanced about 200 yards across the open to the line of the Layes brook. And still the British remained along the line they had reached in the morning.

Later in the afternoon the German companies in Corps and Divisional reserve, began to arrive on the battlefield. By 4 p.m. the 4th and 7th Companies of the 15th Regiment in Corps reserve at Fournes had reinforced the right and right centre, between La Russie and Mauquissart, and half an hour later two companies (3rd of the 56th and 4th of the 57th Regiments) with three machine guns from Divisional reserve at Le Marais advanced through the southern part of the Bois du Bièz and filled the gap between the left of the two Jäger companies and Les Brulots. When the British attack was resumed between 5.30 p.m. and 6 p.m. it was therefore faced by exactly double the strength it had to contend with in the morning assault.

During the evening the German line was further reinforced along the Layes brook in the Bois du Bièz–Les Brulots sector by four companies from neighbouring regiments farther south, one each from the 56th, 57th, 104th, and 133rd Regiments. The Crown Prince Rupprecht of Bavaria, commanding the Sixth Army, in his diary entry on the following day writes that it was a mistake to continue to reinforce a line which actually lay in front of the line of the strong-points. He would have preferred a weakly held front line based on the strong points, with the local reserves kept back under cover till an adequate force for the counter-attack had been assembled; even, he adds, if the British had broken through this line they would only have offered more favourable conditions for the counter-attack. In these words the Crown Prince Rupprecht unwittingly predicted, or had a glimpse of, what was to be a main feature of the mobile defence-in-depth of 1917.

But be that as it may, the defence had so far worked according to General Falkenhayn's plan; the rallying line pivoted on the strong-points (*Stützpunkte*) was now in a position to block any further advance either to front or flanks. For the Germans the crisis was past; the problem now was to recapture the front breastwork.

5

The 11th was misty all day and the British artillery was unable to range upon, and the infantry accurately to locate, the new German line of defence and its pivotal strong-points. Misty or not, this same situation was to recur again and again throughout the war; the difficulty of attacking a second position after the first assault had been held up. On the previous evening First Army headquarters had ordered the continuation of the attack the following morning on the lines of the original plan, that is, the fan outwards and advance on to the Aubers Ridge. This order meant an assault on an unlocated position held more strongly than had been the original front breastwork for which days of preparation had been given, and the account of the fruitless efforts to comply with this order may be read in the British official narrative.

Owing to the cutting by German artillery fire of all communications back from the front battalions, messages had to be sent by runners taking two to three hours, so that the direction of the battle by Corps commanders ceased to function throughout the morning. When, about midday, hearing that the morning attack had been checked, they decided to continue the frontal attack by both corps at 2.15 p.m., their orders to that effect did not reach the various brigade headquarters till a few minutes before the hour of assault, and battalions and companies not till an hour or more later. The afternoon attack therefore ended in a disjointed affair without result, except further losses. The fact that at best the advance could only penetrate still farther into the fatal bottle-neck was apparently not appreciated. Despite these failures on the 11th, and reports from the front line commanders that without effective artillery preparation the prospects of an infantry assault were negligible, Sir Douglas Haig, the First Army commander, ordered the offensive to be resumed at 10 a.m. the following morning (12th). Before that hour, however, the Germans delivered their counter-attack.

6

The German VII Corps commander (General von Claer) when, at 10 a.m. on the 10th, he heard of the loss of Neuve Chapelle, ordered its recapture to be undertaken as soon as the allotted corps and divisional reserves arrived on the battlefield. The village had no tactical value, but this order was in accordance with the underlying principle of rigid defence that no foot of ground was to be lost, and if lost was to be at once recaptured. At the same time he asked Sixth Army Headquarters for assistance and the 6th Bavarian Reserve Division, in Sixth Army reserve near Lille, was thereupon ordered to move forward to the Aubers Ridge. The leading brigade[1] (14th) left its billets in Tourcoing at 3 p.m. and was railed to Don, four miles east of Herlies, which it reached that same evening, and there rested.

At 9 p.m., when General von Claer realized that the troops in the battle-line were insufficient both to hold the line and make the counter-attack, he placed the leading Bavarian brigade at the disposal of 14th Divisional commander to be in position in the Bois du Bièz by 6 a.m. to participate in the counter-attack. The instruction was to assault the new British line with the bayonet at dawn without artillery preparation, in the belief that the British battalions would not have had time to consolidate the new

---

[1] At this period the normal division had two brigades each of two or three regiments (each of three battalions). Already, however, many divisions, such as the 14th mentioned in a previous footnote, were being organized into one infantry brigade of three regiments, the brigade commander commanding the infantry of the divisions.

line for defence. This belief was never put to the test, for although the two Bavarian regiments marched out of Don at 1 a.m., there were unexpected delays in an intensely dark night, and the new day was already beginning to dawn when they reached Halpegarbe, a march of six miles, and it was considered too light to advance down the forward slope of the ridge to the Bois du Bièz, their assembly position. The assault was therefore postponed, the Bavarians being withdrawn to Herlies and Illies.

The first of the long succession of counter-attack divisions which were to be sent against the British in the three following years had therefore arrived too late, as did so many of its successors, for the immediate counter-attack (*Gegenstoss*). The British would now have time to consolidate the new line in daylight, and only a deliberate and methodically prepared counter-attack (*Gegenangriff*) could hope to dislodge them and recapture the village.

Crown Prince Rupprecht of Bavaria, the Sixth Army commander, in his diary entries for the 11th and 12th March 1915, tells of the divided opinions as to how best this should be carried out. At first he himself had thought General von Claer's demand, on the 10th, for a whole division as reinforcement, overestimated the British strength, but he changed this opinion when, at 2 p.m. on the 11th, he was shown a captured copy of Sir Douglas Haig's Special Order of the Day (see above), to the effect that forty-eight British battalions were engaged. In addition to the 6th Bavarian Reserve Division sent up overnight from Lille to the Aubers Ridge he thereupon ordered the 86th Brigade (seven battalions) to be sent forward from Roulers to Don that same night, and also all available (twenty) howitzer batteries to be lent immediately to General von Claer by neighbouring divisions. After giving these instructions he went to General von Claer's headquarters at Marquillies. He arrived just after the Corps order for the counter-attack had been issued, according to which the attack was to be delivered at dawn in a manner similar to the previously prepared *Gegenstoss*, except that it was to be preceded by a half-hour bombardment of the British front line, in addition to a heavy shelling throughout the night on the British position, on Neuve Chapelle village, and the approach roads. To the Crown Prince Rupprecht, it seemed that such a task, added to counter-battery work, was beyond the power of the few field and heavy batteries of the 13th and 14th Divisional artillery to fulfil effectively. He pointed out the risk of making such an attack against a prepared position with so scanty artillery preparation, and suggested postponing the attack a further twenty-four hours, till dawn on the 13th, until the artillery reinforcement now arriving could take effect. To this General von Claer replied that the British, with another twenty-four hours at their disposal, would be able to make their new line so strong that an attack taking a week or more to prepare would be necessary to recapture the village and the original position. Moreover, he doubted if the present line could be held for that additional twenty-four hours, as the British were still attacking, and to confirm that statement he telephoned, there and then, to the 14th Divisional headquarters at Illies, who replied in agreement. On hearing this, the Crown Prince Rupprecht gave his consent to von Claer's plan, although others present, according to General von Krafft, his chief of staff, thought that the 14th Divisional commander if, instead of being asked for his opinion, he had been simply ordered to hold on another twenty-four hours to allow for an effective artillery preparation, could and would have done so. General von Krafft adds that the general impression was that the attack was being made with undue haste and that its prospects were very doubtful.

7

On the British side it was fortunate that while the Corps commanders were trying to give expression to Sir Douglas

Haig's urge to continue the advance, the front battalion commanders had taken the more practical step of organizing the defence of the ground gained. Daybreak on the 12th found them ready, and the half-hour German bombardment that preceded the counter-attack at 5 a.m. fell wide and behind, leaving the front line practically undamaged. A mist covered the German approach till within about sixty yards, but the full fire-power of the British defence then swept it, and against it the German advance could make no headway. Opposite the Bois du Bièz, from where the Bavarians attacked, listening-posts gave the warning, and in this sector southwards to the La Bassée highway twenty carefully sited machine guns gave evidence of their quick and devastating stopping-power in the defence. The counter-attack failed on the entire front, and whereas on the 10th the German casualties had been about one-fifth of those of the British, the proportion on this day was reversed.[1]

The British defence against this counter-attack was the real victory of Neuve Chapelle, and it was essentially a battle won by the efforts and common sense of subordinate commanders on the spot. Corps headquarters knew little about it until some hours later. It was not until 3 p.m., ten hours afterwards, that the First Army commander began to realize the extent of the victory and gave orders to exploit it by means of another general attack, sending forward the 2nd Cavalry Division to co-operate. But the moment for exploitation was long past, and the attack only led to further British losses and nothing gained. It was, however, the final effort. The First Army commander appreciated that further efforts to break through in the Neuve Chapelle sector could be of no avail and decided to establish the position as a new defensive line, ordering it to be wired and secured against attack.

[1] The total British losses during the battle are given as 11,652 and the German total as 8,600 (of which about 1,700 were missing and prisoners, mostly captured in the opening assault).

That order, issued at 10.40 p.m., ended the battle. The Germans decided to cut their loss and accept a local defeat.

I have described this action in some detail as it provides a comprehensive base from which to start.

Chapter II

AUBERS RIDGE: 9th May 1915

The battle of Neuve Chapelle had only been an added proof that until some method of overcoming the German machine-gun nest could be evolved, there would be small hope of advancing to any great depth into the German position, or of 'fanning-out' behind the German front line. As a result of that battle, however, British G.H.Q. made only one constructive effort, which was to provide 'infantry artillery', consisting of batteries of trench mortars and mountain guns carried on armoured cars, to be attached to infantry brigades; they were to support the assault closely and assist in destroying any machine-gun nests and strong points. It was a beginning, but it was not enough. There was no attempt at a change of infantry tactics, no effort to limit that solid target of frail human bodies offered by successive lines of men, all walking across no-man's-land simultaneously and unprotected, and which offered such a quick harvest to a few machine-guns. Nevertheless British G.H.Q. was sufficiently optimistic to write on the 4th April, three weeks after the battle, that 'the outstanding lesson of Neuve Chapelle is that by careful preparation in details and a thorough registration by artillery, it appears that a section of the enemy's front line can be captured with little loss'.

On this confident assumption the plan for the next offensive on the 9th May against the Aubers Ridge was based. Once again massed man-power was to attempt to force a

42

way through a position defended by skilfully placed fire-power. Two sectors of the German breastwork on either side of the old Neuve Chapelle battlefield were to be assaulted, a front of 2,400 yards by the I and Indian Corps from the Rue du Bois and a front of 1,500 yards opposite Fromelles by the IV Corps. After forcing two breaches in the German breastwork at those places, 6,000 yards apart, the two columns were to spread out and advance concentrically, joining up on the Aubers Ridge about 3,000 yards distant.

I

Experience at Neuve Chapelle had taught the Germans that a single narrow breastwork was inadequate to hold back the 'amateur army of tennis-players', and they had set to work like beavers to strengthen the barrier on the whole British front.[1] The breadth of the barbed-wire entanglement was doubled or trebled, and the five-foot broad breastwork was built out to fifteen or twenty feet across, with frequent traverses and a parados; and the two machine guns in a battalion sector were sited in V-shaped box-emplacements at ground level under it. The history of the 57th Regiment mentions with what care the regimental commander had himself selected these machine-gun sites so as to sweep no-man's-land from flanking positions.[2]

By degrees, too, General Falkenhayn's programme of construction was being carried out, and the building of a

[1] References for the German defence are: *Das Infanterie Regiment 55*, Schulz (1928); *Das Infanterie Regiment 57*, Castendyk (1936). Both have been published since the British official account (1915, vol. II) was written.
[2] The statement that a battalion sector had two machine guns needs explanation. A German regiment of three battalions had normally three machine-gun sections, each of two guns. They were either kept together as a machine-gun company or allotted by sections to battalions. In the case in point, the 3rd Battalion of the 57th Regiment, for example, had two companies in the front line, one in support at Rue du Marais, and one in reserve at La Bassée, but the machine-gun section (two guns) allotted to it was with the two front companies.

second breastwork was nearing completion. This second breastwork had at its base a number of dug-outs, each for twenty to thirty men, which were the living-rooms (*Wohngraben*) for the front garrison. It was about 200 yards behind the front breastwork, close enough to man it by way of communication trenches in time to meet an assault, and yet sufficiently far from it to prevent the burst of a shell on one affecting the other. The front breastwork, or trench, became in fact a line of sentry-posts and the second was for the piquets; but it was still the first which had to be garrisoned on alarm and held at all costs. So began the double front trench system which now became orthodox throughout the German defences on the Western Front.

Behind again, and 700 to 1,000 yards distant from the front breastwork, was the line of concrete machine-gun nests (*Stützpunkte*) about 1,000 yards apart, as at Neuve Chapelle, and they were to act as the rallying centres if the front were broken through; for example, facing the Rue du Bois assault frontage were machine-gun emplacements at La Tourelle, at the Ferme du Bois (*Apfelhof*) and at the Ferme Cour d'Avoué (*Wasserburg*) (see Sketch 2).

Another feature of the Falkenhayn programme which was nearly completed was the construction of communication trenches to connect the front breastwork with the living-in trenches (*Wohngraben*), and thence leading back to the support companies. Near the front these communication trenches were soundly built, easily convertible into a flanking fire trench, and with occasional concrete shelters, but farther back they consisted only of a double row of wattle-hurdles to give cover from view.

The disposition of the German garrison was similar to that at Neuve Chapelle.[1] So also was the scheme for defence, except that the new communication trenches were

---

[1] Each front battalion normally had two companies (about 280 rifles) to garrison its front breastwork on a frontage of 800 to 1,000 yards, one company in support about 2,000 yards back, and its fourth in reserve 2,000 to 4,000 yards behind again.

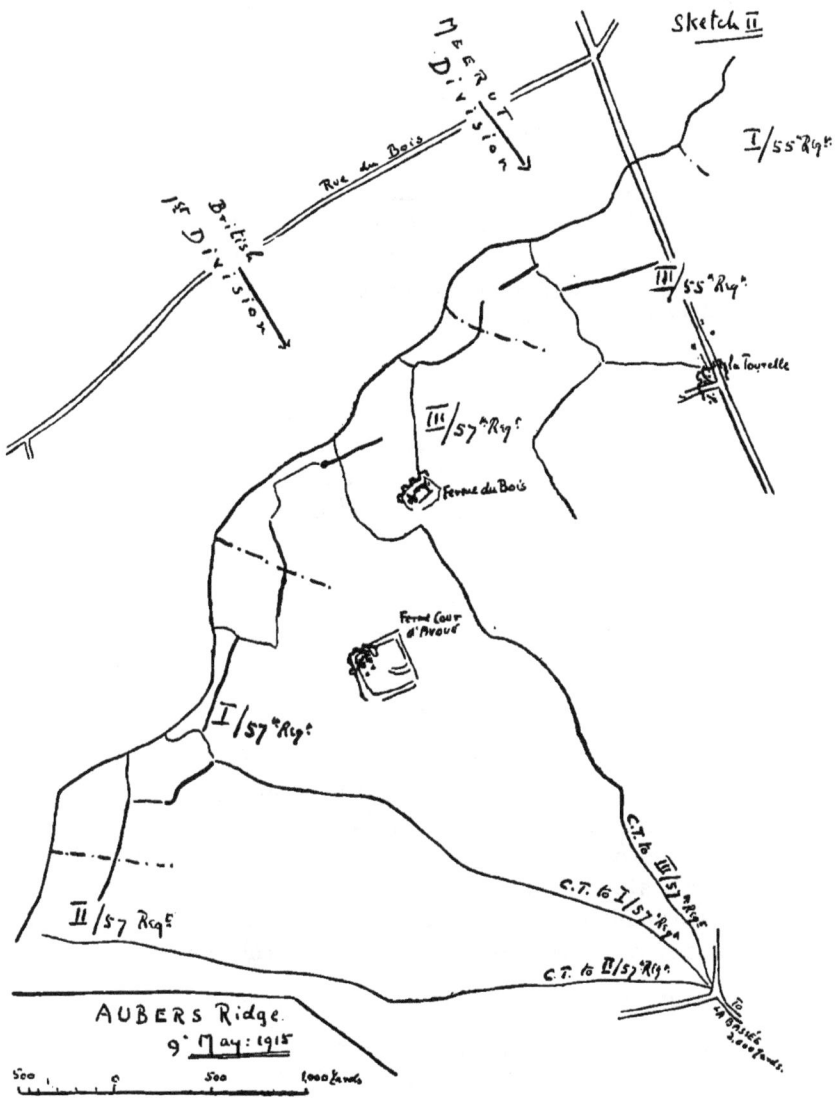

Sketch II

I/55ᵗʰ Rgt.

III/55ᵗʰ Rgt.

la Tourelle

MEERUT Division

Rue du Bois

British 1ˢᵗ Division

III/57ᵗʰ Rgt.

Ferme du Bois

Ferme Cour d'Avoué

I/57ᵗʰ Rgt.

II/57ᵗʰ Rgt.

C.T. to III/57ᵗʰ Rgt.

C.T. to I/57ᵗʰ Rgt.

C.T. to II/57ᵗʰ Rgt.

AUBERS Ridge.
9ᵗʰ May: 1915

500   0   500   1000 Yards

designed so that the support companies might occupy any convenient one in the event of an assault breaking-in, and thereby make it easier to block the flanks. The majority of the supporting artillery, six to twelve four-gun field batteries and a proportion of heavy (foot) artillery batteries, behind each division were on the Aubers Ridge about Lorgies and Gravelin, 2,500 to 4,000 yards behind the front line.[1]

All this work on the German defences had not passed unnoticed by the British front garrison who had watched and listened to its progress by day and by night, but British G.H.Q. kept to its belief, announced after the Battle of Neuve Chapelle, that 'with careful preparation a sector of the enemy's front line can be captured with little loss'. The British official account says that some of the regimental officers expected a much greater success than Neuve Chapelle 'because we have learnt its lessons and shall know what to avoid this time'. But whatever lessons may have been learnt, they had not been applied and, tactically, the battle was to be fought on similar lines. The major difficulties, which Neuve Chapelle had shown might be expected when massed man-power enters a position defended by intelligently applied fire-power, had not yet been faced.

2

No cloud shaded the dawn of Sunday the 9th May 1915 on Aubers Ridge. Skylarks circled to greet the rising sun and peace reigned supreme while the German sentries drank morning coffee after their night's watch. Shortly before 4 a.m. a squadron of British aeroplanes flew over the German position. Twenty minutes later four shells from a British heavy battery screamed overhead and burst

---

[1] The Rue du Bois attack described in this chapter was within range of approximately the same German artillery as took part in the Neuve Chapelle battle, that is, the 7th, 22nd, 43rd and 58th Field Artillery Regiments and the 7th Foot (Heavy) Artillery Regiment.

far behind. That interlude was followed by half an hour of quiet when suddenly, at about 5 a.m., the British bombardment opened with a mighty crash. A hundred years ago Schopenhauer wrote that the crack of a waggoner's whip was the most accursed noise he knew to 'paralyse the brain, cut the thread of reflection and murder thought'. Since then mankind has progressed rapidly. This sudden burst of fire from 600 British guns blasted all thought away. It sent up fountains of earth high into the air, and a few direct hits tore great holes in the German breastwork. The shells burst almost without cessation making a continuous rhythm of paralysing noise. Soon, above and along the German front line, lay a high cloud of smoke, dust and splinters so thick that sight could not penetrate it. Except for a few sentries the garrison ran back, though not before losing many of their number, along the communication trenches, and took refuge in the concrete shelters there. But before the forty-minute bombardment had finished they noticed that its bark was worse than its bite, and began to return to their posts in the front line.

Many British officers and men foresaw trouble when occasionally during the bombardment a light breeze dispersed the cloud of smoke covering the German front line and they saw the Germans looking over the battered breastwork with rifles ready and bayonets fixed. There was no question of surprise this time. Numbers of shells were seen to be falling short and great stretches of the breastwork and wire entanglement were intact.[1] The bombardment had been no more intense on each yard of this much stronger position than at Neuve Chapelle, and it was clearly far more inaccurate owing to worn-out guns and bad ranging. But no cancellation order for the attack was received.

When, at 5.30 a.m., the bombardment began its final

---

[1] The British official account states that 'despite the doubled or trebled strength of the German defences the weight of metal per yard of front used was no greater than at Neuve Chapelle'.

intense phase of ten minutes, the leading companies clambered out into the open of no-man's-land to take up a forward line prior to the assault. At 5.40 a.m. the assaulting lines, about fifty yards apart, began to cross the 200 yards of flat open ground between the opposing breastworks; and although the men of each line were extended to the usual three paces interval the succession of lines offered a dense target.

3

The conditions for both the attacks, from the Rue du Bois, south of Neuve Chapelle, and from Fromelles, north of it, were very similar, and it will be sufficient to describe that from the Rue du Bois as example.

The first assault was to be carried out by two divisions, one each of the 1st and Indian Corps. The 1st Division had its 2nd and 3rd Brigades each on a frontage of 800 yards and each with two battalions in front (1st Northamptonshire, 2nd Royal Sussex, 2nd Royal Munster Fusiliers, and 2nd Welch). The Meerut Division assaulted with its Dehra Dun Brigade, with three battalions leading (1st and 1st–4th Seaforth Highlanders and 2nd–2nd Gurkhas), also on a frontage of 800 yards. The right of the assault (1st Division) was to pass through the Ferme Cour l'Avoué, and the left (Meerut Division) was to be astride the Estaires–La Bassée highway past La Tourelle (see Sketch 2).

According to the accounts given in the histories of the German 55th and 57th Regiments, which faced the attack by the 1st and Meerut Divisions from the Rue du Bois, they saw, when the bombardment had lifted to the back area and the smoke had cleared, three lines of British and Indian troops already in no-man's-land, with a fourth clambering over the British breastwork and two more in rear. The sun had risen; it was behind the Germans and shone in the faces of the attack, so that 'there could never before in war have been a more perfect target in more ideal conditions of light than this solid wall of khaki men, line behind line. There was only one possible order to give, "Fire till the barrels burst." ' Facing the German 57th Regiment, the first line was already only fifty yards from the German breastwork when it was mown down by bullets; a few British reached the wire entanglement, where they were shot and remained hanging on it. The second line was enfiladed by the flanking fire of a machine gun on the left flank and was shot to pieces. The third line, advancing in small groups, came under the combined fire-power of the machine guns and rifles of the front battalion, as well as being enfiladed by a machine gun on the right flank, and was practically annihilated. The fourth wave, clambering over the breastwork, was effectively dealt with by the German supporting field artillery batteries.

The attack was repulsed by the German front companies unaided, and it was already beaten when the support companies, moving across country in loose formation, reached the second breastwork (*Wohngraben*) in readiness. Only at a few gaps in the front breastwork had the attackers succeeded in entering the position, and these were quickly dealt with in close fighting. For example, on the right, at the point of junction of the 55th and 57th Regiments, about fifty men broke in of whom eight were taken prisoners and the remainder killed.[1] Some of the Indians also broke through in places and rushed at the German garrison flourishing knives, but they too were killed with the bayonet or taken prisoners.

4

Within ten minutes the attack was over, but at 6.5 a.m., hearing of the failure, the commanders of the 1st and Meerut Divisions ordered another attack after a further forty-five minutes' artillery preparation. The Germans,

[1] This probably refers to parties of the 1st Northamptonshire and 2nd R. Munster Fusiliers.

seeing renewed preparations behind the British breast-work, gave a sign, by propping up a large red board, to their artillery and supporting infantry that another attack was imminent. Broken machine guns were replaced and reinforcements were sent up; for example, the 3rd Battalion of the 57th, which had most suffered in the regiment's sector, was sent a company (5th) to replace casualties. The second British bombardment was no more effective than the first, and the renewed attack, at 7 a.m., was therefore met by as strong a resistance. The sun was warm now, and the machine-guns became red-hot and the gunners serving the batteries at Halpegarbe, Lorgies, Illies, and Gravelin streamed with sweat; and this second attack, delivered in a similar manner as the first, also failed with heavy loss. The commander of the Meerut Division suggested a third attack for 8.20 a.m., but fortunately, on hearing from the 1st Division commander that two hours would be needed to reorganize before the division could co-operate, it was postponed.

The G.O.C. First Army, Sir Douglas Haig, when he heard of the failure of these attacks, and not realizing the facts of the situation, ordered the whole operation to start again at twelve noon, but on learning that fresh brigades would have to be put in, and that the trenches were congested with dead and wounded, he postponed the hour to 4 p.m.

As the sun lowered in the western sky the Germans, who thought the British must have had enough punishment (*die Nase voll*) for one day, were amazed to see them coming across once again in broad daylight, even with pipers (1st Black Watch) playing. When the smoke of the bombardment had cleared the leading British troops were in some places close up to the German wire, and the whole of no-man's-land, says the history of the 57th Regiment, was again filled with extended lines of men following closely behind one another. On the front of that regiment the leading line succeeded in getting through the battered wire-entanglement and then over the German breastwork, where followed close fighting with bayonets and hand-grenades. All the rear lines were, however, mown down by enfilade fire from three machine guns on the left flank and rifle fire from the right of the 1st Battalion (see sketch), as well as by the artillery fire of the 43rd Field Artillery and of two batteries of the 7th Foot Artillery Regiments. Without support, those British troops who had broken into the German position were soon overpowered. On the greater part of the attack frontage the German breastwork was not crossed. By 6.30 p.m. the battle was over. Under cover of darkness many British wounded and unwounded who had lain out in no-man's-land throughout this hot summer's day were able to return.

The losses of the British 1st and Meerut Divisions during the day's battle were together 6,340 all ranks, while the German 57th and 55th Regiments which had opposed them give their casualties as 300 and 602 respectively, chiefly due to artillery fire. Those of the 8th Division, which had attacked simultaneously in a similar manner and with no better result, farther north opposite Fromelles, were 4,680 all ranks.

The diary of the German 57th Regiment refers to the magnificent courage (*ungeheurer Bravour*) with which the British had pressed their attacks, a sight which had aroused great admiration. Amazement is expressed at the repetition of the attacks in broad daylight once the first attack had so completely failed, but the Germans had at least been shown another aspect of the British character to that of an amateur army of tennis-players. They had been given a glimpse of the struggle ahead before they could be in a position to enforce their will upon that character and win through to victory.

5

The tragedy of Aubers Ridge effected a complete change in British tactics. The First Army commander, Sir Douglas

Haig, decided to 'depart definitely from the procedure of the previous British attacks. He proposed to follow the French method of a long, methodical bombardment of the German defences, followed by an attack with objectives limited to a few hundred yards', and 'in order to wear down the power of resistance and shake the morale of the enemy this bombardment should last at least two or three days and be carried on continuously day and night'.[1] This new conception of a battle was sanctioned by the British Commander-in-Chief, Sir John French, in a letter dated the 14th May, which added: 'As the element of surprise will now be absent (owing to the long artillery preparation) it is probable that your progress will not be rapid.' Sir John French's addition was in keeping with the opinion of General Joffre, the French Commander-in-Chief, whose instructions for the subsequent battles show that he foresaw an offensive as a lengthy and slow business; *l'artillerie conquiert, l'infanterie occupe*, and repeating the process till the enemy was gradually worn down by 'attrition'.

In short, surprise was abandoned, and the long bombardment and so-called 'war of attrition' began. The consequence was that the artillery now became the chief weapon of offence, while the infantry arm, dethroned from its place as queen of the battlefield, became its kitchen-maids or 'moppers-up', and any method of procedure was accordingly regarded as a matter of minor importance. For this reason alterations urgently needed, such as a drastic overhaul of the chain system of command and the working out of a new doctrine for the infantry attack to meet the challenge of the German defence organization, received little or no attention.

The decision of British G.H.Q. was however less than half the answer to the experiences offered by the battles of Aubers Ridge and Neuve Chapelle. They had shown clearly enough what is fully appreciated by the least of God's creatures, that surprise is, on the contrary, a first

---

[1] *British Official History*, 1915, II, p. 47.

essential in an attack, and that a second essential is the
need for covering fire, lack of which had enabled the Germans to fire at their ease, unmolested, into the succession
of British lines advancing simultaneously towards them.

6

The need for covering fire for an infantry assault was not
a new idea. In the British army before the war, it was the
guiding principle in company and battalion training in an
attack that progress could only be made against a position
by one-half of a platoon or company covering by fire each
successive rush of the other half. Many will remember on
Aldershot Command manœuvres at that time the indigna-
tion felt and often expressed by regimental officers when,
for example, at the sham battle of Shrivenham, and again
during an attack on Stow-on-the-Wold, brigades were
ordered to, and did, advance in successive lines of companies without any covering fire, right up to entrenched
positions. On inquiry, however, they were told that the
reason was to show the visiting Secretary of State for War
(Mr. Haldane) the size of the British army, and that if we
had attacked as we had been trained he would scarcely
have seen anyone. And yet, although the gratification of
Mr. Haldane could no longer be given as an excuse, the
array for the British offensive on Aubers Ridge on the
9th May 1915 was remarkably similar to that for those
sham attacks on Stow-on-the-Wold and the village of
Shrivenham.

Conditions were undoubtedly different against an enemy
strongly entrenched, as were the Germans, at 200 yards'
distance compared with those of company training at
Aldershot, and an attack by short rushes at Aubers Ridge
was doubtless impracticable. But there were other ways of
obtaining covering fire for those defenceless assaulting lines.
On that same sunny morning, the 9th May 1915, a French
infantry captain, André Laffargue, taking part in the

simultaneous offensive which the French Sixth Army was making farther south to capture the Vimy Ridge, had an inspiration. He was in the front line of assault; his company, suffering heavy losses, had succeeded in overrunning the German garrison of the front trench system and capturing the ruins of Neuville Saint-Vaast just beyond it. It was then 11 a.m., and his own and the neighbouring company had together only eighty men left. They were approaching the cemetery on the Thélus road beyond the village, which was unoccupied, and the whole of the bare slope ahead of them rising towards the crest of the Vimy Ridge seemed empty of the enemy. At that moment two German machine guns opened fire from the base of a windmill, a few hundred yards south-east of the cemetery; it was a machine-gun nest, or *Stützpunkt*, similar to those which the British had encountered about 1,000 yards behind the front line at Neuve Chapelle. Those two machine guns were clearly the only opposition in the great open space ahead of them, but they sufficed to stop the advance. Captain Laffargue tried to signal back for artillery support, but when it came after a long delay it was on the wrong target and wide of the mill. For four hours the two companies lay exasperated, waiting for some means with which to destroy those two machine guns, until German reinforcements began to arrive by a communication trench and gradually reoccupied the cemetery position. At that hour, too, a French battalion at last arrived in support, but it also was held in check by the same two guns. The following morning another French battalion came up, but it too was checked, after a short and very costly advance, mainly by the same two guns.

The effect of this experience on an intelligent man was such that he wrote a pamphlet, 'L'Etude sur l'attaque', demanding a new method of attack. The problem he faced was identical to that which had confronted British G.H.Q. both at Neuve Chapelle and Aubers Ridge, but the solution he offered was vastly different, almost the direct opposite. He advocated every effort to obtain surprise, and he considered that the infantry arm could remain queen of the battlefield if more suitably equipped and given improved tactical methods.

He maintained that heavy and field artillery, firing at 3,000 to 5,000 yards' range, was inadequate to destroy the front trench system, and asked that they should be supplemented by a quantity of heavy trench mortars and torpedoes (*torpilles aeriennes*) to be used from the front trench system. At close range these, he contended, would have a more accurate and devastating effect than high-explosive shells from distant artillery, and could, he believed, destroy the German front trench system and stupefy the garrison very quickly, so as to give surprise to the assault. To take full advantage of this surprise, he advocated that the first wave of the attack should press through without a check to distant objectives, to include at least the enemy's artillery positions, instead of limiting the objective to a few hundred yards, which he considered would be to sacrifice lives to no purpose; this method was in direct opposition to the British system of 'leap-frogging', with long delays and changes of leaders. More revolutionary, however, was the organization he advocated for the actual assaulting waves of infantry. He fully appreciated the value of an assault in line. 'To have experienced the influence of an alignment in those first critical minutes of an assault is sufficient to appreciate its capital importance . . . to drag on with it any hesitating individuals, to restrain the too impetuous and to give to all that warm and comforting feeling of mutual confidence.' But he urged that there should be only one line at a time above ground in no-man's-land.

In the unusual instance of the assaulting distance being less than a hundred yards he believed that a front trench system properly prepared for assault might be captured in a single rush by this line of assault; but if, as was generally the case, the distance was greater, he demanded, above

55

all, that the first line of assault must be assured of covering fire; it was impossible to guarantee that every machine gun in the front trench system would be demolished by the preliminary bombardment, and he had seen the devastation even a single gun well served could inflict. To give this covering fire he recommended that from each platoon a couple of groups of steady and experienced men, *groupe de tirailleurs*, should advance about fifty yards ahead of the first line of assault. These groups were to be trained to fire as they advanced, and they should be equipped each with a light machine gun, or automatic rifle, a rifle-grenade weapon, hand-grenades, and gas-bombs. Each group would be allotted the narrow sector in front of it to watch as it advanced, and was to concentrate on any point of resistance it saw in that sector. After crossing the front trench system this formation was to press straight ahead, leaving to lines in rear the work of clearing the dug-outs. The *groupes de tirailleurs* would then adopt a method of *infiltration* into the depth of the position, pressing on through gaps found, making use of communication trenches, depressions in the ground, and any available cover. By this means he expected they would be able to take under fire, from a flank or from behind, the German machine-gun crews who were protected by shields from frontal fire, but who formed a vulnerable group target from any other direction. The machine-gun nests (*Stütz-punkte*) were to be located as soon as possible, and light trench mortars and mountain guns were to accompany the first line of assault for the purpose of destroying them by shell or screening them by smoke bombs; in addition, sections of field artillery were to keep in as close observed support as possible of the leading waves of the attack.

In this manner he hoped that a repetition of his experience in front of the mill at Neuville Saint-Vaast would be avoided, and that the *groupes de tirailleurs* would be able to pass beyond the line of *Stützpunkte* and into the enemy's battery positions. Contrary to the official French doctrine of using machine guns only to support attacking infantry from a distance or to consolidate a captured line, a policy which he called '*non-sens*', he demanded that they should follow in close support of the *groupes de tirailleurs* as arrowheads of the attack (*un dent de l'attaque*).[1]

He believed that if such a method of attack was adopted on a wide front a break-through (*trouée*) of the German position on the Western Front was practicable. The *groupes de tirailleurs* would lead the way through the crust of the German defence, but as soon as that was accomplished the infantry arm would come into its own as the supreme weapon of offence for capturing and occupying the hinterland. For this reason he advocated that the mass of the infantry should be trained for open warfare, and not so much for position warfare, as was then being done.

7

Captain Laffargue's pamphlet did not influence the French training manuals, although French G.H.Q. distributed it to the French army for information early in 1916, and it was printed in a small paper-covered book by the Librairie Plon in Paris, during that summer. Neither did it have the slightest influence on British training; it was not even translated into English. British G.H.Q. had, in fact, already at its disposal ideas which far outstripped in originality those of Captain Laffargue. Colonel (now Major-General Sir E.) Swinton's proposal, for example, in October 1914 for armoured machine-gun destroyers or 'tanks' on caterpillar-wheels to precede the infantry advance offered an even greater chance of maintaining surprise for the attack and enabling the infantry to penetrate the hard crust of the German defence; the first experimental tanks, cumbersome though they were, could cross

---

[1] This system of infiltration is also mentioned in the pamphlet written by Captain Laffargue a few months later in 1916, 'Conseils aux fantassins pour la bataille' (Librairie Plon, Paris, 1916).

broken country at two to four miles an hour, and were therefore admirably adapted to act as armoured *groupes de tirailleurs* to cover the infantry assault. But the 'tank' idea was ignored by British G.H.Q., no assistance being given to those who tried to press it, and when, eventually in 1916, the first of their kind were allowed to arrive in France their tactical employment was left to men so lacking in vision that their great value of surprise was lost.

For many months Captain Laffargue's work remained one of the many ideas floating about in 1915 on the same subject, waiting for someone with responsibility to embody them. In the early summer of 1916, however, the Germans found a copy of his pamphlet in a captured French trench, and it was seized on by those in authority as being a concise expression of a doctrine which exactly corresponded to the course they themselves had been trying to follow by cumbersome and slow degrees. The pamphlet was at once translated into German and issued as an official German training manual, eventually becoming the basis of General Ludendorff's text-book for the 'attack in position warfare'. It was with an elaboration of Captain Laffargue's doctrine of 'infiltration' that the Germans so effectively broke through the British position in March 1918 and the Chemin des Dames position in the following May; and his ideas have remained the foundation of the German training manual for attack to this day.[1] There will be occasion to refer again to Captain Laffargue's work in a later chapter, but it will suffice to add here that it was also destined to take a prominent share in the development of the German defensive battle.

---

[1] Ludwig Renn, a German company commander on the Western Front at this period, states (p. 110) in his book *Warfare*, a translation of which has recently (September 1939) been published by Faber & Faber, that 'in 1916 infantry regiments were trained for front-line service according to the theories of Captain Laffargue, a French officer who had written a book on his experiences as an infantry officer at the front, which was literally translated into German and used as a tactical manual for infantry operations'.

8

With this rough outline I have tried to emphasize two opposite schools of opinion which appeared at this stage of the war as a result of the decision of British G.H.Q. after the battle of Aubers Ridge; whether the infantry was to have the covering fire and support of artillery and every form of mechanized aid to help its own skilfully organized forward movement, or whether the artillery and every form of mechanized weapon were to have the infantry to 'mop up' what they intended first to conquer; whether in a few words, fire-effect and movement should work simultaneously together, or whether fire-effect should be followed by movement. British G.H.Q. and French G.Q.G. adopted the latter, fire-effect followed by movement, while German O.H.L. kept to the doctrine which all armies had previously followed, fire-effect combined with movement; and that distinction is still, to this day, the fundamental difference between the latest (1939) training manuals of the French army, on the one hand, and of the German, on the other.

Chapter III

FESTUBERT: 16th May 1915

On the 16th May, seven days after the battle of Aubers Ridge, the new doctrine of a long bombardment was applied by the British First Army on the same ground as the Rue du Bois attack on the 9th, with an extension southwards of 850 yards to about Festubert. During the three previous days the artillery, with carefully observed fire following a definite programme, had attempted to destroy completely the German defences with 26,000 shells on a bombardment frontage of 5,000 yards, which was double the infantry assault frontage. The German front breastwork was obliterated, but a number of machine guns at its base, which only a direct hit could destroy, remained serviceable; and many of the dugouts under the second breastwork (*Wohngraben*) survived.

The German disposition had not appreciably altered, each British division (about 10,000 infantry) being faced by approximately three German companies (about 450 rifles and three or four machine guns). As an encouragement Sir John French told General Haig, the First Army commander, a few days before the battle: 'The strength of your Army is far superior to the hostile forces in front of you: the enemy has few or no reserves, other than local, which he can bring up.'

During the night and early hours of the 15th–16th May, the infantry assault was delivered by three divisions. The objective was limited to the La Quinque Rue road, 1,000 yards distant, which was also approximately the line of the German strong-points (*Stützpunkte*).

On the left of the assault frontage controlled bursts of fire at hourly intervals during the first part of the night, intended to mislead the enemy, only resulted in keeping him on the alert, and when, at 11.30 p.m., the 5th and Garhwal Brigades of the 2nd and Meerut Divisions assaulted they were detected by light-balls and a searchlight and their lines raked by machine-gun and rifle fire before they could cross the 300 yards of no-man's-land. Only the right (6th) brigade of the 2nd Division was successful; advancing in silence, the leading half-companies reached the remnants of the German breastwork before almost a shot was fired, thence passed on and captured the German support trench (*Wohngraben*). There they halted, ready to continue the advance at daybreak. On the right, too, the 7th Division, which attacked at daybreak, was partially successful, although an occasional German machine gun, appearing out of the débris of the front breastwork, caused heavy losses.

On the whole, however, the front line had been overrun in many places, but subsequent fighting showed how effective a resistance could be offered by a few scattered parties of Germans in ditches and shell-holes in the open; difficult to see, these detachments checked any further considerable advance, and succeeded both in blocking the flanks of the break-in and holding it in front, as had happened at Neuve Chapelle. The successful opposition of these isolated shell-hole garrisons marks the beginning of the idea of an 'invisible garrison' (*die Leere des Gefechtsfeldes*) which was to play such a prominent part in the later defensive battles of the war.

The German 14th Divisional headquarters, realizing that the original front breastwork had been so battered as to be of little further use for a line of defence, ordered a new breastwork to be constructed connecting the strong-points (*Stützpunkte*), and to it the German survivors withdrew. By dawn on the 17th, with the arrival of reinforcements, the strength in fire-power along the new alignment was almost double that which opposed the first assault. Three days passed before the British batteries had located this new defence line, by which time it was sufficiently strong to need as heavy a preparatory bombardment to destroy as that previous to the first assault. The British casualties in this operation, in which four divisions became involved, amounted to over 16,000, as against a German total of about 5,000.

The battle had demonstrated the importance of surprise, even though a defence system might appear to be shelled to pieces. It might also have indicated that the long bombardment procedure was not the answer to the problem set by the German defence organization; and the 'attrition', both of man-power and ammunition expenditure, was still on the debit side for the attacker.

Chapter IV

LOOS: 25th September 1915

During that summer (1915) there was a respite in the fighting, and the Germans were able to continue carrying out General Falkenhayn's original programme of construction. The front-trench system, the communication trenches, and the strong-points were greatly strengthened, but most important was the construction of the rearward line demanded in his memorandum of the 25th January. Any opposition to such a line had been abandoned after the experience of Festubert, which proved that the British and French supplies of guns and munitions had increased sufficiently to level a wide sector of the front breastwork or trench, and that a second or reserve line for reserves to occupy out of effective range of the mass of the enemy's field batteries was an urgent necessity.

The new reserve line was therefore sited 2,500 to 3,000 yards behind the front line, in order that a forward move and a fresh deployment of the mass of the enemy's artillery would be necessary to prepare it for assault, and wherever possible it was sited on a reverse slope (*Hinterhang*). Formerly the rule had been to site a fire-trench on a forward slope with good observation and a good field of fire, and the front line on the Western Front had been so sited for most of its length. But the experience gained in the spring defensive battles both in Artois and Champagne had shown that trenches so sited gave too easy a target for the enemy's artillery and that they could be quickly demolished by the rapidly increasing strength of the enemy's munition

63

supplies. The experience of those battles had also shown that the fire-power of a machine gun was so rapidly destructive that an infantry assault could be checked by machine guns with a field of fire of only 150 to 200 yards.

The reserve line was therefore sited on a reverse slope, if possible, out of view of the enemy's ground artillery observers, and a few hundred yards behind a crest-line. It was strongly wired in front, and until the front line had been captured and the enemy's batteries had moved forward there was little possibility of either wire or trench being destroyed in a wholesale manner. At intervals of every 1,000 yards or so was a concrete machine-gun nest or strong-point (*Stützpunkt*) sited so as to sweep the intervening ground between them. In addition, in some sectors, such as in Champagne, the intermediate line of machine-gun nests (*Stützpunkte*), 1,000 yards behind the front line, had been joined up by a continuous trench, and this was called the intermediate (*Mittel-* or *Zwischen-*) line.

Another lesson learnt by the Germans during these spring battles of 1915 was that the best way to employ in the defence their numerical inferiority of artillery was to concentrate its attention chiefly on the enemy's infantry, first by shelling their assembly trenches with deliberate aimed fire, and secondly by increasing to an intense bombardment when an attack seemed imminent, and finally when the attack started, signalled by rockets (*Leuchtpatronen*) sent up by the front line troops, by laying a barrage of shell in front of the attacked sector of the front line; the batteries on the flanks co-operating with flanking fire wherever possible. From this experience resulted the classification of the German artillery fire into three kinds for a defensive battle, *zerstörungs-* (disturbing), *vernichtungs-* (destructive), and *Sperr-*(barrage)*feuer*.

I

In the trench maps prepared by the Intelligence section

of British G.H.Q. in August 1915 these innovations, including the trace of the new Reserve Line discovered from air-photographs, were clearly shown. The problem facing an assault was therefore seen to be much more formidable than that at Festubert, and the expressed opinion both of Sir John French, the British Commander-in-Chief, and of Sir Douglas Haig, the First Army commander, was that it would be best to refrain from any more big offensives until Kitchener's new divisions had been pulled together and the munition factories in Great Britain and France had found their stride.

The plan of General Joffre for two French offensives from Artois and Champagne on the 25th September in which the British were to co-operate was, however, most optimistic. There was now such an increased quantity of guns and munitions available that he believed a hurricane bombardment such as would utterly destroy the German defence system was practicable, and that the subsequent assault by a mass of infantry assembled in great depth, all rear formations moving forward simultaneously with the front line of assault, would prove irresistible. Theoretically the French offensive in both sectors was to be a continuous forward movement of successive lines of infantry at fifty paces' distance, so that there would be a constant flow of men supporting and carrying the assault forward through every obstruction. General Joffre believed that both the German front and reserve defence lines could be broken through in this manner by the first assault, and divisions were to be ready in reserve, preceded by a strong force of cavalry, to rush through the gap. The cavalry were given a line in Belgian territory fifty miles away as ultimate objective, and success was to be followed at once by a general advance of the French and British armies on the entire Western Front.

The British were asked to co-operate with the French offensive in Artois by attacking north of Lens, on the front of six miles between Loos (inclusive) and the La Bassée canal; but as Sir John French did not wish his armies to become involved in offensive operations except in favourable circumstances, which he did not consider existed in this sector, he offered to co-operate at first by artillery fire only until the French advance south of Lens had neutralized the German artillery in the Lens area. Under pressure from Lord Kitchener at home, due to the general situation and that on the Russian front, Sir John French was, however, compelled in the latter part of August to abandon opposition, and to co-operate with the French offensive by a simultaneous infantry assault.

2

The country here was very different to that at Neuve Chapelle and Festubert in the low-lying plain of French Flanders. Broad rounded spurs reach out north-eastward from the Artois plateau and merge into the low-lying plain which is bounded approximately on its southern side by the La Bassée canal (see Sketch 3). The opposing British and German trenches, south of the canal, lay across these spurs, and in the air photographs, the excavated chalk subsoil gave them the appearance of lines of sea-foam on a beach. But although every detail of the German position and of the strong-points was disclosed, that knowledge did not affect the difficulty of ensuring that every machine gun in a vast area of ground was put out of action before the assault across those bare downland slopes, which were devoid of any cover.

The outlook was, however, altered by a decision in August to assist a possible British assault by discharging a cloud of gas from cylinders to be placed in the front line, and which would immediately precede the assaulting infantry. Experiments had been conducted ever since the German gas-attack at Ypres on the 3rd May, and sufficient gas-cylinders were now available.

Sir Douglas Haig, commanding the First Army, which

was to carry out the offensive, witnessed a demonstration of this 'chlorine wave' in perfect wind and weather conditions at Helfaut on the 22nd August, and he was completely converted. His enthusiasm is easy to understand. It is as if he had suddenly seen that attractive German vision of enveloping a large part of the opposing force, whether in attack or defence, in a cloud of some soporific essence and putting it temporarily to sleep, long enough to disarm it; and the sleeping army would awake to find itself a harmless crowd of unarmed men. That vision is not necessarily a fairy story—some such essence which laughs even at gas-masks may yet be found; but in 1915 chemical science still lagged behind, and the best it could offer was the lung-destroying or death-dealing 'chlorine wave' as a substitute, which however possessed the same magic possibilities. It reduced the science of war to its simplest possible form, and put into the shade proposals such as those of Colonel Swinton and Captain Laffargue.

At a conference with his divisional commanders a week later Sir Douglas Haig told them that with the assistance of a gas-cloud he believed in the possibility of a successful offensive. Given a favourable wind blowing eastwards at about twenty miles an hour he considered that the gas would compensate for inadequate artillery support and permit an attack on a wider front than the available artillery alone warranted. Since the gas should be effective up to a distance of two miles he hoped that both the German front and reserve defence lines would be broken through in the first rush of the six assaulting divisions. He emphasized the weakness of the German garrison, the disposition of which had not materially altered since Festubert, except that supports for the front-line garrison tended to be nearer.[1] The situation was that each of six British assault-

---

[1] Each regiment had a sector of about 2,800 yards. Two of its battalions garrisoned the position and the third was in reserve about four miles back. The two front battalions each had two companies in the front trench system and two in support, 2,000 yards back near the

ing divisions was confronted by only two German companies in the front trench-system, which might be overrun
before the local supports and reserves could come to their
assistance; further, he estimated that the entire German
position could be broken through before the larger, and
known nearest, German reserves, a division at Allennes
and one at Douai, seven and twelve miles distant, could
reach the battlefield. For this reason he asked that a 'violent and continuous action' be maintained throughout the
assault, so as to take full advantage of the effect of the gas
cloud. He also counted on having three more divisions,
including the 21st and 24th of the XI Corps, placed at his
disposal by Sir John French from G.H.Q. reserve to assist
in exploiting the break-through and joining hands with the
French beyond Lens.

There was an alternative scheme, in case the wind should
not be favourable for the gas cloud on the morning of the
assault. In such an event only two divisions were to attack,
without gas-support and with limited objectives, and the
bigger attack with gas would not take place until the wind
was favourable, or not at all: the alternative plan allowed
a margin of three days in order to secure a favourable wind
for the bigger attack.

3

Although the British offensive was preceded by a four
days' artillery bombardment by 37 heavy (and siege) and
482 field guns and howitzers firing over 255,000 shells
(22,000 heavy and 233,700 field), it is evident that the
entire British plan depended on a suitable wind on the

reserve line, or, if shelter was available, in the intermediate area. For
example, the 157th Regiment, in the centre, had four companies in
all (about 700 men) holding the front trench system facing the assault
of the British 15th and 1st Divisions, with two support companies at
Hulluch (south) and two at Loos (north); its third battalion was at
Vendin le Vieil (three miles east of Hulluch) and the regimental
battle-headquarters was in the Loos brewery.

morning of the 25th September. The wind had dropped overnight and the indications pointed towards a change to the south; so that in the early hours of the 25th, being told that the wind would probably freshen about dawn, Sir Douglas Haig ordered the big attack to be delivered with gas at sunrise (5.50 a.m.).

The little care with which this most important decision, which of the alternative plans to use, was made is also noticeable in Sir Douglas Haig's ingenuous confession that at 5 a.m. when he went out of the porch of his château at Hinges there was almost a calm, but he asked his A.D.C. to light a cigarette and the smoke floated towards the north-east, so he allowed the order for the full gas-attack to hold good.

The sun rose behind a cloud-covered sky. The wind did not increase; it was scarcely perceptible, and from the south-south-west.

4

The consequence was that the gas-cloud, instead of being driven eastwards by a steady twenty-mile-an-hour breeze, drifted slantwise up the opposing front trenches, which lay roughly on a north-south line (see Sketch 3). Opposite the 47th and 15th (Scottish) Divisions, on the right, the gas had travelled better than elsewhere, owing possibly to the downward slope into the Loos valley, and the advance of the assaulting infantry was also covered by a smoke cloud from batteries of Stokes mortars. The 47th captured and passed on beyond the German front-trench system with comparatively little loss; and although the Scottish battalions of the 15th were also successful, severe casualties were suffered from the fire of two German machine guns before the front-trench system was penetrated.

South of the Vermelles–Hulluch road, in the centre of the assault, the gas was ineffective. The German front

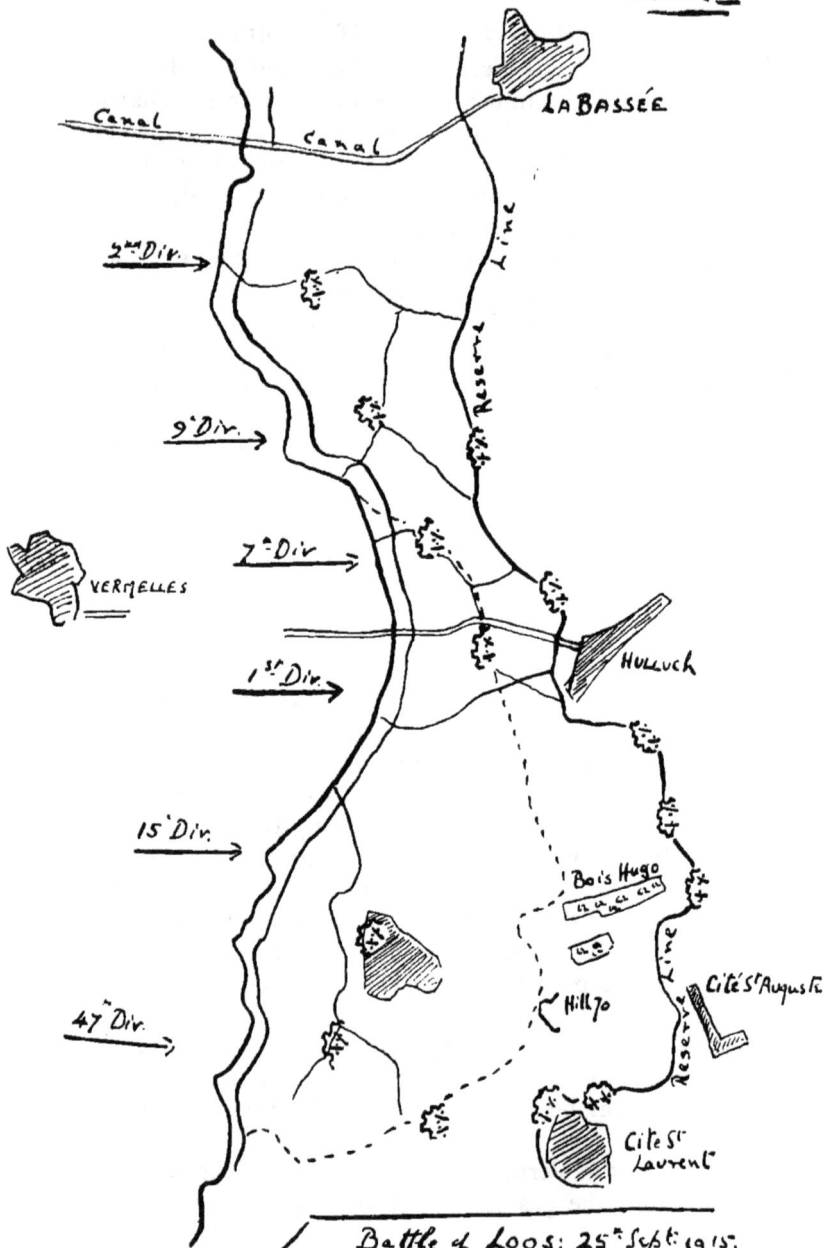

Sketch III

Canal   Canal   LA BASSÉE

2ⁿᵈ Div.

Reserve Line

9° Div.

7ᵗʰ Div.

VERMELLES

1ˢᵗ Div.

HULLUCH

15ᵗʰ Div.

Bois Hugo

Cité St Auguste

47ᵗʰ Div.

Hill 70

Reserve Line

Cité St Laurent

Battle of LOOS: 25ᵗʰ Sept. 1915.

1,000 500 0   1,000   2,000 Yards.

----- = German front line 10 Oct. 1915

trench here was well placed, just behind the crest of the Lone Tree Ridge; the wire entanglements had been little damaged. The gas began to drift back into the British trenches, which here ran north-eastwards, and put the front lines of assault out of action. The initial momentum of the offensive here was therefore broken and two German companies (157th Regiment) held out till the afternoon against a succession of onslaughts.

On the front of the 7th Division the gas hung about in no-man's-land, and the assaulting infantry, almost suffocated, had to remove their gas helmets to get breath, many being thereby overcome by the fumes. Nevertheless the attack here, as on the front of 9th Division farther north, was partially successful and penetrated into the intermediate area of the German position.

On the front of the 2nd Division the gas also stayed about the British front line, causing a large number of the men assembled for the assault to be violently sick and unable to take any further part in the battle. The situation was such that one brigade (6th) had to report that 'the gas was a complete failure, but our men suffered heavy casualties and are not in a position to attack again'. Where certain battalions were able to get forward into no-man's-land they found the Germans ready, and the experience of Aubers Ridge on the 9th of May was repeated.

The failure of the gas to do more than stupefy the garrison of the German front trench in a few sectors left the problem of penetrating deep into the position the same as before, and the situation eventually stabilized in front of the German strong-points (*Stützpunkte*), either those in the intermediate area or in the Reserve Line. Two phases, however, in the subsequent advance of the 15th (Scottish) Division through Loos deserve some attention in so far as they affected the development of the defensive battle.

The two companies of the German 157th Regiment which faced the 15th Division had at once called for assistance and in reply the support companies in Loos village went forward and quickly became disorganized in the fighting against greatly superior numbers about the front line. This was an instance of the need for a change in the method of supporting the garrison of the front trench system, a change which was already receiving the attention of the German authorities. Repeated experiences such as this had proved that to follow the customary procedure of sending supports forward at once to reinforce the front line generally only resulted in increasing the casualty list, and that it was better for the supports to wait in their support-positions until the front line had been broken through, if at all, and then to demoralize by fire those parts of the attack advancing towards them, prior to an immediate counter-attack to regain the lost sector of the front line.

The early entanglement of the Loos supports in the front-line fighting left the village practically undefended, and it fell an easy prey to the 15th Division, whose leading battalions then pressed up on to Hill 70 and across the summit. It was here that the second lesson was learnt. The reserve line followed a contour of the reverse slope of Hill 70 about 800 yards from the summit, covering Cité Saint-Laurent and Cité Saint-Auguste (see Sketch 3). The men of the 15th Division came streaming over the summit and down the reverse slope unsupported by artillery fire, so that a few German machine guns hurriedly placed in the reserve line were able to annihilate them at their leisure. Over a thousand men of the 15th Division were caught on this bare reverse slope, unable to move forwards or backwards, and were all eventually killed or taken prisoner. The action on Hill 70 confirmed for the Germans the value of a reverse-slope position, and also that of keeping a few machine guns in the Reserve Line.

5

The reports from the British front divisions over-estimated their successes, and Sir Douglas Haig, eight miles away, accepting them, sent forward two reserve divisions, the 21st and 24th of the XI Corps, handed over to him by Sir John French during the morning. They were newly arrived from England, all of the first hundred thousand volunteers and of the best that England possessed, but they were only half-trained and had inexperienced commanders and staffs. Sir Douglas Haig now ordered them to 'break down entirely the tottering German second line of defence (Reserve Line) and press on to objectives beyond it'. At 2.35 p.m. he confirmed this order in greater detail by an instruction to General Haking, the XI Corps commander, to 'push forward at once between Hulluch and Cité Saint-Auguste and occupy the high ground between Harnes and Pont à Vendin and the crossings of the Haute Deule canal there' (which was over three miles beyond the German Reserve Line). It was dark and streaming rain before these two divisions had reached the original British front trenches but Sir Douglas Haig repeated his order in a message at 11.30 p.m., and ordered the advance to be continued the following day. The conforming XI Corps order to its two divisions was given out by General Haking at 1 a.m. on the 26th from Corps headquarters at Nœux-les-Mines, four miles from the battlefront. The attack was to start at 11 a.m. and would have to cross 2,000 yards of open down-land on a slope facing the enemy before reaching the German Reserve Line (see Sketch 4).

There was no convenient reverse slope in this sector for the German Reserve Line, and instead it had been sited along the rim of the saucer-shaped depression that lies between Hulluch and Hill 70; both it and the strong wire entanglement in front were clearly marked in the British trench maps. The Corps commander considered it essential that the two commanding positions, Hill 70 and Hulluch village, which flanked the Reserve Line here, should be captured before the attack was delivered. Attempts to do so in the early hours failed, showing that the German reserves from Allennes and Douai had arrived overnight,

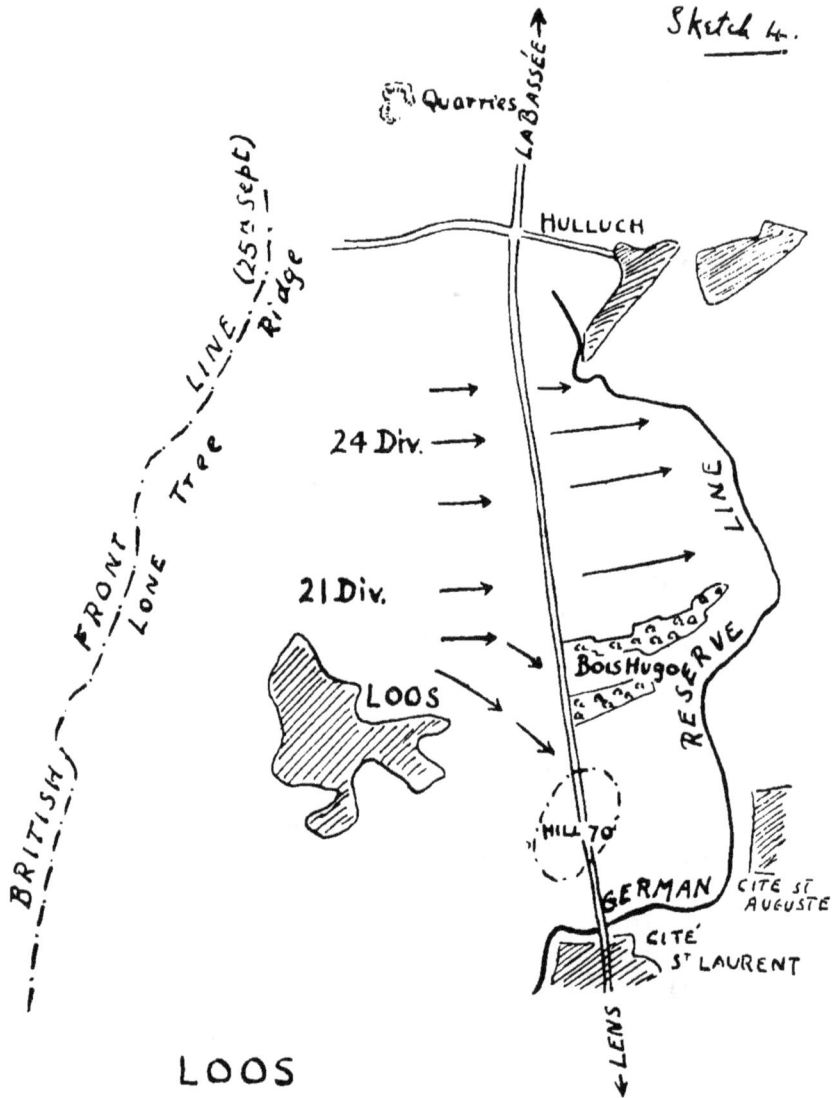

Sketch 4.

Quarries

LA BASSÉE

HULLUCH

BRITISH FRONT LINE (25th Sept.)

Lone Tree Ridge

24 Div.

21 Div.

LOOS

Bois Hugo

RESERVE LINE

HILL 70

GERMAN

CITE ST AUGUSTE

CITE ST LAURENT

LENS

LOOS
26th SEPTEMBER 1915

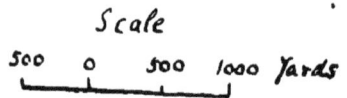

Scale

500   0   500   1000 Yards

as predicted by the British Intelligence Section of G.H.Q. several days before the battle. General Haking, however, still hoped, at 10 a.m., that the division on his left (1st) would take Hulluch, and he allowed his orders for the attack to stand. Unfortunately the information, known at Corps headquarters early in the morning, that both Hill 70 and Hulluch were strongly held by the enemy and that the intervening stretch of the German Reserve Line which the 21st and 24th Divisions were about to attack was therefore also probably garrisoned, was not passed on to the men for whom it was of vital importance, namely the battalion commanders concerned.

In the hour that followed, between 10 and 11 a.m., a series of events occurred which altered the whole prospects of the attack. First, the batteries which were to prepare the Reserve Line for assault had taken up wrong positions in the morning mist and the artillery preparation consisted only of a few ranging shots that fell wide of the mark. Secondly, at 10.30 a.m. the Germans counter-attacked some advanced troops of the 21st Division who had gone forward overnight to a wood (Bois Hugo) close in front of the German Reserve Line, and they recaptured the wood. This counter-attack and its subsequent fire-effect led to a general retirement of the leading brigade of the 21st Division at a moment, 11 a.m., when the general advance was due to begin. Thirdly, the attack by the 1st Division on Hulluch was, owing to a misunderstanding, postponed at the last moment till noon.

None of these happenings was known to General Haking, four miles away at Noeux-les-Mines, till after midday. In other words, owing to his distance from the battlefield, he did not realize until an hour after the attack he had ordered had begun that what he knew to be the essential conditions for its success were lacking.

These two divisions had been told that 'in no conceivable circumstances would they be put into this, their first, battle unless and until the Germans were absolutely smashed and

75

retiring in disorder'. By 11 a.m. it would have been clear to an observer near the battery positions on Lone Tree Ridge not only that the Germans were not smashed but that the two best-trained veteran divisions in the world could not capture the German Reserve Line in the circumstances. One of the brigade commanders of the 21st Division tried to stop his battalions, but the Corps order was to attack. No cancelling order arrived from Corps headquarters, and the two doomed divisions, less one brigade which fortunately remained in reserve, advanced in columns of battalions in extended lines towards the German position.

It was a dull afternoon, clear but overcast. The history of the German 15th Reserve Regiment states that 'ten columns of extended lines of infantry were counted between Hulluch and Hill 70, and each column had about a thousand men, all advancing as if carrying out a parade-ground drill'. The first sight of such a mass of the enemy caused consternation among the Germans, but, as there was no covering fire and the British artillery had almost ceased to shell, the consternation gradually turned to amazement. 'A target was offered to us such as had never been seen before, nor even thought possible.' German machine guns opened fire at 1,500 yards' range, but the columns crossed the Lens road regardless of it, and moved on past the southern front of Hulluch, between the village and Bois Hugo, with the right of the 21st Division towards Hill 70. 'The entire front', says another German history (26th Regiment), 'was covered with the enemy's infantry.' The Germans 'stood up, some even on the parapet of the trench, and fired triumphantly [*jauchzend*] into the mass of men advancing across the open grassland, and a six-gun battery in Hulluch village shelled them over open sights. Never had machine guns had such straightforward work to do, nor done it so effectively; with barrels burning hot and swimming in oil, they traversed to and fro along the enemy's ranks unceasingly; one machine gun alone fired 12,500 rounds that afternoon. The effect was devastating. The enemy could be seen falling literally in hundreds, but they continued their march in good order and without interruption. The extended lines of men began to get confused by this terrific punishment, but they went doggedly on, some even reaching the wire entanglement in front of the reserve line, which their artillery had scarcely touched. Confronted by this impenetrable obstacle the survivors turned and began to retire.'

In the terrible ordeal of those few hours the two divisions lost 385 officers and 7,800 men. There would have been more, but the Germans, in the words of the history of the 15th Reserve Regiment, were 'nauseated by the sight of the massacre on what became known as the "field of corpses of Loos [*Leichenfeld von Loos*]" ', and 'when British survivors began to retire no more shots were fired at them for the rest of the day, so great was the feeling of compassion and mercy after such a victory'.[1] The Germans might have followed up those survivors in an attempt to recapture their original front-trench system, but as it had been shelled to pieces by the preliminary bombardment it was decided, as at Festubert, to abandon the idea.

Once again the German defence system had not been put to a really severe test, but, as on Hill 70 the previous day, this affair had demonstrated the value of a Reserve Line and also of the presence in it of a few machine guns. According to a German machine-gun history, the battle of Loos was 'the birthday of the idea of siting the heavy machine guns at the back of the position',[2] which, during 1917, was to become a main feature of their employment in the defensive battle.

[1] Forstner, *Das Reserve Infanterie Regiment 15* (Berlin, 1929), pp. 226–32.
[2] Von Hoppe, 'Die Taktik der Maschinengewehre', *Militär Wochenblatt* (October 1936).

6

The fighting continued spasmodically till the 13th October, but did not materially alter the fact that only another small salient, or *Ausbeulung*, had been made into the German position (see Sketch 3). The German casualties for the battle of Loos, up till the 10th October, are estimated in the *British Official History* from German authorities as less than half (441 officers and 19,393 other ranks) those of the British (1,721 officers and 41,669 other ranks), and of these the Germans lost about 5,000 killed compared with 16,000 British killed, or never heard of again.

So ended that daydream of Sir Douglas Haig on the afternoon of the 22nd August, when he first saw the chlorine wave.

7

It may seem strange that Sir John French should have been relieved of his command after the battle of Loos, and Sir Douglas Haig appointed British Commander-in-Chief in his place. Sir John French had hoped that as few infantry as possible might become involved in the battle, and he is therefore rightly blamed for allowing his better judgement to be overruled by Sir Douglas Haig's demand for two of the three divisions in G.H.Q. reserve; but it was Sir Douglas Haig who had ordered the full gas-cloud attack, with so slight a wind to carry it, and it was he who had given that order to the 21st and 24th Divisions. There was, however, a deeper reason for the change of Commander-in-Chief. Sir John French's previous optimism had cooled, and after the Loos offensive he openly stated his doubts as to the successful termination of the war. Sir Douglas Haig, on the other hand, had supreme confidence in the British Army, and his confidence in himself was such that he has written that he believed he had a divine mission to win the war for England. Sophisticated minds might ridicule such a claim. The fact, however, that he did eventually lead a victorious British Army to the Rhine seems to justify a belief that supreme faith of such rock-like substance as his may be the most valuable asset of all in a commander.

Part II

FOUNDATION OF A DEFENCE
IN DEPTH

———

Chapter V

THE CHAMPAGNE BATTLES:
September–October 1915

The chief of the Operations Section of German O.H.L. was Colonel Tappen, but throughout most of 1915 he was away with General Falkenhayn at Pless, the eastern branch of O.H.L., from where the German offensives against the Russians during the spring and summer of 1915 were conducted. His representative at Mézières, the Western Front branch of O.H.L., throughout that period, was Lieut.-Colonel von Lossberg. As this is the man who was destined to direct the further development of the German defensive battle up to the end of the war, and will be the chief character in the remaining chapters of this book, it will be well to give a short account of him.

Colonel von Lossberg belonged to an old Thüringian family with a long military record. In 1887, at the age of nineteen, he joined the 2nd Guard Regiment zu Fuss, being the third generation of his family in that regiment, and became a company and then a battalion commander in it. For four years he was an instructor at the *Kriegsakademie* (Staff College), and in 1913, as a lieut.-colonel, he was appointed chief of staff to the XIII Corps. In that capacity he took part, at the outbreak of the war, in the advance through the Ardennes, and later, in the October battles against the British south of Ypres. After a short spell with his Corps on the Russian front at the end of 1914 he was, in January 1915, appointed deputy-chief of the

83

Operations Section of O.H.L., and for the next eight months was cloistered in Mézières.

At that time he was forty-seven years of age, and contemporary accounts in the German Press describe him as 'tall and powerfully built, of smart appearance and with a charming manner'; other accounts add that he was 'beloved by his subordinates', and, as subsequent chapters will show, he was a tiger for work, and indefatigable.

I

The duties of this Operations Section consisted in working out various strategical and tactical possibilities on the Western Front as well as normal routine work. For example, although executive power remained with the eastern branch of O.H.L. at that period, Colonel von Lossberg had had through his hands the various reports of Corps and Armies after the spring battles recommending the advantages of siting the Reserve Line on a reverse slope; those reports had given him opportunity to study the various aspects of that important decision which was made shortly afterwards.

He had in his section about a dozen staff officers, and some of these junior members were evidently progressively minded men, for they were outspoken critics of the doctrine of a rigid defence of a line, which had been enforced by General Falkenhayn, the Chief of O.H.L. Judging by the comparatively few German casualties and by the small loss of ground compared with the British and French objectives, the doctrine had passed its first test with flying colours, but they foresaw evils ahead as soon as the unlimited resources of the enemy in munitions began to take effect on the battlefield. They predicted that the doctrine of rigidly defending the foremost line would lead local commanders more and more to cram the defence garrison into or near to it, in order to hold it at all costs, with a result that the German casualty lists would probably multiply with the enemy's munition output and consequent increased strength of his artillery bombardment. Another point they considered was that although the existing British and French methods of attack by massed man-power in successive lines appeared to them as obsolete as their own rigid defence of a line doctrine, there was always a chance that the enemy might modernize his methods and succeed in breaking through on a wide front the rigidly held line which had such inadequate reserves behind it. Instead of a doctrine which would most certainly tend to increase the density of the front-line garrison they therefore wished for one which would thin it, and at the same time give it depth and resiliency.[1]

These ideas were still in the discussion stage when a document captured in a raid on a French trench near La Ville-au-Bois, north of Rheims, on the 10th May 1915, reached the Operations Section. At first sight it seemed of minor importance; it was merely a local defence organization recommended by the French Fifth Army commander, written ten days previously, for holding the front trench system by the front battalions. But on examination these junior members found in it an inspiration towards a solution for which they had been searching.[2]

2

As this French instruction was the conception from which a new defence doctrine was eventually to grow, I have given a translation of it in full in an appendix at the end of this chapter. Briefly, it advocated the front-line battalions to be disposed as follows: first a line of listening posts not necessarily connected up by a trench, and behind them a line of sentry-groups which was called the first, or outpost, line of resistance. About 200 yards behind, ac-

[1] Bauer, *Der grosse Krieg in Feld und Heimat* (Tübingen, 1921).
[2] Sesselberg, *Der Stellungskrieg 1914–18* (Berlin, 1926), pp. 109–21. Also the chapter on the Hindenburg Line later in this book.

cording to the sketch which was captured with the instruction, was a line of piquets, or front companies, which provided the sentry-groups and listening posts (see Sketch 5). This line of piquets was called the main line of resistance in the event of the first line being broken through or made untenable. About 600 yards behind the main line of resistance was to be a third line consisting chiefly of well-built shelters for the local reserves. The original touch in this instruction was that the main line of resistance, that is the line of piquets, was to be held not by a continuous line of rifles, as was usual, but by a line of strong-points, about 200 yards apart; and these strong-points were to be constructed like miniature forts for all-round defence and capable of offering a long resistance, 'even though surrounded on all sides'. Their garrisons were to hold on at all costs until they could be relieved by a victorious counter-attack by the reserves from the third line. Further, the instruction pointed out that all communication trenches leading back to the third line were to be constructed as fire trenches, as, in the event of an attack breaking-through, they would play a 'chief part' in the defensive battle.

Now whatever may have been in the mind of the French author of this instruction the junior members of the German Operations Section read into it a meaning which exactly suited their purposes, namely to enable them to thin out the front line garrison and to put a more offensive spirit into the rigid or passive defence. They construed it as meaning that a determined attack was almost invited to pass through the line of strong points, which would only serve to break its first impetus, and that the defensive battle proper would take place behind the strong points, in the 600 yards of ground between the main line of resistance and the line of reserve-shelters. Here the attackers would be hemmed in and demoralized by the enfilade fire from the communication trenches, and then counter-attacked and overrun by the local reserves, who would subsequently

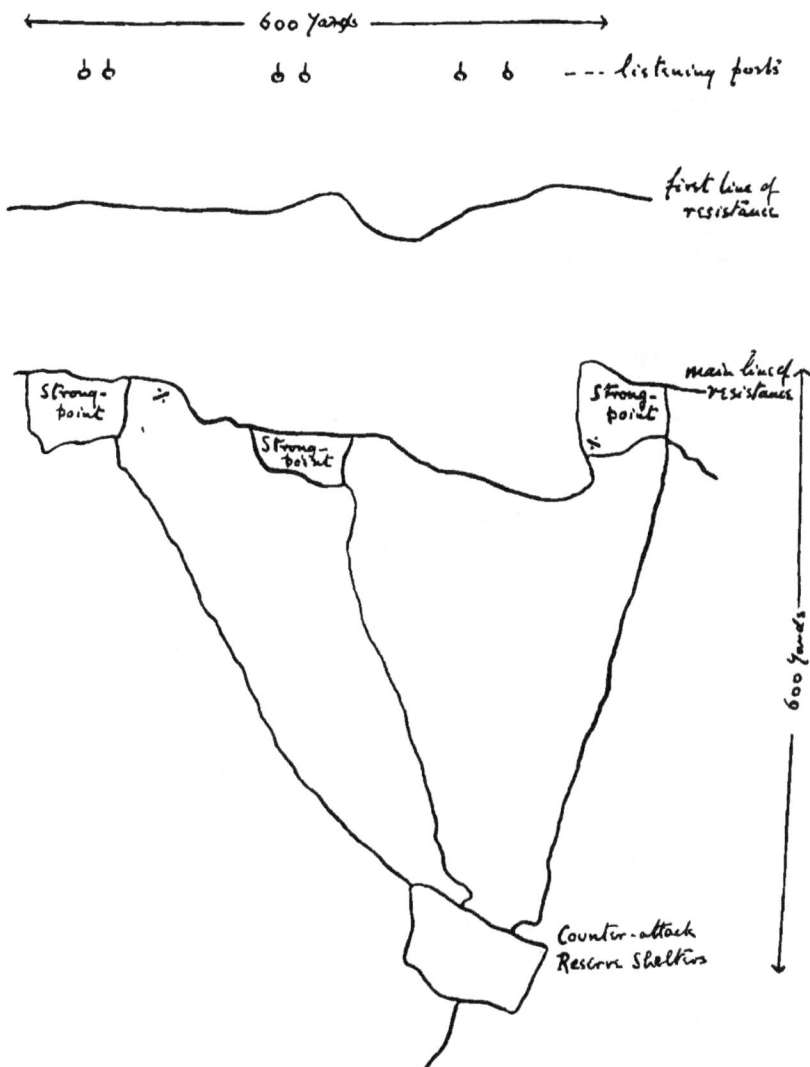

←—— 600 yards ——→

δ δ δ δ δ δ --- listening posts

first line of
resistance

Strong-
point : : Strong-
point main line of
resistance

Strong-
point

600 yards

Counter-attack
Reserve Shelters

To accompany French Fifth Army Instruction
of 30. 4. 15.

SKETCH 5

relieve the beleagured garrisons of the strong-points and reoccupy the line of sentry-groups and listening posts. From this point of view the foremost line might be regarded as an elastic band which an attack would stretch inwards, while the immediate counter-attack by the local reserves would be the spring to take the elastic band back to its normal tension.

Colonel von Lossberg does not appear to have taken much notice of this French document. He firmly believed in the efficacy of the doctrine of the rigid defence of a line, although agreeing that it might result in the foremost line being held too densely with men, but that might be avoided. He rejected, however, any idea of 'elasticity' or of an invitation to enter, and maintained that the garrison of the foremost line should be so disposed that it could best hold the foremost line from the outset, and that that line was to be held at all costs.

The difference between these two opinions can be summed up in a few words: both sides were agreed that the defensive battle should be fought for the foremost line, but whereas Colonel von Lossberg maintained that it should be fought in it, these junior members of his staff thought it might preferably be fought behind it.

In the excellent account of his activities during 1914–18, recently published,[1] and to which the following chapters are indebted for much of their material, the only mention von Lossberg makes of this discussion with the junior members of his staff is that he was 'frequently able to correct some of their highly exaggerated ideas of the capabilities of front-line units and of the general conduct of a battle which were often in direct contradiction to my own considerable experience'; and he adds, by way of excuse for them, that although they were keen and hard-working men, only one of them (Captain Harbou) had had any front-line experience.

[1] Fritz von Lossberg, *Meine Tätigkeit im Weltkriege 1914–18* (Mittler, Berlin, 1939).

This divergence of views may seem a trivial quibble, but it was soon to become the subject for a first-class argument throughout the German Army, from the Commander-in-Chief down to the last-joined private. For the moment, however, it was confined to the dinner-table of the Operations Section in Mézières, and neither side convinced the other. Major (later Colonel) Bauer, Major Bussche, and Captains Geyer and Harbou, continued to hold their own opinion and to build upon it, and Colonel von Lossberg remained adamant.

3

Throughout the eight months which Colonel von Lossberg spent in Mézières he was straining at the leash to return to more active work at the front, and the first opportunity, which came by accident, he seized with both hands. His chief, Colonel Tappen, was still away when the French offensive was delivered on the 25th September and von Lossberg deputized for him when General Falkenhayn explained the situation to the Kaiser, William II, the following morning. A message had come through earlier in the morning from the chief of staff of the Third Army, Lieut.-General von Höhn, that the left corps might have to be withdrawn two miles to behind the Dormoise, and Colonel von Lossberg during his account of the situation on the Champagne battlefront expressed strong disapproval of such an action. Within three hours of that interview he was on his way to replace General von Höhn as chief of staff, a marked honour for a junior colonel of only two months' seniority, as all the other chiefs of staff of armies were at least major-generals.

Before leaving O.H.L. he wrote to his wife: 'I am leaving this place of dusty documents and am going to Champagne, where there is fresh air. There I shall be in my element among soldiers, and shall be able to breathe again.' He was to remain in his element for three years, but there can be little doubt that the foundation of his future fame were the ideas, principally those on the advantages of a reverse-slope position and those of a lightly held but deep defence, which he had consciously or subconsciously acquired during those eight months spent among the dusty documents at O.H.L.

4

The French offensive in Champagne, delivered simultaneously on the 25th September with that in Artois and with the British attack with gas at Loos, had been carried out with twenty divisions in the first line, on a frontage of eighteen miles between Auberive and Ville-sur-Tourbe and with seven more divisions in the second line followed by six cavalry divisions and an infantry division, which were to press on, through the gap to be made in the German position, to distant objectives. To face this mass of assault the German Third Army had five divisions in the line, with a few brigades in reserve ten to fifteen miles away

The French assault was preceded by a cloud of gas, and here, unlike at Loos, the opposing trenches lay east and west, so that the slight south-westerly breeze carried it over the German front trench system and put sectors of it temporarily out of action. A smoke screen which accompanied the gas-cloud also hid the progress of the assault from the German artillery observers, and the previous heavy bombardment of three days' duration had broken most of the telephone cables back to their batteries. By the evening of the first day of battle the French had broken in on a front of two and a half miles on the eastern flank to a depth of about 1,000 yards, where the attack had been held by the line of machine-gun nests along the intermediate (*Mittel*) line; in the centre, north of Perthes and Souain, where the front-trench system had been overrun on a frontage of eight miles, they had penetrated to a depth of over 2,500 yards but were there checked by a thin line of German reserves who hurriedly occupied the Reserve Line. The Reserve Line, for reasons mentioned in the Loos chapter, was on a reverse slope, behind the crest of the high ground which forms the southern side of the Py valley, and, although the trench was only a shallow excavation of little depth, reinforcements which arrived during the afternoon enabled it to be effectively held. For the moment the French offensive was checked, but the Germans had suffered such heavy losses that insufficient troops were available to attempt to retake the lost ground by immediate counter-attack. On the French side there was disappointment at the check, and time was needed to organize another effort to break through the Reserve Line, which was planned for the 27th.

It was during this pause in the battle that Colonel von Lossberg arrived as chief of staff of the Third Army. He left Mézières about 1 p.m.; it was about the hour during which, a hundred miles away, the British 21st and 24th Divisions were being massacred in front of the German Reserve Line between Hulluch and Loos. He reached his new headquarters in Vouziers at 3 p.m., and his arrival was characteristic. He went direct to the room of the chief of staff, and found it empty, as General von Höhn, whom he was to replace, had already left; but, as he entered, the telephone bell rang, and picking up the receiver he heard one of the Corps commanders, who believed it to be General von Höhn, asking whether the withdrawal was to take place that night. Colonel von Lossberg replied at once on his own responsibility that the withdrawal was cancelled. Half an hour later he had explained and received sanction from the Third Army commander, General von Einem, for what he had done; and, after asking permission to spend the remainder of the day visiting the battlefront, he obtained full powers from General von Einem to give on the spot any orders he thought fit to meet the critical situation of the Third Army.

It is interesting to see the reaction of this man to such a

sudden acquisition of complete responsibility for the conduct of a great defensive battle on a frontage of eighteen miles. Within two hours of that interview with the Army commander he had left his car at Somme-Py, and, walking up the southern slope of the valley, was soon 'running from shell-hole to shell-hole' near the front line, the original Reserve Line, in the most threatened sector of the battlefield about Navarin Farm. There he saw for himself the state of the position and of the men holding it, and his observations were to be of fundamental importance for the future of the defensive battle. The existing front line was to be held at all costs, but, he writes, he saw that it was being too densely reinforced, that it should be held lightly, and that the greater part of the garrison should be kept back for the immediate counter-attack; also that the divisional and corps reserves were not sufficiently distributed in depth.

Returning to Somme-Py and going up on to rising ground on the northern slope, he appreciated, looking back across the valley, the extreme value of the long southern slope as a great battle-position, with the new front line a few hundred yards behind the crest of the ridge. A disconnected line of sentry posts would have to be maintained along the crest itself to watch the ground in front, but they would withdraw to the new front line on attack to allow an artillery barrage to be maintained along the crest-line. The site of the new front line on the reverse slope would be difficult for the French to locate, and its range of 200 to 400 yards from the crest was sufficient for machine-gun and rifle fire to check any parts of the assault which escaped the artillery barrage. The extreme importance of enabling a close and intimate touch between the artillery observers and their batteries was especially evident, as he looked at the battlefield from this point of view. The whole of the 3,000 yards of depth of the southern slope, from crest to brook, could be overlooked from this northern side of the valley, and he considered that the artillery

Rough Cross Section of Py Brook valley position - (Champagne: Oct. 1915.

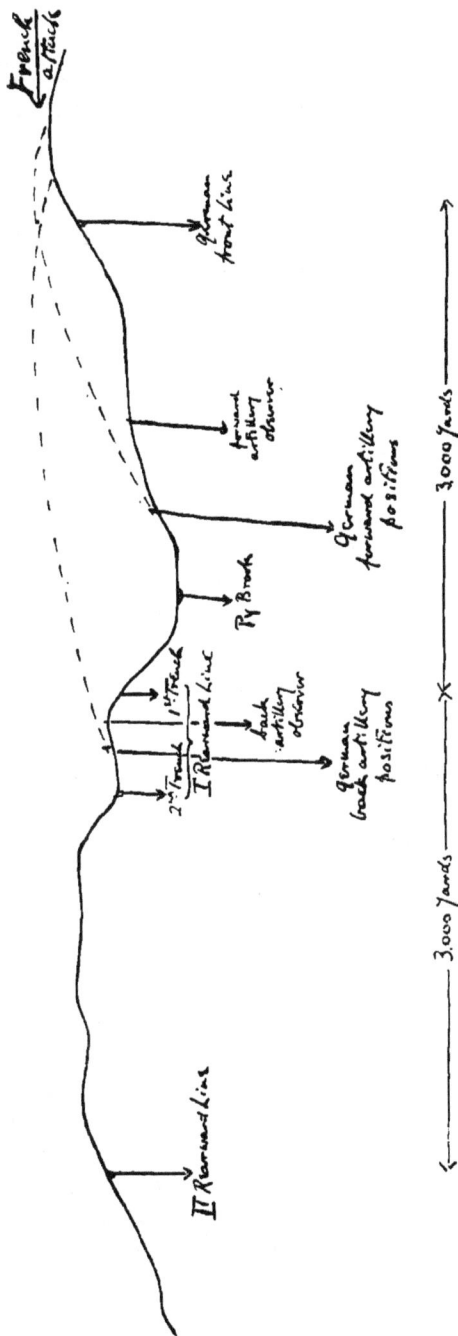

French
attack

German
front line

forward
artillery
observer

German
forward artillery
positions

Py Brook

1st Trench 1st French Line
2nd Trench II French Line

back
artillery
observer

German
back artillery
positions

II Reserve Line

←————— 3,000 yards —————→

←————— 3,000 yards —————→

Heights not to scale

SKETCH 6

observers should be well back near the batteries, or at least sufficiently far from the front line to avoid the effect and confusion of its bombardment prior to an assault. A further French advance down the southern slope would have to be made without the observed support of their artillery, whereas their every movement would be under observation by the German artillery observers. He saw that the first necessity for the defence was to form a strong artillery organization to take advantage of this vital weakness of the attack, and at the same time to give observed artillery support to the immediate counter-attack (see Sketch 6).

The Py valley lay parallel to the German line of defence for several miles, and he writes that owing to the dusk he was unable to see more of the battlefield farther west, beyond Saint-Marie-à-Py, before the continuation of the attack which he believed would take place the following morning. He had, however, in that short space of time, 5 p.m. to dusk on a September evening, seen enough to permit him to 'face with confidence any further offensives in this particularly important sector'. So confident was he of the success of his defence scheme that he ordered that same evening new wooden hutments to be built in the woods on the northern side of the valley to accommodate the garrison during the winter. In addition, as reserves became available, he intended to organize a succession of formations organized in great depth, at 2,000 to 3,000 yards' distance behind one another, which would be able to exert a constant forward pressure, by immediate counter-attack, against any French assault detachments which might break-in through the main line of resistance; each going forward to the position evacuated by the one in front as it moved up to the counter-attack. To give shelter and an alignment for the organization of these various échelons of reserves in depth, he therefore ordered a new Reserve Line, called the 1st Rearward (*rückwärtige*) Line, to be dug north of the Py brook, about 3,500 yards behind the existing front line in those places where the French attack had

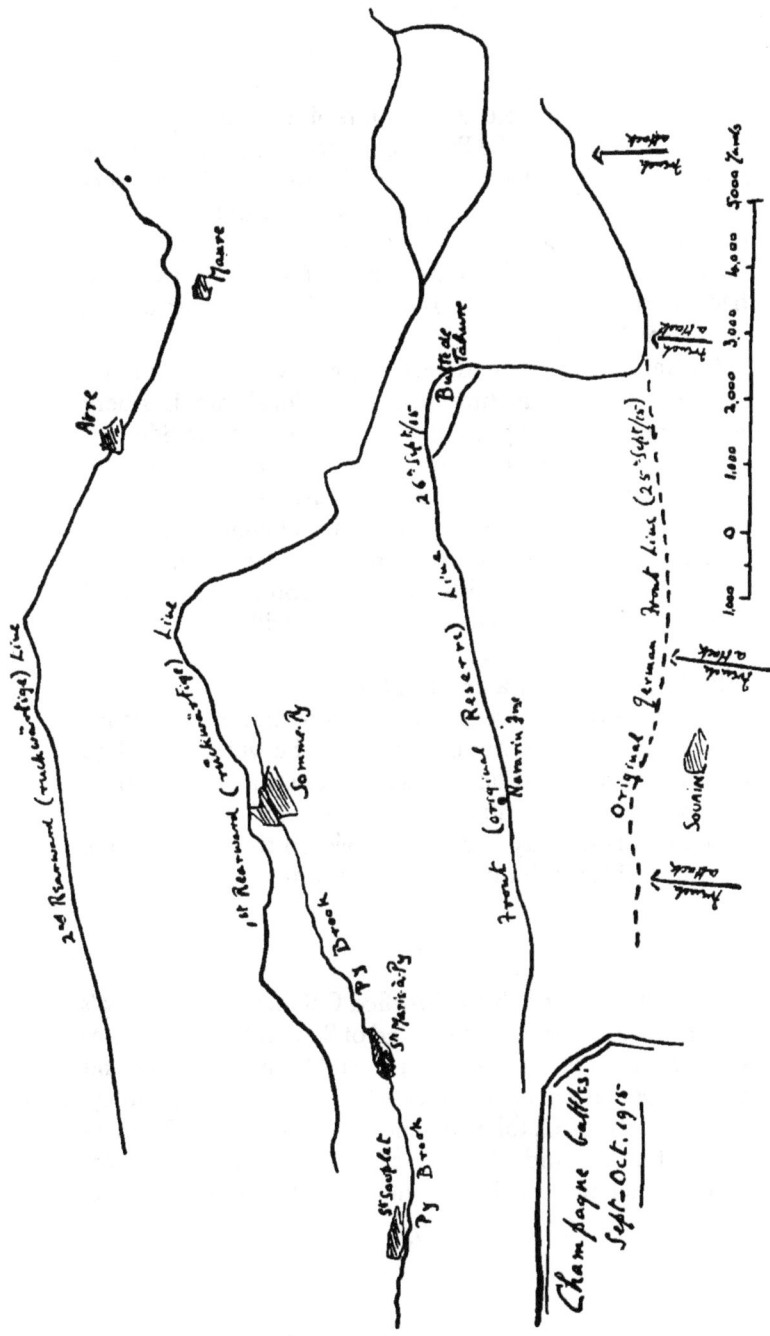

Champagne battles.
Sept.-Oct. 1915

SKETCH 7

2nd Reserve (rückwärtige) Line

Arre

Maure

1st Reserve (rückwärtige) Line

Somme Py

Py Brook

St Souplet

Py Brook

Ste Marie à Py

Front (original Reserve) Line

26°Sept/15

Butte de Tahure

Nanroy 3ng

Original German Front Line (25° Sept/15)

Souain

French attack

French attack

French attack

French attack

1,000   0   1,000   2,000   3,000   4,000   5,000 Yards

nearly reached it, and another, the 2nd Rearward Line, about 3,000 yards behind again (see Sketch 7).

So it was that those evening hours of the 26th September 1915 in the valley of the Py brook witnessed the birth of the idea of a mobile defence-in-depth, just as the village cemetery of Neuville-Saint-Vaast on that sunny morning of the 9th May 1915 saw the birth of the 'infiltration' doctrine for the attack; and the materialization of those two ideas became the principal progressive tactical achievements of the Great War of 1914–18.

Captain Laffargue had been powerless to give any practical effect to his meditations, but Colonel von Lossberg was armed with full powers. He motored on from Somme-Py to some of the corps and divisional headquarters, to each of which he explained his intentions and gave the necessary orders. But they involved a change of doctrine in many respects, which meant his own personal intervention in a multitude of different ways, and it is evidence of the exceptional courage, energy, and will-power of this man that he should have accomplished such a task successfully in the midst of a great battle.

He writes that he went to bed for the first time since his arrival at Vouziers at midnight on the 28th, two days afterwards; and that he slept so soundly that, although by an open window, a French air-raid failed to wake him, although about sixty bombs dropped on the village, some bursting within a hundred yards of him.

6

The subsequent fighting justified Colonel von Lossberg's optimistic forecast. Up to the end of September success was largely due to the favourably placed German artillery and their observation over the southern slope of the valley, but by early in October defence-in-depth of the infantry was achieved, and the corps and army reserves were ready écheloned back to a depth of five miles to meet the French offensives on the 6th to 8th and 31st October.

The experience gained in those battles was that immediate counter-attacks (*Gegenstösse*) by local reserves, supported by observed artillery and machine-gun fire, were the best means of retaining a hold on the front line, but that they must be delivered before the enemy had time to consolidate a line of defence; if they were too late Colonel von Lossberg, from his own observations, ordered that they should not be delivered, but that a methodical counter-attack (*Gegenangriff*), after a thorough preparation, which might take several days, was then the only procedure to adopt.

It was on these principles that the remaining battles in Champagne during the autumn of 1915 were fought, and successfully; a constant forward pressure during battle by counter-attack reserves écheloned in depth, with the recapture of the foremost line wherever lost, as the permanent objective; and if an immediate counter-attack was too late, then a methodically prepared counter-attack was eventually delivered. In all these counter-attacks the reverse slope on which the front position lay continued to give the defence every advantage. The faith of von Lossberg in the fact that 'we could concentrate our artillery fire by direct ground observation while the French could only use observation from the air' was well founded. In each of these battles the French artillery was unable to support the necessarily uneven progress of its infantry, while the German counter-attacks, delivered with the support of observed and concentrated artillery fire, were able to recapture the lost ground and take a great number of prisoners. The French made no further advance down the southern slope of the Py valley that winter.

An important feature of Colonel von Lossberg's activities during this period was the constant touch he maintained with the front-line units. Any free time he could spare he spent visiting the front-line commanders and in personal reconnaissance of different sectors of the position; he also divided the army front among the officers of his staff and each had to visit the battle area of his sector twice a week and ask the junior local commanders their requirements. These were forwarded to the divisional staffs concerned, and, if reasonable, had to be attended to at once. Colonel von Lossberg mentions that the reward he received for these untiring efforts to ease the privations of front-line units was the grateful recognition he was invariably given on his visits to them. He found this relationship between Army headquarters and the front line invaluable.

APPENDIX

Translation of French Fifth Army Instruction

5th Army. G. St. 3 Bureau.
No. 2043–3.   30.4.15

Construction of a Defensive Position

A. Construction of the Forward Battle Position

The existing front line defences in the Fifth Army sector were built up by degrees during the heavy fighting on our front in September 1914. They were extemporary, and built on no thought-out plan; efforts must therefore be made to improve them.

(*a*) In sectors where an attack is probable the position must consist of three lines of defence.

The first line is for the sentry groups; it must be strongly built but weakly garrisoned, and will be the first line of resistance. In front of it shelters for listening posts will be made.

The second line will form the main line of resistance in the event of the first line being broken through or being made useless for defence. This second line will therefore be strongly constructed, and must have sufficient dug-out accommodation for the garrison.

The third line will consist principally of shell-proof shelters for the reserves.

In this way there will be established a deep defence organization, to be a complete outpost system (line of sentries, outpost companies, and outpost reserves).

The presence of numerous communication trenches, well constructed between these three lines, will play a main role in the event of an attack.

In addition the strong points in the main line of resistance which have to be held at all costs must be strengthened. These strong-points must be turned into miniature forts, which will be able to continue to resist even though surrounded on all sides. They are to be held until they can be relieved by a victorious counter-attack.

(*b*) In the few sectors which are less threatened a single well-built defence line may suffice, but it must have a very strong wire entanglement in front and have as small a garrison as possible.

B. *Construction of a Second Defence Position*

The construction of a second defence position which will be able to offer further resistance can now be proceeded with. It must be completed in every detail and strengthened in insufficiently defended sectors.

This work will be carried out by the reserves in the sector, by labour companies, and by park-battalions who have good training for such work.

> (Signed) d'Esperey,
> Commanding the Fifth Army.

Chapter VI

THE SOMME CAMPAIGN:
July–November 1916

The winter of 1915–16 passed without official recognition being given by either side to any further alteration of doctrine to meet the rapidly changing conditions of a battlefield due to the increasing effect of the mass-production of munitions.

British G.H.Q. and French G.Q.G. continued to pin their faith on Weight of Metal; the artillery was to be the chief arm of offence and the infantry were to be the moppers-up of the battlefield. General Falkenhayn, too, kept to his original decision that the defensive battle was to be fought in the front trench, and that not a foot of it was to be given up; if lost, it was to be regained by an immediate counter-attack, irrespective of its tactical value.

General Falkenhayn's decision to retain the doctrine of the rigid defence of a line unconditionally is reflected in the German position on the Somme uplands, which was to become the main battlefield on the Western Front during the summer of 1916. In this position every detail of his construction programme of January 1915 had been completed, and more strongly than he ever anticipated. The original wire entanglement, five to ten yards in breadth, had now grown into two great belts of entanglement, each about thirty yards broad and fifteen yards apart. Masses of barbed wire of double and treble thickness were interlaced to iron stakes and trestles, three to five feet high, and

made an impassable barrier except for small gaps left here
and there for German patrols to pass through. The front
line, from being a single trench or breastwork, had become
three lines of trench 150 to 200 yards apart, one for the
sentry groups, the second (*Wohngraben*) for the front-trench
garrison to live in, and the third for the local supports.
Traverses ten yards thick had been built across these
trenches at frequent intervals to localize the bursts of the
heaviest shells and mortar bombs, and concrete recesses
had been dug deep into the parapet from which the
sentries could observe either directly or with a periscope.
The dug-outs, instead of being six to nine feet below
ground, as in the spring of 1915, had now been tunnelled
to a depth of twenty to thirty feet and at intervals of fifty
yards, each capable of holding some twenty-five men; and
at each end wooden steps led up a steep shaft to daylight
in the front-trench system. The intermediate line of strong-
points (*Stützpunkte*), about 1,000 yards behind the front
line, had been perfected (for example, the famous *Nordwerk*
and the Quadrilateral, the northern and southernmost of
the line of strong-points shown in Sketch 8). Communication trenches led back to the Reserve, now called the
Second Line, which was as strong and as heavily wired as
the first, and, being out of effective range of the mass of the
enemy's field batteries, would it was believed force the
enemy's artillery to make a new deployment before preparing it for assault. Following the experience of the autumn
battles in Champagne a Third Line, about 3,000 yards
behind again, had been begun in February and was almost
completed before the Somme battles opened. The artillery
arrangements had been equally carefully organized. The
whole front was divided into barrage sectors (*Sperrfeuer-
streifen*) and every officer in the front line was supposed to
know the batteries which were ready to form a barrage in
front of his trench and also those detailed to take on any
targets suddenly appearing on his front. To ensure co-
operation an extensive telephone system, which for five

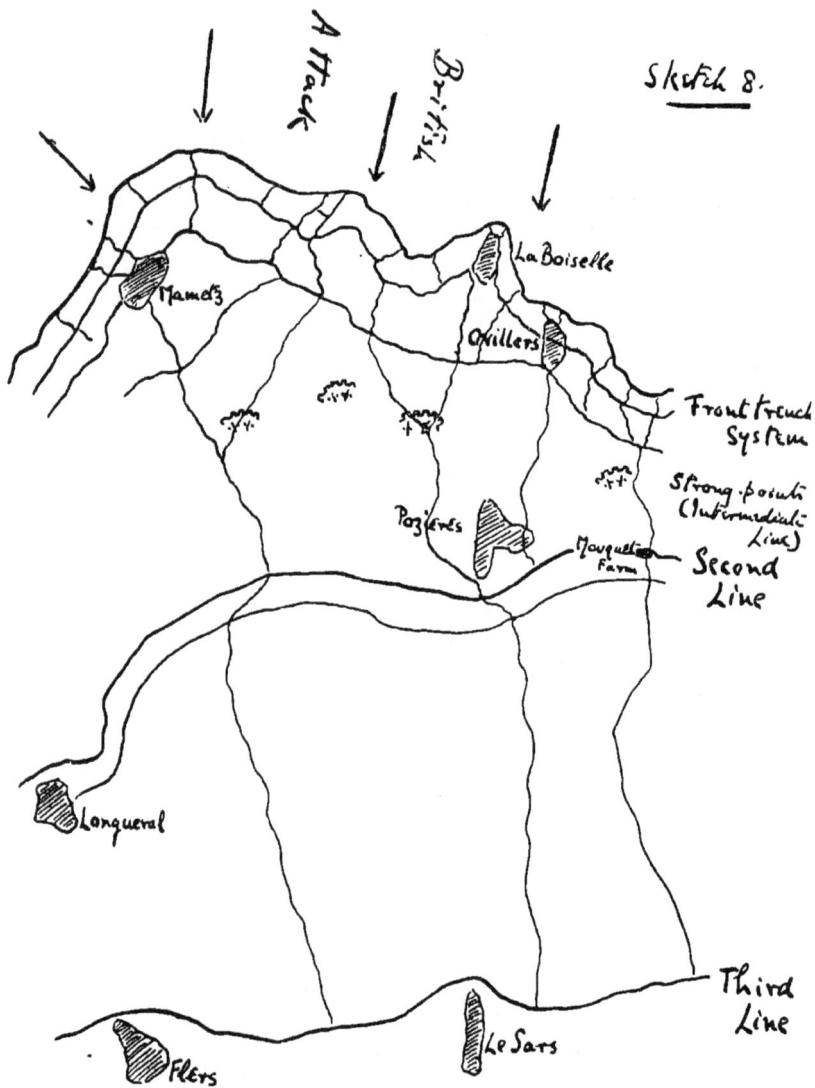

Sketch 8.

Attack British

La Boiselle

Mametz

Ovillers

Front trench System

Strong points (Intermediate Line)

Pozières

Mouquet Farm

Second Line

Longueval

Third Line

Flers

Le Sars

Sector of Somme Battlefront
1st July 1916

0   1,000   2,000   3,000   4,000   5,000 Yards

miles behind the front line was buried at a depth of six feet or more below the surface, connected the front trench direct with the batteries.

Although the position was of such apparent strength, it had two inherent weaknesses which, to the despair of many at O.H.L., General Falkenhayn took no steps to remedy. Firstly, the front-trench system was on a forward slope where it had been sited in the autumn of 1914, at a time when a long and wide field of fire was considered essential and when artillery observers were posted in the front line. It was therefore in full view of the enemy's ground observers, to whom the excavated chalk subsoil gave all the evidence they required. Secondly, the front defences were, as the junior members of the Operations Section had predicted, garrisoned more densely than ever, with the supports and reserves closer at hand; the custom of removing from their appointments commanders who failed to retake a lost sector had further increased this tendency to place the bulk of the defence garrison as near the front trench as possible.[1] For example, at Neuve Chapelle in March 1915 a front-line regiment had its support battalion 2,000 yards behind the front breastwork, and its reserve battalion 2,000 yards behind again; whereas on the Somme battlefront at the end of June 1916 the normal disposition of a front-line regiment was to have two battalions in or near the front trench system and its third battalion partly near the strongpoints in the intermediate line and partly in the Second Line, that is all within 2,000 yards of the front line and the bulk within 1,000 yards of it. The fact that these supports and reserves were in deep dug-out shelters was not likely to prevent a far greater proportion of losses once the battle began.

The combined result of these two defects was that the bulk of the defence garrison was in a forward-slope position, so placed that it would receive the full brunt of the great accumulation of the enemy's artillery ammunition

[1] Bauer, *Der grosse Krieg in Feld und Heimat* (Tübingen, 1921).

directed by observed fire on clearly marked trench lines. This, the critics maintained, was due to General Falkenhayn's persistence in the doctrine of holding the front line rigidly by obsolete methods. The improved methods begun by Colonel von Lossberg the previous autumn to achieve the same purpose, that is by holding the front line thinly and, if possible, on a reverse-slope position, had not been adopted.

In addition, General Falkenhayn's reputation had suffered a bad setback through his conduct of the attack on Verdun in February. It was directed on the east side of the Meuse only, whereas, Colonel von Lossberg writes at the time of the preliminary conference: 'there was scarcely one among those present who did not see that an attack on the east bank alone must very soon come under a heavy French enfilade artillery fire from the west bank.' Moreover, the attack frontage was too narrow, and he adds that he 'could not imagine an attack so planned had much chance of capturing Verdun'. The effort was, however, made and the fighting for the fortress continued all through the summer without success; the battle gradually losing its original purpose to capture Verdun and becoming one of wearing down the French Army.

Towards the end of May, when preparations disclosed the project of a great British and French offensive astride the Somme, General Falkenhayn had intended to meet it with a powerful counter-offensive which he hoped would give the British Army a knock-out blow; but owing to the great losses sustained by the Germans during the Verdun battles this scheme had to be abandoned and replaced by that of a passive and rigid defence; in other words, by an elaborated continuation of the previous defensive battles.

I

The plan for the offensive undertaken by the French and British armies on the Somme uplands in July 1916 was

again an optimistic one. The impressive ammunition supplies which had accumulated during the winter and spring
banished the idea of 'attrition', and it was believed that no
living creature could exist under the hail of shells and
clouds of gas with which it was intended to drench the
German position. The intention, therefore, was to make
another attempt to break-through in the old manner.

The British Fourth Army was to assault on a frontage of
fourteen miles between the French left at Maricourt, on
the northern bank of the Somme, and Serre, north of the
Ancre. It was then to press forward eastward across the
rolling uplands of the Somme, a great open expanse of
chalk downs, and secure the line Bapaume–Guillemont, an
advance of six to seven miles. From here it would advance
to the Bapaume–Péronne road, keeping touch with the
French, who were to co-operate on the right by an assault
on a frontage of nine miles and a subsequent advance of
about the same distance, to a front Sailly–Saillisel–Péronne.
Three British cavalry divisions were to be ready to take
advantage of any gap made and to push through to
Bapaume, ready to wheel northwards behind the enemy's
flank and rear, but the establishment of a position on the
Bapaume–Péronne road would conclude the first stage of
the operation. Efforts would then be made to work northward up the German defences between the Ancre and Arras
and to press on eastward down into the plain of Douai,
capturing the important rail and road centres of Douai
and Cambrai.

The offensive was to begin with a prolonged bombardment lasting five days, the infantry assault to be delivered
on the 29th of June. On the 28th, however, the French
reported that their preparations were not complete and at
their request, and for the additional reason of the bad
weather, the infantry assault was postponed for forty-eight
hours.

For the preliminary bombardment on the British front
and for covering the attack 1,513 guns and howitzers had

been placed in position behind the battlefront, averaging a field gun to every twenty yards and a heavy gun to every sixty yards of front. Over two million shells were collected in the ammunition dumps behind the battery positions and 1,628,000 were actually fired by the British artillery during the preliminary bombardment and the first day of the assault.

The Germans had seven divisions in the front line, with four in reserve, against the assault of seventeen British and French divisions in the front line, followed by fifteen more divisions in support. Their inferiority in artillery and air-craft was still greater. The British and French had of each of those arms over three times the strength of the Germans in the sector attacked, and ten times the amount of artillery ammunition, according to German estimates.[1]

In order to give some idea of the effect of a long bombardment by the mass of metal the British had accumulated behind the Somme battlefront on a position such as the Germans had created by the end of June 1916, I have made a short summary of several German accounts.[2]

2

The night of the 23rd–24th June passed quietly and day broke clear with the promise of a Sunday of blue skies.

The Germans in their deep tunnelled dug-outs in the front line had finished their morning coffee and the night sentries had been relieved when suddenly, at 6 a.m., a great mass of shells burst with a thundering crash on and along the whole front. The day sentries, looking out from

[1] Von Lossberg, p. 250.
[2] Gerster, *Die Schwaben an der Ancre* (Heilbronn, 1920); Junger, *In Stahlgewittern* (Berlin, 1922); *Die Bayern im Grossen Kriege, 1914-18* (Bayerischen Kriegsarchiv, Munich, 1923); Gerster, *Das Württemberg, Res. Inf. Regt. Nr. 119 im Weltkrieg, 1914-18* (Stuttgart, 1920); Holtz, *Das Wurttemburg, Res. Inf. Regt. Nr. 121 im Weltkrieg, 1914-18* (Stuttgart, 1922); *War Diary of the German 55th Res. Inf. Regt. from the 24th of June to the 2nd of July 1916*, captured during the Somme fighting.

their bomb-proof shelters towards the British trenches, saw no movement there, and the British wire entanglements appeared normal, showing that no immediate attack was to be expected. Above the German lines, however, hung a mass of small white clouds as the shrapnel burst, their bullets clattering into the German trenches and on to the roofs and walls of the ruined villages near by. This violent tornado lasted some hours, until about midday the shelling changed to a steady, carefully aimed fire, as if the British batteries were competing with one another in a shooting tournament, but during the afternoon the strength of the bombardment increased again, the rumbling of heavy batteries mingling with the noise of the field guns. Towards evening the sky clouded over and a light rain fell, laying the dust and making the ground about the trenches, churned up by the shells, a sea of mud.

During the following day, 25th June, the fire of the British heavy batteries increased, and whereas on the previous day nine-tenths of the fire had been shrapnel or from guns of small calibre, the heavy batteries were now in the majority. Their shells crashed into the German trenches, the ground shook and the dug-outs tottered. Here and there the sides of a trench fell in, completely blocking it. Masses of earth came tumbling into the deep dug-outs, obstructing the entrances to many of them. By evening some sectors of the German front line were already unrecognizable and had become crater-fields.

From the intensity of the fire in certain places, particularly astride the Ancre, north and south of Thiepval, about Ovillers, Fricourt, and Mametz, it could be roughly foretold at which points the British intended to assault, and that night the brigade and divisional staffs made their defensive preparations accordingly and ordered the Second Line to be garrisoned by reserves. The fire slackened somewhat during the night, but early on the 26th increased again. In the early hours, about 5 a.m., clouds of chlorine gas crossed no-man's-land from the British trenches north of

the Ancre towards Serre and Beaumont, and again, about
11 a.m., a thick, yellow-brown mist of gas and smoke moved
from the British line towards Fricourt on the southern part
of the front. The dense fumes reached the German position
and, being heavier than air, filled every crevice in the
ground. They crept like live things down the steps of the
deep dug-outs, filling them with poison until sprayers
negatived their effect. At midday the bombardment increased to a still greater intensity in the central sector
about Thiepval, and then suddenly stopped as if preliminary to an infantry assault. The German sentries, looking
towards the British trenches, saw, however, no sign of
infantry, but instead another dense cloud of gas moving
slowly towards them. This, together with the previous
bombardment, led them to believe an infantry attack to
be imminent. Gas-masks were hurriedly put on, and the
men climbed up out of the earth and lined the edges of the
craters and what remained of the German front trench.
Red rockets gave the signal to the German artillery, which
quickly placed a barrage of shells in no-man's-land to
check a possible infantry advance behind the gas, but the
yellow fumes passed over the German line, closely followed
by reddish-brown smoke clouds. The battle area was
enveloped in a dark, muddy fog, but as there was still no
sign of an infantry attack the men crawled back again into
the depths of the earth.

During the afternoon aerial torpedoes (such as Captain
Laffargue had advised in May 1915), fired from heavy
mortars in the British front line, made their first appearance. Coming down almost perpendicularly from a great
height, these monsters bored deep into the ground and
then burst. Tons of earth and great blocks of chalk and
rock were hurled into the air, leaving craters, some twelve
feet deep and fifteen feet in diameter. Only deep dug-outs
of great strength could stand the shock, and the weaker
ones were crushed to atoms with all they contained. The
Germans, who up till now had endured the inferno almost

with indifference, began to feel alarmed. Every nerve was strained as they sat listening to the devilish noise and waited for the dull thud of the next torpedo as it buried itself in the ground, and then the devastating explosion. The concussion put out the candles and acetylene lights in the deepest dug-outs. The walls rocked like the sides of a ship and the darkness was filled with smoke and gas fumes.

A fresh note, too, now mingled with the thundering of the heavy guns, as the shells from a British rival to the German 'Big Bertha' shrieked through the air against the redoubts and principal strong points in and behind the German lines. A hail of shells of lesser calibre was also poured into the villages near the front, such as Miraumont, Irles, Grandcourt, Courcellette, Pys, and Pozières, the ruin of which was quickly completed. The roofs and walls of the cottages collapsed, blocking the streets, and the foundation of the roads was torn up, the deep craters preventing any traffic along them. Some of the villages near the front were also badly affected by the gas that swept over them from time to time; shrubs and plants were withered by it; rats, mice, moles, and much else came out of holes and corners and lay dead about the place; civilians with streaming eyes and choking for breath implored the Germans to give them gas-masks, but instead, they were compulsorily transported from the danger zone. As the cellars gave little cover against the heaviest shells the villages were also gradually evacuated by most of the troops sheltering in them.

The 27th and 28th June brought a similar picture of continuous devastation, which was increased by heavy rains. The bombardment continued to appear without method, an intense and apparently wild shelling, then carefully observed heavy artillery fire by individual batteries, then trench-mortar bombs and aerial torpedoes or gas attacks, or again a sudden tornado of shells, with occasional periods of complete quiet. During calm intervals at night patrols would move forward from the British trenches across no-man's-land to inspect the damage done and to see if any Germans were still alive. Some of these patrols were captured and, from statements made, it was concluded that a combined French and British attack was to be delivered on both sides of the Ancre and the Somme at 5 a.m. on the 29th June.[1] At that hour the whole German line stood to arms, all units were ready at their posts, reinforcements had been brought up during the night, and the artillery ammunition supplies replenished. The morning, however, passed in comparative quiet and no attack developed. In the afternoon the British bombardment was resumed with all its former violence, swelling at times to gigantic proportions and then falling off, only to concentrate the more intensely on some small sector of the front. Then suddenly it would begin again along the whole line and move slowly eastward towards the rear defences, settling for a time on the villages, redoubts, and battery positions. The British gunners, whom the Germans imagined sweating through the heat of the day at their work of destruction, appeared to be indefatigable. Now and again the storm of shells would be followed by a gas attack with occasionally a small infantry advance, as if once more to test the strength of the German defences. In most cases, however, the trench garrison had sufficient warning from the sentries with their periscopes, either in the concrete recesses, or, if those had been destroyed, from the dug-out entrances, and a heavy machine-gun and rifle fire greeted the attacks. Few reached the German position.

The 30th June was a repetition of the previous six days. The German front defences no longer existed as such. Wire entanglements had been swept away; iron stakes and posts dotted along the front, with thick strands of barbed wire

---

[1] In the regimental history of the 119th Reserve Infantry Regiment it is stated that this information was given by a Polish Jew (British Regiment not given), captured by their 10th Company. The 29th was the original date of assault, until postponed the previous day.

knotted around them, were all that remained to mark the position of this first, and exceedingly strong, protection of the front-trench system. The trench itself had gone. A succession of shell-craters replaced it, and half-closed holes in the earth marked where the exits from the deep dug-outs had still been kept open. The steps down to them were, however, buried in the fallen earth and stones, so much so that it was difficult to get a footing to climb up the steep slope to daylight. In some cases both entrances to a dug-out had been completely blocked up, and since there was no underground gallery to connect one dug-out with another the men inside were suffocated.[1] The look-out shelters and bomb-proof observation posts were now a heap of ruins, a mass of twisted steel rails and broken blocks of concrete. All the communication trenches had also been blocked, and many of them completely destroyed.

The colossal expenditure of money, guns, ammunition, and human energy had done its work and the German position seemed ready for assault. Every yard of ground had been churned up and churned again, the land being reduced to a desert of mud and shell-craters. Woods were uprooted and slashed to pieces, houses and cottages were razed to the ground and their ruins crushed to powder, so that whole villages were no longer recognizable. In spite of the devastation and chaos on the surface, the defenders in those of the deep underground dug-outs still intact had, however, survived the ordeal. For seven days and nights they had sat on the long wooden benches or on the wire beds in the evil-smelling dug-outs, some twenty feet and more below ground. The incessant noise and the need for constant watchfulness had allowed them little sleep, and ever-present, too, had been the fear that their dug-outs might at any time become a living tomb from which escape would be impossible. Warm food had seldom reached them

[1] As a result of the experiences during this bombardment, the German dug-outs were afterwards connected in series by underground galleries.

during the bombardment, so that they had had to live on the supplies, three dumps each of 2,000 rations in each company sector, as well as supplies of chocolate and mineral waters, previously stored in the front line.

After a restless night, during which the British artillery concentrated its fire chiefly against the rear defences and communications, the 1st July broke clear and cloudless. With the first light of day British aeroplanes filled the air and captive balloons ascended all along the western horizon. The early hours between dawn and sunrise were comparatively quiet apart from isolated shell bursts. At 6.30 a.m., however, a bombardment of an intensity as yet unparalleled suddenly burst out again along the whole front. At first it was most severe in the centre, about Thiepval and Beaumont, but it quickly spread over the entire line from north of the Ancre to south of the Somme. For the next hour continuous lines of great fountains of earth, rocks, smoke, and débris, played constantly into the air and, as one German describes it, it seemed as if all the fiends of the infernal regions had been loosed to tear up and destroy the entire district. The giant explosions of the heaviest shells were the only distinguishable noises in the continuous thunder of the bombardment and the short, regular intervals of their bursts gave it a certain rhythm. All trace of the front-trench system was now lost, and, with only a few exceptions, all the telephone cables connecting it with the rear lines and batteries were destroyed, in spite of the six feet of depth at which they had been laid. Through the long trench-periscopes held up out of the dug-outs could be seen a mass of steel helmets above the British parapet. The storm-troops were evidently ready, standing shoulder to shoulder and there was little doubt that the infantry assault was imminent. The Germans in their dug-outs, each with a beltful of hand-grenades, therefore waited ready, rifle in hand, for the bombardment to lift from the front trench to the rear defences. It was of vital importance not to lose a second in reaching the open

before the British infantry could arrive at the dug-out
entrances.

3

At 7.30 a.m. the storm of shells ceased as suddenly as it
had begun an hour earlier. In broad daylight under the
cloudless blue sky of a midsummer morning the assault
began. 'No braver or more determined men ever faced an
enemy than those sons of the British Empire who went
"over the top" on the 1st July 1916,' writes the British
official historian. 'Never before had the ranks of a British
army on the field of battle contained the finest of all classes
of the nation in physique, brains, and education. And they
were volunteers, not conscripts. If ever a decisive victory
was to be won it was to be expected now.'

The sudden cessation of the terrific bombardment also
acted as a signal for the Germans that the assault was
imminent, and the German accounts mentioned above give
a good idea of it from their point of view. The Germans at
once clambered up the steep shafts to daylight and ran to
the nearest craters, singly or in groups. Machine guns with
their heavy ammunition boxes were pulled up out of the
dug-outs and hurriedly placed in position, and a rough
firing line was thus established. The various German
diaries, as also statements made by German prisoners taken
at the time, show that the shell-craters were considered as
good or better for defensive purposes than the original
trenches; in the trenches their position was known, but
when they lay among the craters it was impossible to locate
them. The defence was also made more mobile, as the men
could rapidly take up fresh positions in other shell-holes
either in front, in rear, or facing the flank.

It seems, from reading the German accounts, that the
success or failure of the attack depended in great measure
on the closeness with which the advancing lines of infantry
followed the artillery barrage, an arrangement which
apparently was not carried out uniformly by the British

assaulting divisions. In some cases, particularly opposite Thiepval and on the southern part of the front about Montauban, Mametz, and Fricourt, the leading assaulting lines had advanced fifteen to twenty minutes before the conclusion of the first period of the bombardment and lay out in the open close to the German position, so that when, at 7.30 a.m., the artillery lifted from the front trench they reached the entrances to the German dug-outs before the Germans had had time to clamber up out of them. Where this was done the assaulting lines were able to enter the German front-trench system with little loss. In other parts of the front, however, the infantry advance did not leave the British front trench till the first artillery lift, at 7.30 a.m., and the Germans were thus given time to get into position among the shell-craters.

In the Thiepval sector, for example, the history of the German 99th Regiment states that the British overran their position in the first rush, and that before the Germans had time to emerge from their dug-outs, British sentries were standing on guard at the entrances with apparently no inclination to descend into the unknown world beneath, and contenting themselves with throwing down hand-grenades and stink-bombs from time to time.

On the other hand, the history of the 119th Reserve Regiment in the Beaumont Hamel sector tells a very different story. It says that wave after wave of men rose from the British front trench and began to move forward as if on parade, their bayonets glistening in the sun. Eight waves in all were seen advancing across the 300 yards of no-man's-land, carrying with them plank bridges and steps for crossing the German trenches, but before the leading wave had reached the line of the German entanglement the German companies to right and left were able to get out into the open. Such a hail of bullets from machine guns and rifles was poured into the solid mass of advancing lines that it was checked almost immediately, and the supporting columns were unable to leave the British front trench.

This fire was intensified by cross-fire from machine guns firing over the heads of the front-line defenders.

Similar is the account given by the 180th Regiment in the Ovillers sector. While the Germans were clambering out from the dug-outs and taking up their positions in the craters near by, a series of extended lines of British infantry began to move forward from the British trenches. The first line appeared to continue without end to right and left. It was quickly followed by a second line, then a third, and a fourth. They came on at a steady, comfortable pace, as if expecting to find nothing alive in the front trenches and only perhaps a weak resistance in the second and third line trenches. Some 'appeared to be carrying Kodaks and stopping to take photographs which would perpetuate the memory of their triumphal march across the German defences'. The front line, preceded by a thin line of skirmishers and bombers, was now half-way across no-man's-land. 'Get ready!' was passed along the German front from crater to crater, and heads peered over the crater-edges as final positions were taken up for the best view and machine guns were mounted firmly in place. A few moments later, as the leading British line approached, the rattle of machine-gun and rifle fire broke out along the whole line of craters and a hail of lead swept into the advancing lines. Some fired kneeling so as to get a better target over the broken ground, while others stood up in the excitement of the moment, regardless of their own safety, to fire into the crowd of men in front of them. Red rockets sped up into the blue sky as a signal to the artillery and immediately afterwards, a mass of shells from the German batteries in rear tore through the air and burst among the advancing lines. Whole sections seemed to fall, and the rear formations, moving in closer order, quickly scattered. The advance rapidly crumbled under this hail of shells and bullets. All along the line men could be seen throwing their arms into the air and collapsing, never to move again. Badly wounded rolled about in their agony, and others less severely injured crawled to the nearest shell-holes for shelter. The British soldier, however, in the words of the author of *Die Schwaben an der Ancre*, has no lack of courage, and once his hand is set to the plough he is not easily turned from his purpose. The extended lines, though badly shaken and with many gaps, now came on all the faster. Instead of a leisurely walk they covered the ground in short rushes at the double, halting for a moment where the ground gave cover. In places the leading troops had reached within a stone's-throw of the German crater-line, and, while some Germans continued to fire at point-blank range, others threw hand-grenades among them. The British bombers answered back, throwing grenades into the craters, while the infantry rushed forward with bayonets fixed. The noise of battle now became indescribable. The shouting of orders and the shrill British cheers as they charged forward could be heard above the violent and intense fusillade of machine guns and rifles and the bursting bombs, and above the deep thunderings of the artillery and the shell explosions. Again and again the extended lines of British infantry broke against the German defence like waves against a cliff, only to be beaten back and then to be brought forward again by fresh waves of men, which in their turn were decimated and checked by a hail of lead. It was an 'amazing spectacle of unexampled gallantry, courage, and bulldog determination on both sides'. By the evening, however, the attack had come to a standstill, and the 180th Infantry Regiment was still in possession of the whole of the trace of its original front-trench system.

Just as the weather conditions were similar to those of that sunny May morning the previous year on Aubers Ridge, so had been the course of the battle on the greater part of the front, and for similar reasons. As then, there had been no surprise; the long bombardment had given ample warning of the exact frontage of assault, even if the actual day or hour was not known. As then, too, there was no covering fire worthy the name, to support the infantry. Both Sir Douglas Haig and the army commanders emphasized at various conferences before the battle that 'nothing could exist at the conclusion of the bombardment in the area covered by it', and the conclusion drawn was that the assault need not be a race for the German dug-out entrances, but 'something to be carried out at leisure'. Such lack of imagination is astonishing, considering that the depth of the German dug-outs out of shell-reach was known, and that the German powers of endurance had already been demonstrated on many occasions. Neither was the barrage of shells which was to go in front of the assault a substitute for covering fire; it was by time-table and unobserved, so that it moved irrespective of any checks to the infantry advance; the German machine guns beyond it fired through it, and those nearer took shelter until it had passed. The plan of attack therefore suffered once more from being based on a doctrine of fire-effect preceding movement, instead of fire-effect combined with movement.

By the evening of this first day of the Somme campaign, on a fourteen-mile front of assault only three miles of the German front-trench system had been occupied, and the remainder the Germans still held. The British casualties during the day were 57,470, including over 19,000 killed, or died of wounds. The German casualties during the bombardment and first day of the battle are not ascertainable, but the number of British killed on that first day alone was more than the entire garrison of the German front-trench system before the battle.

The *British Official History*, in its summing-up of the battle, says that 'for this disastrous loss of the finest manhood of the United Kingdom and Ireland there was only a small gain of ground to show', and it considers with good cause that the reason 'greater success was not gained was as much due to faulty tactical direction from the General Staff, and lack of experience in the higher ranks, as to rawness in the lower ranks'.

4

During the offensive on the 1st July the French had reached and occupied the Second (Reserve) Line in the sector west of Péronne. German Second Army headquarters, the frontage of which included that of the entire Franco-British offensive, thereupon decided to abandon the Second Line there and to use the reserves to occupy and hold a new and shorter line behind it. General Falkenhayn arrived at the Second Army headquarters late in the afternoon, and on hearing of this order expressed his displeasure, as it was contrary to the principle upon which his conception of the defensive battle was based, namely that 'not one foot of ground must be given up, and if lost must be retaken by immediate counter-attack at all costs'. He made the chief of staff, General Grünert, responsible for the order, and, though not cancelling it, decided to replace him by Colonel von Lossberg, to whom this second opportunity therefore came in a very similar manner to the first.

The offer of this new appointment reached Colonel von Lossberg by telephone at 11.30 p.m. that evening, and he was asked to go at once to Mézières to see General Falkenhayn, who had returned there. Arriving in Mézières at 1 a.m., he requested from General Falkenhayn a promise that the attacks at Verdun would be stopped at once in order that sufficient supplies and reinforcements should be available for the Somme defensive battles, which were certainly only beginning. After considerable hesitation General Falkenhayn, on shaking hands, gave this promise, but as Colonel von Lossberg mentions in his book, it was not kept, and the attacks on Verdun continued until General Falkenhayn was relieved of his command two months later. The failure to keep it was to affect the entire conduct of the defence during the early Somme battles.

Colonel von Lossberg arrived at Second Army headquarters in Saint-Quentin at 5 a.m. in the morning, by car from Mézières. He asked permission from General Fritz von Below, the Second Army commander, to spend the day visiting the battlefront and obtained full powers to give on the spot any instructions he might find necessary for employing the few reserves available. At 7.30 a.m. he left by car to visit some of the divisional headquarters, and then went on to Hill 110 north of Péronne, which lay under heavy artillery fire. This commanding position overlooked a wide panorama of the Somme district, which he now saw for the first time. There was no definite battlefield such as that offered by the valley of the Py brook in Champagne in the previous September; the country here was a rolling upland, with chalk subsoil, dotted with numerous small woods, and with well-built villages and farms. North of the river, where the British lay, it was, however, well suited to both frontal and flank observation and fire-effect for artillery; also he considered that the conditions were good for an infantry defence, especially as the many villages would be adaptable for a determined resistance; but he could see for himself the great superiority held by the enemy in the air, and watched their low-flying aeroplanes machine-gunning German infantry incessantly and unmolested. After spending an hour on Hill 110, he visited a number of front-line units farther north, and to all he repeated that every foot of ground was to be contested, and that in no circumstances, even such as the heaviest bombardment or an infantry attack with greatly superior numbers, was ground to be abandoned. This order which had been applied successfully throughout the Champagne battles, was also to be the basis of the defence during the Somme campaign.

It was late in the evening before he arrived back in Saint-Quentin, and after discussion with General von Below it was agreed that the defence should be conducted as during the Champagne battles; that is, the foremost line was to be held thinly but determinedly to the last, and wherever lost the defensive battle was to be fought offensively by immediate counter-attack (*Gegenstösse*) by the supports and reserves until recaptured. If the immediate counter-attack failed to dislodge the invader a deliberate counter-attack (*Gegenangriff*) after careful preparation was to be delivered. A special order was issued to this effect, adding that every leader was to see that his men were imbued with this instruction, and that an enemy advance could only be over dead bodies.

During his first day's visit Colonel von Lossberg had decided to overhaul the entire system of communication. The telephone system back to army headquarters from the battlefront was inadequate; laid too near the front, many of the cables were already broken in several places, and he ordered a new line to be laid out parallel to, but out of effective artillery range of, the battle line, with branches leading forward to the various battle-headquarters. He gave special attention to the artillery command organization, and ordered that where possible the divisional field artillery and heavy artillery commanders in each divisional sector should have their battle-headquarters near to one another. He also impressed the need for siting the artillery observation posts some hundreds of yards behind the foremost line instead of in it, an improvement introduced during the Champagne battles.

5

In the early Somme battles the difficulty of the defence was chiefly lack of reserves. Although Colonel von Lossberg frequently, during telephone conversations, reminded General Falkenhayn of his promise to stop the battle for Verdun, the reply was always evasive, and so long as that battle continued so long was the supply of infantry, artillery, aeroplanes, and munitions to the Somme area quite inadequate. Reinforcements arrived spasmodically and had to be sent up piecemeal by battalions, or even companies, to fill gaps in the line wherever needed, so that the organization of an échelon of reserves which had been effected so successfully in the later Champagne battles was not practicable. The result was that divisions could not be relieved when they needed it and so lost most of their best men; a loss which was far-reaching and irreparable so long as the war lasted.

On the 17th July the Somme battlefront was divided into two, the Somme river forming approximately the dividing line. The Second Army took over the southern half, and a new First Army was formed to fight the battle in the northern half, from the Somme northwards to Monchy-au-Bois, a frontage of over twenty miles. This First Army, to which most of the headquarters of the Second were transferred, including its commander, General Fritz von Below, and its chief of staff, Colonel von Lossberg, was destined to carry the main burden of the Somme campaign.

6

After the failure of the 1st July, Sir Douglas Haig decided to return to the idea of 'attrition', the artillery conquering a small area of ground by a thorough bombardment and the infantry occupying it. There was consequently no element of surprise in the British attacks, and the Germans had ample time to take the necessary precautions. They had learnt, for example, that it was safer to avoid trenches and for small groups of men to live in shell-holes with a waterproof covering; so that, as the British artillery continued to concentrate their fire mainly on trench lines and believed strong points, a large proportion of the shells was wasted and the British infantry were killed in thousands doing their menial task of 'mopping up' ground which had not been conquered by the artillery.

The 'kitchen-maid' aspect of the infantry arm adopted by Sir Douglas Haig and the senior British commanders was further exemplified by the manner in which the first tanks were employed on the 15th September, a later offensive of the Somme campaign. They were sent on ahead to carry out independent tasks irrespective of the progress of the infantry advance, and the infantry were to 'mop-up' whatever they chose to conquer. In practice, with such orders, neither could support the other, and most of the tanks which reached their distant objectives remained as valuable German captures and disclosed their secrets. The fire-effect of the tanks, like that of the artillery, had preceded the infantry movement instead of co-operating with it, and failed in its purpose.

The limited objective attack had, however, made the defence more difficult. As the German front line was almost incessantly under artillery fire, it had gradually become a crater-field of shell-holes. No dug-outs were left, the wire entanglements disappeared, trenches became impassable, and even the second line of little value as shelter. For this reason the position had lost its shape; instead of a front-trench system there was only a foremost line of occupied shell-holes, with supports and reserves in more shell-holes farther back or in any available cover. When attacked, the foremost line of shell-holes, thinly held by small groups of men, often in twos and threes and about twenty yards apart, with an occasional machine-gun crew, was frequently overrun by the first impetus of an assault, and the assaulting infantry were then themselves able rapidly to take up a line of defence along a row of shell-holes a few hundred yards farther on before the immediate counter-attack (*Gegenstöss*) by the German local reserves could be organized and reach them.

The German remedy to counter these offensives with limited objectives was to deliver a well-prepared deliberate counter-attack (*Gegenangriff*) periodically on a wide front to recapture the more important tactical points, such as Longueval and Poziéres, which had been lost. Colonel von Lossberg planned a number of counter-attacks of this kind during the early Somme battles, but most of them had to be abandoned owing to the lack of adequate reserves of men, artillery, and ammunition.

7

During the periods between battles attempts were made to connect up the occupied shell-holes by a trench for intercommunication, but such a trench was quickly seen by the enemy's air observers, and it was generally evacuated when a bombardment began, the garrison occupying shell-holes a few hundred yards away, generally in front. In this way the infantry, no longer tied to one place, acquired freedom of movement. The foremost line, though it had to be held at all costs, became really a zone or defended area within which the front units moved as the situation demanded.

The system of defence from shell-holes had the advantage that the enemy's artillery had no recognizable target in the isolated shelters and machine-gun nests. It had to batter a whole area of ground, using an immense quantity of ammunition, instead of a known and easily located trench-line. The importance of trench-lines as rallying centres was, however, appreciated and as soon as labour was available, the construction of a new series of back lines and switch-trenches was begun. The siting of these trenches was carried out according to Colonel von Lossberg's experience in the Champagne battles. Especial attention was given to the position of the artillery observers. Previously these had generally been near the front line of infantry, but now the artillery observation line was the first to be selected and the main infantry line of resistance was placed 500 to to 1,500 yards in front of it, and if possible 200 to 400 yards behind a crest-line on a reverse slope which the artillery observers could overlook. A short field of fire had been found sufficient to stop an attack with machine guns and rifle fire, and along the crest itself were only shelter-pits for infantry observers or listening posts. A similar line was prepared 2,000 to 3,000 yards farther back, and as this line would probably be close in front of the mass of the field battery emplacements supporting the main line of resistance it was called the artillery protective line (*Artillerie Schutz Stellung*). In this way, should an attack penetrate to the back of the forward defended area of shell-holes it would be confronted by a new deep position ready for occupation by reserves. A large number of labour companies were employed to assist in all this construction work.

The rallying lines of the Champagne battles had therefore become carefully sited defensive positions demanding a long artillery preparation and a most determined and well-supported infantry to attack, and the influence of the Py valley position can be recognized in these back positions of the Somme battlefields.

An incident which had the effect of hurrying on their construction is worth mention as an example of German methodical procedure. About midnight on the 14th July Colonel von Lossberg was rung up on the telephone from two different report centres, both saying that British troops had broken through between Longueval and Bazentin and were near Flers, which was two miles behind the front line. There had been a British offensive that morning, and as the infantry had broken into the position to a depth of 2,000 yards on a frontage of 6,000 yards, the news seemed very possible. He at once ordered three divisions, two from the south and one from the north of Flers, from reserve about sixteen miles distant, to move by motor-lorries and block the northern and southern flanks of the break-in and, if necessary, attack. Two more divisions were also ordered forward from more distant places to be in a position early the following morning to co-operate in a combined counter-attack from front and flanks, to be arranged by the Corps commander concerned. He also sent two staff officers by car, one to the north and one to the south of Flers, to find out the facts. It was not till

10 a.m. the next morning, after a sleepless night, that to his great relief (*fiel ein Stein von der Seele*) the two officers telephoned back to say that the break-through was by 500 English prisoners of war who, captured during the day, were on their way back under escort to Flers, and had been mistaken for armed troops. The interest of this affair is that it was the first occasion on which measures were definitely taken to meet a break-through, and it shows that such an occurrence was to be met in the same way as had been a break-in to a lesser depth, for example at Neuve Chapelle.

8

The development of these defended areas of shell-holes as a foremost line made very difficult the problem both of control of the front-line units and that of their food and ammunition supply. The Germans, even before the war, had gone a long way towards breaking up the chain system of command and giving more initiative to subordinate commanders, and Colonel von Lossberg now carried that idea a stage further. He found that on an average during these battles a message took eight to ten hours to reach the front line from divisional headquarters, and for this reason it became essential to increase greatly the power of the front battalion commanders (*Kampf-Truppen-Kommandeur*). They were given as full a control over their sector of the battle-area as has a captain over his ship, and their decisions were to be accepted, by superiors and subordinates alike, as final and unquestioned while the battle lasted. They not only commanded their own battalions, but also automatically took charge of all reinforcements which arrived in their sector, irrespective of rank or seniority. The task of the regimental (English, brigade) commanders was chiefly to keep their front battalion commanders supplied with ammunition, and to have the reserves ready in the right place for the immediate counter-attack, if required.

It was, however, on the divisional commander that the fullest responsibility for the conduct of the battle rested. He was given control of all available forces in his sector, including field and heavy artillery, with the exception of heavy batteries engaged on special tasks, such as long-range objectives, and the aviation units which were under Army or Corps headquarters. His chief means of influencing the battle was by ensuring that both his own reserves and those placed at his disposal by higher authority were allotted and sent forward to subordinate commanders at the right place and time, but it was to be left to those subordinates to make local arrangements for the employment of those reserves on the battlefield as the situation demanded. It was, however, the divisional commander, acting on the reports from his front battalion commanders, who decided the course of the battle. There was, in fact, no chain of command left, as it had only those two links. The relation of the Corps commander to the divisional commander during a battle was very similar to that of a regimental to a battalion commander.

Another important innovation in the system of command was the placing of each Corps headquarters on a permanent basis. It became a group of three or four divisions, but the divisions were constantly changing, passing in and out of the group, although the Group, or Corps, Staff and its sector remained unchanged; so the XIV Corps, for example, under General von Stein, became the *Gruppe Stein*. From this development it followed that the division, which moved intact with its headquarters, became the independent battle-unit of the German Army.

Already in the early Somme battles the system of defending a zone or defended area, combined with a deep defensive position behind it, had taken practical shape; and the break-up of the chain system of command enabled a mobile defence to be conducted within these deep defended areas.

9

The development of this organization in depth was based almost entirely on the result of personal observation. Colonel von Lossberg spent so much of his time away from his headquarters that he left all the routine work to a deputy. Every morning he accompanied General von Below, the First Army commander, on visits to one or more corps or divisional headquarters, but he evidently regarded these formal drives, which, as he mentions rather impatiently, were in a closed car, as a waste of time; it was in the afternoons, when he went back to the battle area alone in an open car, 'from which I could see what was going on', that he did his work. He also writes that frequently he was in the foremost shell-hole positions about daybreak, which was the time the British usually attacked. There can have been few Army chiefs of staff during the war who made such pilgrimages; he mentions it to point out the necessity for studying the state of the men holding the foremost line, so as to discover for how long a division could safely be expected to hold out, exposed to those exceptional conditions of weather and unremitting bombardment in which they had to live. His observations on such occasions, which no other method could replace, were largely responsible for the fact that a division was never asked to do the impossible and that every British attack during those Somme battles came up against an opposition ready to offer a stubborn defence. The importance which he himself attached to this matter is shown by the fact that in his book the several sketches of the Somme battles are devoted almost exclusively to show the system of divisional reliefs; and the immensity of his task may be understood by the fact that during the five months of the Somme campaign, July to November, there were 146 reliefs of divisions, over a million men in infantry alone, in and out of the twenty-mile battlefront of the First Army (48 divisions put in once, 43 twice, and 4 three times).

10

On the 28th August, while the Somme campaign was still at its height, General Falkenhayn was superseded as Chief of O.H.L. by Field-Marshal Hindenburg, with General Ludendorff as chief of staff. The attacks on Verdun were at once stopped, so that more troops and material might be available for the Somme, and the later Somme battles took on a different aspect.

The German inferiority in guns and aeroplanes became less marked. For the first time during the Somme battles German aeroplanes began to adopt offensive tactics and fought over the British lines; it was found possible to allot one artillery flight with a protective flight to each infantry division, and two or three reconnaissance flights, including one for photographic reconnaissance, to each group of three or four divisions. The number of heavy batteries was greatly increased, and the field batteries were able to diminish their barrage frontage from 400 yards per battery in the early battles to 200 yards, an improvement which greatly assisted the front garrison both to hold the line and for immediate counter-attacks.

There may be seen also at this time the formation of an échelon of reserves such as Colonel von Lossberg had organized for the Champagne battles the previous autumn. By degrees he was able with the extra divisions, freed from Verdun, to form a first line of relief divisions (*Ablösungs-divisionen*), ten to fifteen miles back, ready to relieve the front divisions whenever necessary.

As a result of this increased defensive strength the German counter-attacks, both immediate and deliberate, became stronger and more frequent, and the British advance more difficult and costly.

11

In these later Somme battles Colonel von Lossberg was

able to test and improve, on a far greater and more diverse
scale, the method of a defence-in-depth which he had experi-
mented with so successfully during the Champagne battles.

The foremost line had to be held rigidly, as before, but
it was held thinly and every use was made of flanking and
overhead machine-gun fire and of artillery barrage support to enable the weak garrison to fulfil its difficult task.
But the strength of the defence lay in the deep defended
area behind the foremost line. The supports and local
reserves were distributed about that area in dug-outs and
shelters on the reverse slopes of undulations or wherever
cover was available, with their machine guns so sited that
they could surprise and demoralize by fire the attacking
lines preparatory to the immediate counter-attack. The
custom of reinforcing the front line with the supports was
abandoned, as further experience continued to show that
it only led to heavier losses. Instead, the supports, the local
reserves, and the corps and army reserves became échelons
of formations distributed in depth, each at about 2,000
yards' distance, ready to exert a constant forward pressure
during the battle by a series of immediate counter-attacks
until any lost ground was retaken.

It followed that the defensive battle developed into a
mobile action within the confines of a deep zone, with a
widely distributed garrison ready to take advantage of any
situation. Trenches came to be regarded in a different
light. They were carefully sited rallying lines, but they
were primarily used for living in during calm periods, for
shelter against the weather, for communication, and for
bringing forward troops, rations, and ammunition. When
an attack appeared imminent, they were generally abandoned, and a line of shell-holes occupied a short distance
in front to escape the artillery barrage. Although German
orders captured by the British showed that this was being
done, the British artillery did not take it into sufficient
account in their bombardments, and the assaulting infantry frequently encountered a heavy fusilade from German

infantry and machine guns lying unharmed in shell-holes well in front of their imagined front line.

The framework of the new defensive position was therefore no longer a line of trenches, but rather the concealed machine-gun nests and dug-out shelters distributed about a deep defended area. Defence in depth was obtained by a deep distribution of the defence garrison rather than by the defence of successive trench lines.

The author of that notable work *Kritik des Weltkrieges* claims that this development was the one and only 'pearl of wisdom' (*Perle der Weisheit*) which shone above the shambles of battlefields on the Somme uplands in the autumn of 1916. That statement is probably true enough, but it should be qualified. The development of the German defence had been governed chiefly by the need to keep pace with the growth of the material strength of the enemy in artillery and munitions. The methods with which the enemy had employed that wealth of material were, according to many German authorities, contrary to all the tenets of the science of war; the name of *Materialschlacht* given to the Somme battles was generally used by the Germans with the sarcastic interpretation that they were battles fought by the enemy with material, but without brains. But be that as it may, the German development had been evolved to meet a special form of attack which had not varied, namely fire-effect preceding movement, and it is very doubtful whether that development would have followed the same lines if it had been faced by a form of attack in which, for example, fire-effect was combined with movement, and therefore in which surprise and covering fire for the infantry were the chief essentials. This important aspect of the development of the German defensive battle will become more apparent in the later chapters.

12

That 'pearl of wisdom' was given expression in a pamphlet entitled 'Erfahrungen der I Armee in der Somme-schlacht' ('Experiences of the First Army in the Somme Battles'), and Colonel von Lossberg has described with what care he compiled this record of experience at the request of General Ludendorff. It was arranged in two parts, tactical and administrative, and although each of the directing officers of the headquarters staff had a share in it, Colonel von Lossberg was its principal author and editor. For some weeks in December and January he spent 'several hours every evening discussing its features with his collaborators'; and, as his battlefront visits occupied most of his mornings and afternoons, he writes that during this period he 'found little time for sleep'. Throughout the Somme campaign, in fact, his telephone orderly calculated that he did not average more than four hours' sleep at night, but he himself admits that he had the gift of being able to sleep at odd moments, especially during his frequent car-journeys.

The result of this burning of midnight oil was printed on the 30th January 1917, and it crystallized the idea of a mobile defence in depth on a practical basis. It was to affect vitally the German defensive battles for the remainder of the war.

13

The Germans give their casualties in the Somme campaign as 465,000 against the British and French total of 623,000 (419,000 British and 204,000 French). These figures, even allowing for some difference due to the German custom of excluding lightly wounded in their totals, compared with the corresponding totals in the preceding defensive battles showed an increasingly heavy proportion of German casualties, and it was the flower of the German Army which was gradually being lost. The losses in guns were equally severe, due to the British counter-battery work. The majority of the casualties, too, were due to artillery fire, the ten to one superiority in ammunition supplies having its inevitable effect.

General Hindenburg and his chief of staff, General Ludendorff, believed that, with the steady increase of the ammunition supply which was to be expected from the British and French ammunition factories, backed by unlimited resources in raw materials, the introduction of a new defence doctrine for the German Army was essential. It seemed to them that the rigid defence not only of a foremost line but even of a foremost zone would soon be too costly a doctrine to continue. This change of outlook brings us to the Hindenburg Line.

Chapter VII

THE HINDENBURG LINE

When the Hindenburg-Ludendorff régime took over from General Falkenhayn at O.H.L. on the 28th August 1916, the strategical framework of the war was very similar to that in January 1915, when General Falkenhayn made his first defence construction programme. The Russians had not yet been defeated and Roumania had joined in, so that Germany still had to maintain nearly half of her armies on the Eastern Front (on 25th January 1917 the Germans had 122 divisions on their Eastern and 133 divisions on their Western Front). The holding of so large a proportion of German divisions during these critical years, thereby enabling the armed strength of the British Empire to be mobilized and developed, was Russia's great and vital contribution to the final victory.

General Ludendorff was consequently faced by the same inability to take any serious offensive operation on the Western Front; and he decided to remain on the defensive there until Roumania had been defeated and Russia was forced to abandon resistance.

I

One of the first orders (5th September) of the Hindenburg-Ludendorff régime, after taking over the direction of O.H.L., was for the construction of rear lines of defence on the Western Front. They were to be similar to the rallying

133

positions (*Eventual-Stellungen*) on the Russian front, but with two differences. Facing the Russians, who attacked with masses of infantry and comparatively little artillery support, these back lines had been sited several miles back on a forward slope with a wide and unobstructed field of fire and with good artillery observation from it. On the Western Front, of a more solid and continuous character, the new back lines were to be only so far in rear as their immediate purpose required, and owing to the greater destructive power of artillery the front trench system was to be sited on a reverse slope wherever possible.

In the following months five such positions were traced, four being named after heroes of Teutonic sagas. The *Flandern* Line was to run from the Belgian coast along the Passchendaele Ridge and behind the Messines salient to the Lille defences; the *Wotan* Line was to carry on from there southwards to Sailly, behind the Loos–Vimy–Arras battlefields of 1915 and the Somme battlefields of 1916; the *Siegfried* Line, from Arras by way of Saint-Quentin–Laon to the Aisne, east of Soissons, was to cut out the great Noyon salient; the *Hunding* Line, from the Somme, near Péronne, to about Etain, east of the Meuse and north-east of Verdun, was to be behind the Champagne battlefields; and the *Michel* Line, from about Etain to Pont-à-Mousson on the Moselle, was to cut out the Saint-Mihiel salient. General Ludendorff expressly stated as late as the 13th November 1916 that there was no immediate intention of retiring to these back lines, and that they were to be regarded only either as 'precautionary measures' (*Sicherheitskoeffizient*) or to be used to shorten the line to economize in man-power (see Sketch 9).

Of these five lines the Siegfried, which, by cutting out the Noyon salient, would release the greatest reserve of man-power, was the first to be tackled.[1] It was to run as

[1] At an important Western Front conference at Cambrai on the 8th September 1917, which is referred to later in the text, Lieut.-General Fuchs, a corps commander, advocated the construction of a

directly as the ground permitted from the front line at Arras to rejoin the front line south of Laon, passing west of Saint-Quentin and west of Laon. This new line, about ninety miles long, would shorten the front by nearly twenty-five miles. Its general course was traced out by the 19th September, and the order for its construction to begin was given by Crown Prince Rupprecht of Bavaria, commanding the Army Group, on the 27th; the general idea being to provide accommodation for a front garrison of twenty divisions (one division to every four and a half miles). The technical direction was under an engineer, Colonel Kraemer, from O.H.L., assisted by General Lauter as artillery adviser, and 12,000 German and 3,000 Belgian labourers, in addition to 50,000, chiefly Russian, prisoners of war, (141 labour companies) were assembled for the work.

The other four lines remained paper propositions until the end of the year. The trace of the Wotan Line was decided by the 4th November but its construction was not to begin until the Siegfried, or, to give it its original popular German name, by which it will continue to be called throughout this chapter, the Hindenburg Line was completed.

2

As late as the 21st January there was still no thought of a withdrawal to the Hindenburg Line unless forced by urgent necessity,[1] but by that date it was considered

line from Arras to west of Laon to shorten the front by forty kilometres and so spare ten or more divisions, with which, with other reserves, he recommended an offensive to be made from Alsace or southern Lorraine. The idea of the offensive was dropped, but that for shortening the front was accepted (*Militar Wochenblatt*, 27th February 1937).

[1] General Ludendorff's memorandum after his inspection of the Western Front (*Gesamteindruck der Westreise*), dated 21st January 1917: *German Official History*, xi, p. 509.

roughly ready for occupation. It was not until a week later, on the 28th, that a message to O.H.L. from the Crown Prince Rupprecht of Bavaria, in whose sector the line lay, definitely proposed it. This message was to the effect that the condition of the trenches in the Somme battle area on the front of the First Army, particularly on either side of the Ancre, was such that it was doubtful whether they could be defended, or made suitable for defence, against another prolonged offensive, and it concluded by recommending a withdrawal in the near future to the Hindenburg Line. On the following day General Ludendorff reported that both for political and military reasons a voluntary withdrawal to the Hindenburg Line could not be sanctioned, but that he was in favour of a withdrawal on a smaller scale to a line Arras–Quéant–Sailly, that is, to the northernmost sector of the Hindenburg and southernmost of the Wotan Lines, which would cut out the Somme battle area (see Sketch 9). In reply it was pointed out that the Wotan Line had not yet been begun and its southernmost sector, Quéant–Sailly, although only about twelve miles in length, could not be ready before the end of March.

On the day following this reply (30th) General Ludendorff in a telephone conversation with General von Kuhl, the Crown Prince Rupprecht's chief of staff, showed an inclination to agree to the greater withdrawal, the *ganzer Entschluss*. He was influenced by the fact that it would free a greater number of divisions and artillery (thirteen infantry divisions and more than fifty heavy and a proportionate number of field batteries) for an offensive he was planning in support of the Austro-Hungarian Armies (against Italy); also by the fact that it would give about eight weeks' respite before the French and British could bring forward adequate artillery to prepare another offensive. This influence was strengthened by serious delays in the delivery of munitions which came to light during conversations in Berlin on the 1st and 2nd February, showing that it was

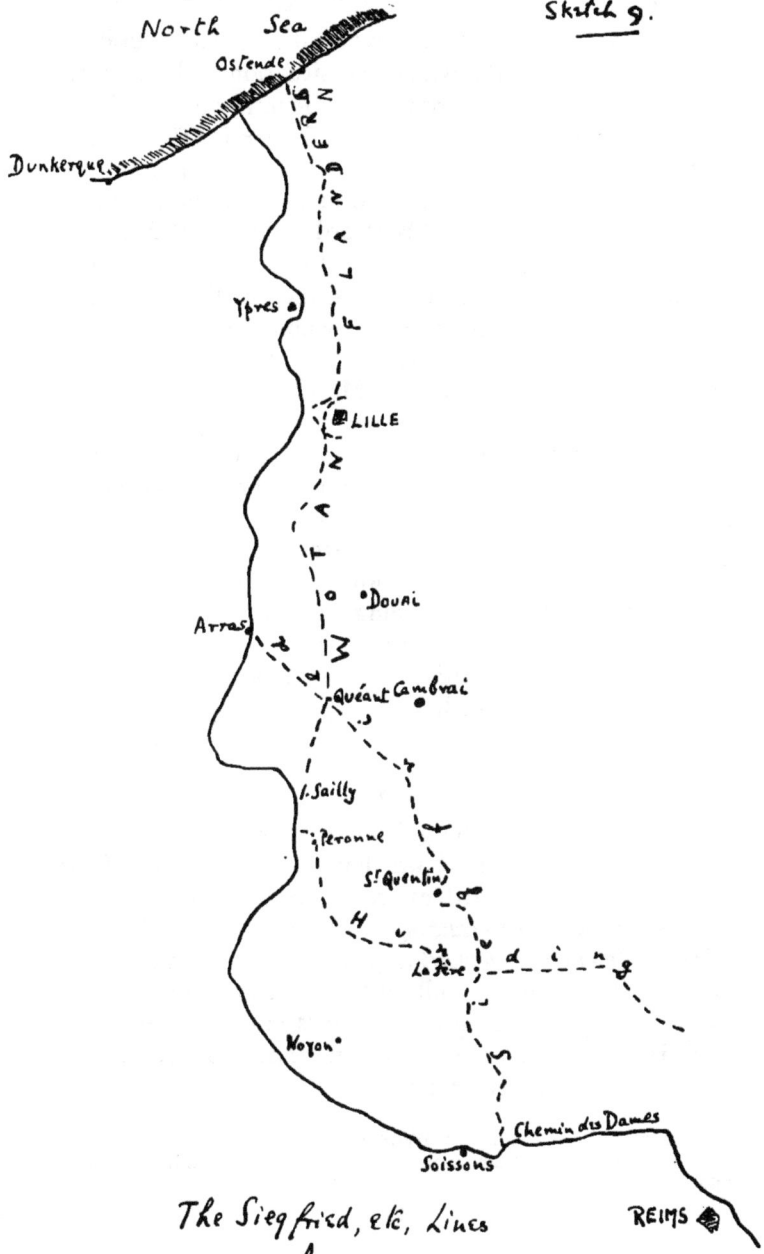

North Sea

Sketch 9.

Ostende

Dunkerque

Ypres

LILLE

Douai

Arras

Quéant Cambrai

I. Sailly

Peronne

St Quentin

La Fère

Noyon

Chemin des Dames

Soissons

REIMS

The Siegfried, etc, Lines
January 1917

10 5 0   10   20   30 Miles

far below both orders and expectations. The munitions problem, vital for the whole war situation and for operative decisions, was, according to General von Kuhl, the factor that finally forced General Ludendorff's decision, for, above all, time was needed to replenish munition supplies, especially of guns and artillery ammunition.[1]

On the 4th February O.H.L. ordered the withdrawal to the Hindenburg Line, and it was to be carried out over a period of five weeks starting from the 9th February. The name *Alberich* was given to the whole movement and a calendar of *Alberich* days worked out, according to which the period 9th February–15th March was to be employed in devastating the area to be evacuated (a procedure strongly opposed by many senior German commanders, including the Crown Prince Rupprecht and General Gallwitz), while the actual withdrawal was to take place during the three days 15th–18th March.[2]

During those five weeks, however, that is, during the period between the order being given and its completion, all that part of the new Hindenburg Line south of Quéant, against which the British were to advance, was to be completely transformed.

3

When the Hindenburg Line was traced, the O.H.L. instructions for it laid down that it was to consist of two trenches about 200 yards apart, the front one for the sentry garrisons (*Sicherheitsbesatzung*) and the second as the main line of defence (*Hauptverteidigungslinie*), with dug-out accommodation for the bulk of the front garrison. Massive wire entanglements up to 100 yards in depth were to be laid in front of this trench system, and, in addition, concrete emplacements for machine-gun shelters were to be

---

[1] Hermann von Kuhl, *Der Weltkrieg* (Berlin, 1929).
[2] In places on the Somme battlefront the withdrawal began earlier for local reasons.

built in front of and behind it. Wherever possible, that is, wherever artillery observation was available from points farther back commanding it, this trench system was to be placed on a reverse slope, a *Hinterhangstellung*, behind the lie of the ridges and folds of ground, its garrison needing a field of fire of only a few hundred yards.

These instructions were in accordance with the experience gained during the Champagne and Somme battles, but it is evident that the experts from O.H.L., General Lauter and Colonel Kraemer, who were responsible for siting it, either did not agree with or ignored them. A visit to the original Hindenburg Line shows that the requirement for efficient artillery observation, on which Colonel von Lossberg had placed such emphasis, was neglected more often than fulfilled. For the greater length of it the artillery observation posts were actually in or even in front of the front-trench system; and to give them a wide horizon, that front-trench system had been sited either near a crest-line or on a forward slope or at the back of a long reverse slope. Great stretches of the Hindenburg Line were, in fact, sited on principles already obsolete for the Western Front.

4

On the evening of the 5th February, the day after the issue of the *Alberich* calendar for the withdrawal, the First Army commander, General von Below, and his chief of staff, Colonel von Lossberg, visited the headquarters of the Army Group at Cambrai. Their mission was to tell the Crown Prince Rupprecht of Bavaria that they wished to reshape the Hindenburg Line. They explained that the later Somme battles had shown conclusively the supreme importance not only of siting the front-trench system on a reverse slope but also of possessing artillery observation points behind and overlooking both it and the probable battlefield; also that these observers should be at least 500 yards behind the front-trench system, or otherwise the dust, smoke, and moral effect of the enemy's bombardment, added to the risk of breaking all means of communication, would make their work difficult, if not impossible. They pointed out that the First Army sector of the line, the thirty-five miles stretch between Quéant[1] and Bellicourt (north of Saint-Quentin), did not adequately satisfy this condition. For this reason they wished to construct a new line 2,000 to 3,000 yards in front of the existing Hindenburg Line. The latter would then become the Second or artillery support line (*Artillerieschutzstellung*) and it already had, in their sector, 1,200 concrete or mined dug-outs, sufficient for 14,000 men, which was about the requirement for sheltering local reserves. The new front line was to have, like the Hindenburg Line, a front-trench system of two trench lines, about 200 yards apart, sited on a reverse slope, and they asked for the necessary labour and material to construct in and about it mined dug-outs for 24,000 men and concrete dug-outs for 500 by the 15th March, the day of the withdrawal (the remaining deep mined dug-outs to be replaced by shallow concrete ones as time and labour permitted). They asked for three divisions of infantry and 15,000 labourers for this work.

As First Army headquarters was at Bourlon, they had been alongside the Hindenburg Line throughout its construction, crossing it almost daily in visits to the various corps headquarters nearer the Somme battlefront, but, Colonel von Lossberg explained, they had not previously mentioned its defects owing to the fact that an immediate

---

[1] The First Army northern boundary at this time was at Croisilles, five miles north of Quéant, but the Wotan Line was to join the Siegfried at Quéant, and these two were regarded as the future main defence line. Also it was foreseen that the expected British offensive would probably include the Croisilles–Quéant front and that there might not be time to make the desired alterations. The British Arras offensive in April 1917 therefore came up against the original Hindenburg Line, sited on rigid defence principles, and not the improved Hindenburg Position.

withdrawal had not been contemplated. Now that the withdrawal had been ordered they considered the reconstruction to be urgent.

At this interview the forward shift (*Vorverlegung*) of the line was proposed for the centre sector only, but during the next two days permission was asked for the whole of the First Army sector as far north as Quéant, the junction point of the Wotan Line.[1] The Crown Prince Rupprecht doubted if the work could be completed in time; and First Army headquarters therefore asked if the *Alberich* calendar could be altered, delaying actions to be fought in the rear positions behind the Somme battlefront to give time to complete it, but this was refused. In principle, however, the construction of a forward Hindenburg Line on the First Army front was sanctioned; the Crown Prince Rupprecht inspected the line (27th February) with Colonel von Lossberg and agreed that it was necessary.

If Colonel von Lossberg's experience was to be accepted there could be little doubt about the need for this forward shift. Stand, for example, on that grand stretch of upland about Bonavis, where the highways from Péronne and Saint-Quentin meet on their way north-eastward to Cambrai, and you may appreciate at a glance how it enabled an indifferently sited Hindenburg Line to be converted into an ideally sited Hindenburg Position. The original Hindenburg Line crossed the two highways near their junction, skirting the farm buildings of Bonavis. North of the junction it is still marked by a great sunken concrete shelter near the Ferme de Bonavis, and to the south it turned back along the southern edge of the Bois Lateau. In front of it, 1,000 yards away, the Péronne road crosses the head of two big depressions falling away to north and south, bordered on their farther side, another 2,000 yards

---

[1] The Moulin Sans Souci, north-east of Quéant, was the place of meeting of the new First Army Line, the Hindenburg Line, and the Wotan Line. See *Das Reserve Infanterie Regiment 91*, p. 267 (Kummel, Berlin, 1926).

distant, by the skyline of the La Vacquerie plateau. Both
these depressions offered perfect assembly positions, un-
observable to the defence except from the air, for an attack
on the Hindenburg Line. But by pushing forward infantry
listening posts to the La Vacquerie skyline (the Vacquerie
Line), by siting a new front-trench system (the Banteux
Line) 300 to 500 yards behind it, on the reverse slope
within the depressions and by placing the forward artillery
observers a few hundred yards in front of the original Hindenburg Line, the disadvantages of the original Hindenburg Line became the advantages of the new Hindenburg
Position. The Vacquerie outpost line denied to the attack
ground-observation over the position, whereas the front-
trench system and the depressions were under the direct
observation of the defender's artillery observers in front of
the Hindenburg Line. The attacking infantry pressing forward into it would have to fight exposed to the concentric,
well-observed artillery fire of the defence without the support of the observed fire of its own batteries; in other words
it would quickly become an attack by one arm at a dis-
advantage against a defence by two arms with every advantage. The trace of the outpost (Vacquerie) line, the
front trench system (Banteux Line), and the Hindenburg
Line may be seen to this day (1939) by the upturned chalk
marks on the arable; and it will be noticed that in this
Hindenburg Position are repeated the tactical conditions
of the Py brook valley position which had served Colonel
von Lossberg so well during the Champagne battles in the
autumn of 1915 (see Sketch 10).[1]

[1] Any reader visiting the Hindenburg Line is recommended to con-
sult for further details the generally excellent German regimental
histories. For example, for the Bonavis sector are available the following regimental histories, to which I am indebted for many of the facts
and for Sketch 11 in this chapter.

For the sub-sector north of the Péronne road towards Havrincourt,
the regiments of the 18th Division (31st, 85th, and 86th). For the sub-
sector south of that highway to Banteux, the regiments of the 27th
(Würtemburg) Division (120th, 123rd, and 124th). These garrisoned
the position from April to May 1917.

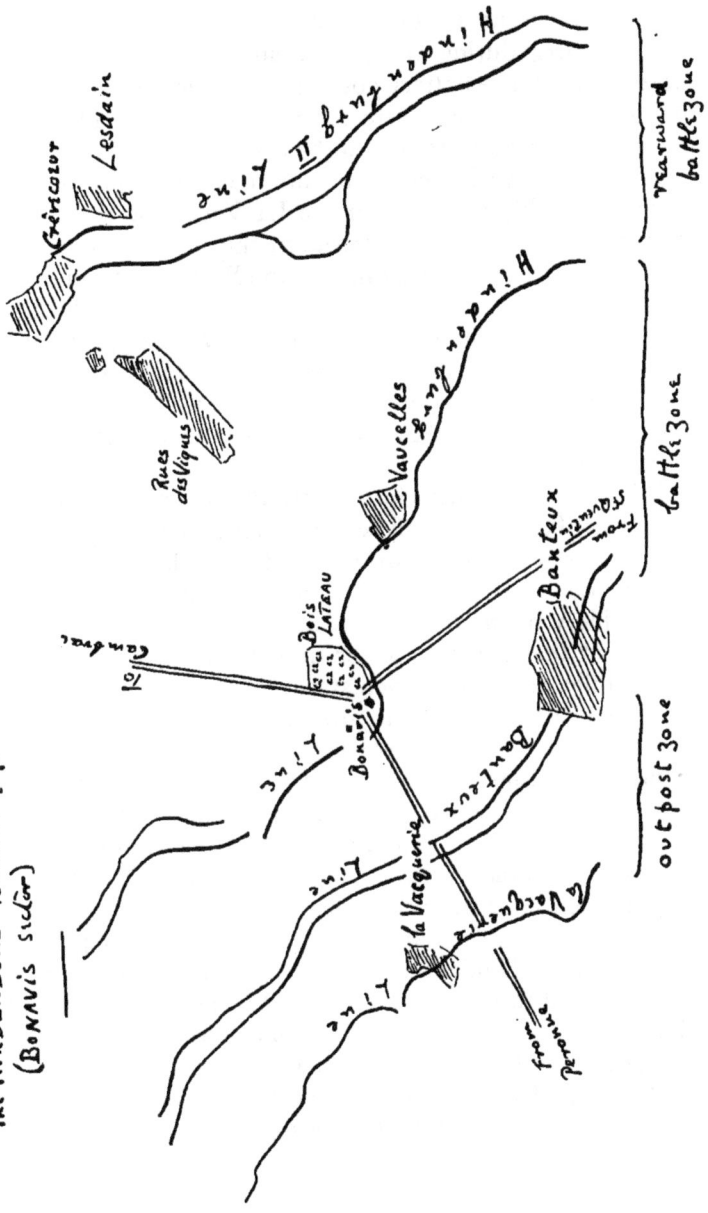

Sketch 10

The Hindenburg Position. 1917.
(Bonavis sector)

Grincourt
Lesdain
Hindenburg Line II

Rues desVignes
Vaucelles
Hindenburg Line

Cambrai
Bois LATEAU
Banteux
From Gouzeaucourt

Bonavis
H. Line
H. Line
Banteux
la Vacquerie
H. Line
From Peronne

outpost zone
battle zone
rearward battle zone

100 500 0 1000 2000 Yards

The artillery, like the infantry, was to be disposed in depth on the basis of detailed instructions issued by Colonel von Lossberg during the period 8th February to 10th March 1917.[1] The battery positions intended for the original Hindenburg Line were scrapped, and, instead, the forward batteries were now to be sited where they could bring an effective fire on and behind the enemy's probable assault-assembly positions on the La Vacquerie plateau. The greater part of the batteries in this sector were east and north-east of Bonavis (and behind Bois Lateau) in the neighbourhood of the Hindenburg Line, the new artillery protective line. The observers were a few hundred yards in front, where they could overlook the Banteux Line and outpost zone, and at the same time were well away from the effect of a bombardment of the front-trench system and its immediate vicinity.

Follow the site of the Hindenburg Position in the thirty-five miles of the First Army sector, and the same conditions, or an effort to make them, will be found, the new front-trench system being sited primarily so as amply to cover the artillery observation posts. South of Bonavis, for example, in the four-mile sector from Banteux to south of Vendhuille, the front-trench system was advanced to the Scheldt Canal, so that the ground about and behind it could be overlooked by artillery observers in the original Hindenburg Line; at the same time an outpost line was occupied which denied to the enemy ground observation of this area. Throughout the length of the Hindenburg Position expression will be found of this fundamental requirement for a defence in depth.

No sooner had the batteries arrived in their new positions along the Hindenburg Line, in mid-March, than they were ordered to reconnoitre a second line of battery positions, according to the normal German custom, in a defensive position, of having battery positions ready to retire to in the event of a break-through. This second line was to be

[1] See *Geschichte des 22nd Res. Feld-Artillerie Regts.*, pp. 187–94.

about 3,000 yards in rear, the distance being governed by the requirement that the mass of the field batteries should be able to lay an effective barrage in front of the front trench of the Hindenburg Line in the event of that line being occupied as a front-trench system (*Eventual-Stellung*).

As soon as labour was available another *Eventual-Stellung* (the Hindenburg II Line) was begun in the neighbourhood of the second line of battery positions. It was not necessarily a protective line for these battery positions, but the essential was that the attack would have to make a new artillery deployment to bring effective fire to bear on it. The Hindenburg II Line became the back line of, and completed, the Hindenburg I position (*Siegfried I Stellung*), a sector of which is shown in Sketch 10, and gave to it a depth of 6,000 to 8,000 yards.

During the war it was the actual crossing of the Hindenburg Line trench system which gave the headlines to the English newspapers, and so the popular, and almost legendary, conception of it has remained to this day that of a continuous trench system fortified with every modern convenience, embedded in shell-proof concrete. In actual fact the Hindenburg Line was a minor feature, namely the Intermediate Line (*Siegfried I Zwischen Stellung*), of the Hindenburg Position, a great defended area several thousands of yards in depth. By the autumn of 1917 a complete Hindenburg II Position (*Siegfried II Stellung*), with the Hindenburg II Line as its front-trench system, had been traced and begun, and even a Hindenburg III Position contemplated. Given sufficient human material and the necessary will-to-victory, there was no finality to such a defence system.

5

The lay-out of the Hindenburg Position followed essentially the ideas of Colonel von Lossberg; it was another stage in a gradual evolution from the Py brook valley position of 1915 through the Somme battlefields of 1916. The method of conducting the defensive battle within it was, however, to be something quite new; and to understand how that came about, it will be necessary to cast back to those dinner-table discussions at Mézières during the summer of 1915 between Colonel von Lossberg and the junior members of his staff.

It will be remembered that the bone of contention was a captured French Fifth Army instruction which the junior members interpreted to mean that the defensive battle might be fought behind, instead of in, the front line. This had led to the idea, with which Colonel von Lossberg had disagreed, that the front line might be considered as an elastic band which an attack could be allowed to stretch, and that the counter-attack reserves would be the spring to take it back to its normal tension.

During the months which followed, after Colonel von Lossberg had left the Operations Section, the junior members had continued to brood over this idea, but whereas the French instruction had applied it to companies holding a front-trench system back to a depth of 800 yards, they contemplated its application to divisions and groups of divisions for the defence of an area ten times as deep. The French instruction had an outpost system of 200 to 300 yards in front of the main line of resistance (the line of piquets and strong-points), but they gave this outpost area a depth of anything from 500 to 3,000 yards, depending on the ground and the relative strength of the defence force, and called it an 'outpost zone'. The ground behind the main line of resistance was where they intended the defensive battle should be fought, and they therefore called it the 'battlezone'; and this battlezone extended back 1,500 to 3,000 yards or more, again depending on the ground. To fight this battle there was to be a line of counter-attack divisions in readiness behind the battlezone, corresponding to the counter-attack reserves in the French instruction, and they would meet the attack as it struggled through the battlezone and defeat it there, and then recapture the battle and outpost zones.

It was important to break up the impetus of the attack to make easier the task of the counter-attack reserves; and for this purpose the French instruction had provided 'miniature forts' along the main line of resistance, but the German version was to dot them about chequerwise in suitable places so as to make them more difficult to locate and to give as many surprises as possible to the attack. These miniature forts the Germans named *Widas* (*Widerstandsnester*) or nests of resistance, and the orders given to their garrisons were an exact translation of those given in the French Fifth Army instruction, namely that they were 'to be able to continue to offer resistance even though surrounded on all sides', and their garrisons were 'to hold out until relieved by a victorious counter-attack', which would recapture the foremost line. Similar, too, were the instructions for making communication trenches suitable to hem in and outflank by fire an attack passing through the battlezone.

6

Side by side with these ideas for a new defensive battle was a movement for abolishing the doctrine of attacking positions by successive lines of men. Already in the summer of 1915 Captains Rohr and Reddemann (formerly chief of a Leipzig fire-brigade), under the supervision of Colonel Bauer of the O.H.L. Operations Section, had worked out the technical details of a special assault battalion (*Sturmbataillon*) which was intended to be a model upon which the entire German Army was eventually to be equipped and trained. It was provided with various infantry guns, light mortars, and flame-throwers (*Flammenwerfer*), and equipped with the first steel helmets and with portable shields, a kind of armour. The capture in the early summer of 1916 of Captain Laffargue's work, *Etude sur l'attaque*, explained in an earlier chapter, gave an additional impetus to the work of these two pioneers, as Captain Laffargue's meditations exactly suited their tactical outlook. During that summer they had accordingly developed the idea of assault-detachments (*Sturm-* or *Stosstrupps*) which were equivalent to Captain Laffargue's 'groupes de tirailleurs', and which were to precede an assault by a process of 'infiltration' into the enemy's position, and overcome any points of resistance by surprise, and from flanks and rear, with their various portable weapons.

It was soon obvious that this organization of *Sturmtrupps* and *Sturmbataillon* was equally suitable for the new defensive battle, which was based upon counter-attack; the *Sturmtrupp* would be the counter-attack unit for the outpost zone, and the *Sturmbataillon* for the battlezone.

7

These junior members of the Operations Section had received no encouragement from General Falkenhayn, but when, on the 28th August 1916 General Ludendorff took charge at O.H.L., they were at once given scope to develop their ideas. With that change of leadership, writes Colonel Bauer, who it will be remembered was the senior of the junior members principally concerned, 'we all felt as if a great weight had been lifted from us' (*wie von einem Alp befreit*). General Ludendorff not only listened to their ideas but accepted them. He agreed that a defensive battle could no longer be fought in the front defended area of shell-holes without excessive casualties, and that it would be better to concentrate attention on fighting it behind out of range and view of the attackers' artillery, where the counter-attack by the defence would have every advantage. Accordingly, he directed these men to write a new defensive-battle text-book. The *German Official History* (vol. xii) recently published (June 1939) states that Colonel Bauer gave the new text-book its main outlines (*vorwärtstreibend und richtunggebend*), and General Ludendorff in his *War*

Memories states that Colonel Bauer and Captain Geyer, who 'combined an exceptional power of expression with a remarkable knowledge of tactics', were chiefly responsible for it.

What was to become famous as General Ludendorff's text-book on the defensive battle was in fact the work of the junior members of the Operations Section whom Colonel von Lossberg, their deputy-chief the previous year, had belittled owing to their lack of any front-line experience, and whom he considered had 'highly exaggerated ideas of the general conduct of a battle'; and the ideas they put into the text-book were the very ideas with which he had so strongly disagreed. Nevertheless, their text-book now became the official training manual for the German Army; and the defensive battle within the Hindenburg Position was directed to be fought accordingly.

The text-book itself, called *Conduct of the Defensive Battle* (*Die Führung in der Abwehrschlacht*), was issued to all German divisions on the 1st December 1916. It has become a landmark in military history, for it laid down for the first time a comprehensive organization for the elastic defence of a deep zone (*Flachenverteidigung*) to replace the rigid defence of a line (*Linienverteidigung*). General Ludendorff wrote an introduction to it, in which he said, 'No longer will the infantryman have to say to himself, "Here I stay and here I die," ' but he was to be allowed freedom of movement within a deep defensive zone. As the new text-book demanded new ideas in the construction of a defensive position a supplementary document was issued as a com-companion to the text-book, and called 'Principles of Field Position Construction' (*Allgemeines über Stellenbau*). These two documents were the theoretical foundation of the 'elastic defence in depth'. The French had given the idea for it on a small scale, but to the Germans must be given the credit for elaborating this *An-sich-herankommen-lassen* (invitation-to-walk-right-in) system, as they call it, in the grand manner.

8

The foundation of the new text-book was the intention to abandon the rigid system of fighting for every foot of ground irrespective of its tactical value. Henceforward the German defensive battle was to be fought for the ground's value as part of a selected position, and the text-book described a selected position as one in which the attacking force will most rapidly 'fight itself to a standstill and use up its resources while the defenders conserve their strength'. The main factors in its selection were to be 'suitable positions and observation posts for the artillery and good communications behind', and the defending infantry were to fight a mobile defence in a series of zones, the front divisions in an outpost zone and a battlezone, instead of a static defence in a succession of trench lines. The depth of these zones would necessarily vary considerably, depending on the character of the ground and the comparative strength of the defending force. In flat, open country or where the defending force was weak, particularly in artillery, the outpost zone might extend back to 3,000 yards in order that the front trench system, or main line of resistance, and the battlezone behind it might be out of effective range of the enemy's field batteries; on the other hand, in hilly or wooded country the outpost zone might coincide with the battlezone, with listening posts a few hundred yards in front of the main line of resistance. In any case, this main line of resistance, the front trench-system, was to be sited on a reverse slope if possible, protecting and at least 500 yards in front of the line of artillery observation posts. Behind it, back to a second line 1,500 to 2,500 yards distant, was to be the battlezone or defended area in which the defensive battle was to be fought out. To give the defending infantry every advantage this battlezone was to be selected as much as possible out of sight of the enemy's ground artillery observers and in fullest view of those of the defence.

The tactical conditions required were, in fact, very similar to those which Colonel von Lossberg had evolved during the Champagne and Somme battles. So it happened that the reshaping of the Hindenburg Line, though primarily to meet the requirements of artillery observation, also gave an ideal opportunity to put into practice on a virgin position, as yet unapproached by an enemy and untouched by a shell, the principles of the new defensive battle text-book.

Take, as an example of the distribution of the infantry, the sector of the 18th Division north of the Bonavis–Péronne road in April 1917, when the defence organization of the Hindenburg Position was nearing completion. Its outpost line lay along La Vacquerie skyline and its main line of resistance, the new First Army line, was about 600 yards in rear, the battlezone extending back about 2,000 yards to the original Hindenburg Line. The divisional sector was divided into three sub-sectors, one to each of its regiments (British brigades). The regimental sector of 3,000 yards, shown in Sketch 11, had two battalions holding the outpost and battlezone and one resting in reserve, three or four miles back. Of the two front battalions, side by side, each had three companies (later two) in the outpost zone and front-trench system and one (later two) in the battlezone and garrisoning the fortified localities or *Widas* (*Widerstandsnester*), of which there were four or five in each battalion sector, dotted about within the outpost and battlezones. These *Widas*, concealed concrete machine-gun shelters arranged for all-round defence and placed so as to be difficult for artillery to find and range upon, were garrisoned by one or two groups (a group equalling one non-commissioned officer and eleven men), with one or two heavy machine guns, and this garrison was to hold its ground at all costs 'even though enveloped on all sides'. The garrisons of these four or five *Widas* required altogether over half a company[1] and six machine guns, leaving

[1] Assuming four one-group and one two-group garrisons per bat-

three and a half companies in each front battalion sector
for a mobile or elastic defence. The reserve, third, battalion
was, on alarm, to march at once from its rest billets and
occupy the Hindenburg Line. This distribution followed
the development already evolved by Colonel von Lossberg,
and the density of the garrison of the outpost and battlezones of the Hindenburg Position in April 1917 was approximately half that of a similar area of the German
position on the opening day of the Somme campaign on
the 1st July 1916. Actually, in order to avoid confusion of
units, it was customary from this period of the war onward
for a regiment to have its three battalions one behind the
other, as front, support, and reserve battalions (*Kampf-
Bereitschaft-* and *Reserve-Bataillon*); but the new text-book,
emphasizing the need for mobility rather than rigidity in
the defence, gave the utmost liberty to divisional and
regimental commanders so long as the three factors of
depth, mobility, and concealment were assured.

9

General Ludendorff's text-book gave a straightforward
account of how the mobile or elastic defence of the outpost
and battlezones was to be conducted. At first, up to the
end of March, the no-man's-land or *Vorfeld* in front of the
front-trench system had been covered only by listening
posts, or by strong points garrisoned in strength (i.e. one
officer and twenty-four men), 400 to 1,000 yards ahead,
holding any commanding artillery observation points from
which the enemy could overlook the battlezone. During
April, however, as labour became available after complet-
ing the main position, a more detailed outpost organization was elaborated and the *Vorfeld* became a *Vorpostenfeld*
(outpost zone). Within this outpost zone the front companies provided six piquets, which between them posted

talion sector, it would need about seventy-two all ranks, and the
rifle strength of a company at this period averaged about 120.

out by day two or four and by night ten or twelve double
sentry posts. In the event of attack these sentry posts were
allowed to fall back on the line of piquets, close behind
which was a line of so-called group nests (*Gruppennester*),
shallow dug-outs in which lay one or more *Stosstrupps*
(*Trupp* was a squad of five men and a leader) from each
company, and these were to assist the piquets to recapture
the lost line of sentry posts by immediate counter-attack
(see Sketch 11).

The construction of the defences and the conduct of the
defensive battle in the battlezone was to be very similar to
that within the outpost zone, only on a larger and stronger
scale. The first trench of the front trench system was the
line of sentry posts for the battlezone, the garrison in the
second trench was the line of piquets, and the support, and
reserves in rear corresponded to the *Stosstrupps*. The fortified localities, as any in the outpost zone, were additional
with their own orders, i.e. to hold on irrespective of the
course of the mobile defence. A minor attack might be held
by the trench garrison, just as a raid might be held by the
line of piquets in the outpost zone, but it was realized that
a massed offensive might overrun, or force back, the garrison of the outpost zone and that of the front trench system.
In such a case the garrison was entitled 'to yield elastically
in face of this hostile concentration of fire and assault, but
only to turn again and counter-attack'.[1] The text-book,
however, made quite clear that this yielding was only to
be of a very temporary nature. The 'detachments of the
trench garrisons who are retiring to the flanks and to the
rear, and the supports lying ready behind the foremost
trenches, whose task must have been so drilled into them
as to become second nature, must counter-attack immediately and recapture the front line'.

From these quotations it will be seen that the defenders,
no longer tied to a trench line, were entitled to fight a
mobile action within the confines of a deep battlezone, to

[1] Beltz, *Das Infanterie Regiment 85* (1925), p. 107.

153

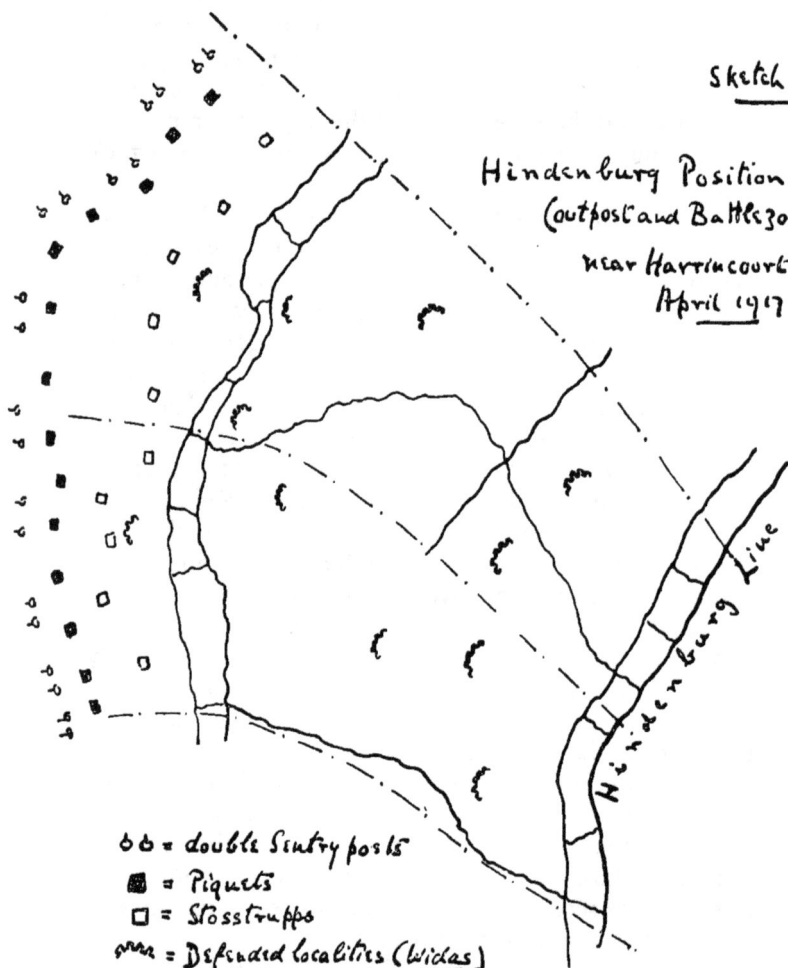

Sketch 11

Hindenburg Position
(outpost and Battlezones)
near Harrincourt
April 1917.

Hindenburg Line

b b = double Sentry posts
▣ = Piquets
□ = Stösstrupps
ᕙᕙ = Defended localities (widas)
—·—·— = Battalion boundaries

500   0   1000 Yards

advance or retire as seemed best at the moment, always
provided that the whole battle and outpost zones were in
their possession at the conclusion of the action. Although
circumstances might compel detachments to retire, a general withdrawal on a wide front was not contemplated, but
rather a yielding of separate detachments giving up voluntarily untenable sectors of the position. These would rally
on the support centres and counter-attack at any favourable opportunity; and their immediate counter-attack
within the position was called the *Gegenstoss in der Stellung*.

The defensive battle was to take the form of a number of
local engagements of this kind, either flank and frontal
counter-attacks over open ground, or bombing attacks
along the front trench system by companies on the flanks
of the break-in, or both combined. The attacker would in
this way meet increasingly numerous and unforeseen ob-
stacles and stronger resistance the deeper he penetrated
the position. He would have to cope with these local
counter-attacks, he would be swept by enfilade or frontal
machine-gun fire from the concealed fortified localities and
communication trenches, he would lose artillery support
owing to the siting of the battlezone out of view of his
artillery observers, and he would soon find himself cut off
from reinforcements by a barrage of the defending artillery.

The critical hour of the attack would now set in, a period
which proved fatal to so many British battalions during the
war. It might last several hours or only a few minutes, but
it was that moment of reaction and weakness when the
attack, disorganized by losses, exhausted by a period of
great nervous and physical strain, and beset with a feeling
of increasing isolation at every step forward into the unknown ground of an enemy's position, begins to waver.
Unless it can by some means be given adequate and well-
timed support to overcome this critical period, success is in
the balance. From the defender's point of view it is the
period when, to quote General Ludendorff's text-book
again, 'the immediate counter-attack acquires decisive

importance. . . . It is the most effective and the most economical method, both of human lives and of ammunition, of restoring the situation quickly and decisively.'

The text-book stresses the fact that both for the defensive organization and for the immediate counter-attack 'the strength does not consist in any way in the number of troops engaged, but in the skill with which they are employed and more especially in the harmonious co-operation of the different arms, and in rapid and energetic action'. In a later paragraph this same idea is summarized by the sentence: 'The defensive battle should not be conducted in a rigid manner by masses of men, but by an elastic defence by means of attacks employing artillery, machine guns, rifle and trench-mortar fire to the greatest extent.'

The text-book foresaw, however, that even these measures might not suffice to check a determined offensive by a great superiority of numbers assisted by the vast supply of mass-produced munitions which the French and British armies had at their disposal. The battlezone might be overrun, leaving within it only the small isolated garrisons of the fortified localities (*Widas*) still holding out, like rocks in the surge of a flowing tide, devastating and disorganizing the lines of attack within their field of fire. The attack approaching the second (artillery protective) line at the back of the battlezone, the original Hindenburg Line in Sketch 10, 'will now be engaged', to quote again from the text-book, 'in fighting the local reserves and fortified localities, and in consolidating its position among a strange system of trenches . . . and the difficult position in which the attacker now finds himself must be utilized without awaiting further orders'. The moment would have arrived for the immediate counter-attack by the foremost units (*Sturmbataillon* or *Sturmregimenter*) of the counter-attack divisions.

It will be noticed that the system for the counter-attacks in each zone is similar, but on a continually larger scale.

In the outpost zone the *Stosstrupp* was to deliver the immediate counter-attack, in the battlezone it was the special task of the support companies and reserve battalions of the front-line regiments, and, if they failed, it was the leading battalions or regiments of the counter-attack divisions which were to deliver it from behind the battlezone. For this purpose they were to be assembled 'close behind the Second Line' prior to an offensive. These regiments, taking forward with them the survivors of the front-line regiments or divisions, would push on through the battlezone, relieve the garrisons of the fortified localities, and without delay recapture the front-trench system and outpost zone. The recaptured position would then be reoccupied in depth as before. This immediate counter-attack from behind the battlezone was called the *Gegenstoss aus der Tiefe*.

Should the counter-attack divisions arrive too late or fail they were to deliver a methodical or deliberate counter-attack (*Gegenangriff*), the preparations for which might take several days, provided that the ground to be recaptured was worth the cost and was essential for the retention of the rest of the position.

In this way the new defensive battle was still to be fought *for*, but not necessarily *in*, the front line: the rigid defensive was to be replaced by the defensive-offensive. It brought up to date the teaching of Clausewitz, Germany's great military philosopher, that the defensive battle should take the form not of a pure defence (*kein absolutes Abwehren*), but of a combination of parry and thrust (*eine Verbindung von Parade und Stoss*); and the counter-attack divisions provided the thrust, the 'flashing sword of retaliation' (*das blitzende Vergeltungsschwert*).

The importance of having a sufficient reserve of divisions on the Western Front, ready to send as counter-attack divisions to any threatened sector, was for this reason fully appreciated, and it was believed that the staging of an offensive by the French or British armies on a scale sufficient to break deep into the new position would give ample warning for their timely arrival. The raising of another twenty-two divisions by the 'Hindenburg programme', in addition to a number of divisions released from the Eastern Front, enabled O.H.L. to form an O.H.L. reserve of forty divisions ready on the Western Front for this purpose in the spring of 1917.

10

General Ludendorff admits that the controversy over his new text-book 'raged furiously' among his own staff, and that he himself 'had to intervene to advocate the new tactics'.[1] But this battle of words was not confined to his domestic circle; it spread to most of the German commands and staffs, down to regiments and battalions, even, according to regimental histories, to the rank and file, those belittled scraps of humanity on whose behaviour and good-will the success of the whole scheme would ultimately depend.

The general principles of the new defence-in-depth appear to have been accepted unreservedly and with great satisfaction, especially as regards the immediate intervention by the counter-attack divisions from behind the battle-zone. It was the text-book's permission to the front trench garrison 'to yield elastically' which became the chief target for criticism. This was directly contrary to the old Prussian defence doctrine, *Halten was zu halten ist* ('Hold what you are ordered to hold'), on which the German Army had been trained since its foundation. In addition many officers, including General Falkenhayn,[2] the ex-Chief of O.H.L., believed that this phrase, together with General Ludendorff's introductory statement in the text-book that 'the infantryman would no longer have to say to himself, "Here I stay and here I die,"' would be interpreted as offering an easy excuse and way of escape

---

[1] Ludendorff, *War Memories*, VOL. I, p. 387.
[2] See General von Kuhl's *Weltkrieg*, VOL. II, p. 10.

from the hell of a modern battlefield, especially by the young and half-trained recruits who were already beginning to replace the heavy German losses in the Somme and Verdun battles.

This revolt seems to have been led by Colonel von Lossberg. At a conference at Cambrai on the 8th September 1916, the first to be held by Generals Hindenburg and Ludendorff after taking over command at O.H.L., it was he who got up and 'objected very strongly' (*sehr scharf aussprach*) when General Ludendorff suddenly broached the subject of the elastic defence.[1] Small wonder that he was annoyed to hear from the mouth of the new chief of O.H.L. the heresy of that elastic-band business which he thought he had crushed to extinction across the dinner-table in Mézières twelve months before. There can be little doubt that the great emphasis which he placed on rigidly holding the foremost line, in his 'Experiences of the First Army in the Somme Battles' mentioned in the previous chapter, was a deliberate intention to counteract the influence of the new text-book. Although issued eight weeks after the text-book, with which it 'assumed in its readers a thorough acquaintance', Colonel von Lossberg's memorandum went out of its way to challenge the instructions given in it for the conduct of the defence by the front battalions. At least six of the twelve sections devoted to that subject stress the fact that the fight must take place *in* the foremost line. During the battles of the Somme, it explains, 'every man was obliged to fight at the point at which he was stationed and the enemy's advance could only be over his dead body'. The only movement allowed to detachments of a garrison was a movement in a forward direction or to a flank, to avoid exposure to heavy shell fire. 'It was owing to this firm determination of every leader to stand and fight that the superior numbers of the enemy were destroyed in face of the steadfast, closely-knit ranks of our front-line troops' (*geschlossenen*, stressed in the German

[1] *German Official History*, VOL. XI, p. 17.

original in double black print, *Reihe unserer Kämpfer*).[1] That word *geschlossenen*, stressed in heavy black print, means literally 'closed' or 'serried', but read in its full context it embodies, as I understand it, the main challenge to General Ludendorff's text-book. It not only stresses the need for fighting the battle steadfastly and unflinchingly in the foremost line, as opposed to General Ludendorff's permission to yield. It also demands cohesion in the defence, with the battalion as the tactical battle-unit.[2] The new text-book, on the other hand, implied a far greater dispersion; the piquets, the *Stosstrupps*, the isolated 'group' garrisons of the fortified localities, the liberal permission to detachments of the front garrison to retire, all conduced to make more and more difficult control of the battle by battalion or even by company commanders. For this reason the text-book had made the group (one non-commissioned officer and eleven men) the official tactical battle-unit, and General Ludendorff, in his *War Memories* (vol. I, p. 387), admits that this was 'a risky business, of the success of which many eminent soldiers were sceptical'. Subsequent experience was to prove fairly conclusively that these critics were justified.

Another important criticism concerned the 'fortified localities' (*Widas*). In the later Somme battles every occu-

[1] It is a pity, and most misleading, that the last words of this important sentence should have become in the British G.H.Q. translation (3rd May 1917): 'that the superior numbers of the enemy bled to death in the face of the serried ranks of our soldiers', with no stress on, or explanation of, the word 'serried', nor emphasis on the meaning of the word *Kämpfer*, which, as a military term, refers to front-line units rather than soldiers. So translated, literal almost to the point of inaccuracy, a reader might justifiably dismiss the sentence as the idle ranting of a die-hard colonel, whereas it was the summing-up in a few carefully chosen words, and by a first-class brain, of the rich experience gained during the Somme battles.

[2] In the course of the Somme battles the chain system of command had been broken up and the battalion commander had become all-powerful in his front-line sector. Decentralization had gone so far, and Colonel von Lossberg's memorandum makes quite clear that he did not consider it advisable to carry it further.

Colonel Fritz von Lossberg
1917

pied shell-hole in the front line, whether garrisoned by a group of men or by a nest of machine guns, had become a fortified locality to be held at all costs. This system, which Colonel von Lossberg's memorandum continued to advise, resembled the French instruction of 1915, referred to above, a front line of fortified localities, rather than scattering them over a deep zone according to General Ludendorff's text-book; behind them would be a mobile garrison ready to take advantage of any situation, and at the disposal of its company or battalion commander. This was in keeping with the principle of cohesion of the defence under the battalion and company commanders, rather than the dispersion under group (one non-commissioned officer and eleven men) commanders which the text-book system entailed.

It is a tribute to General Ludendorff's flexibility of vision that he not only allowed Colonel von Lossberg's memorandum, 'Experiences of the First Army in the Somme Battles', to be circulated, unexpurgated, to all German divisions but even had it incorporated in full in a new *Manual of Infantry Training for War (A.V.F.I.)*. It may be that the opposition had led him to question the wisdom of some of the instructions given in his text-book, and possibly accounts for the statement in his *War Memories* (vol. i, p. 387) that his defensive battle text-book was 'completed' by the *Manual for Infantry Training (A.V.F.I.)* issued eight weeks later, although it contained such a contradictory doctrine for the conduct of the defence within the battle-zone.

These criticisms, important as they were, were however of detail. In general the idea of fighting a mobile defensive battle within a series of zones rather than rigidly in successive lines of trenches was approved, although the difficulty of ensuring that the counter-attack divisions were in the right place at the right time was emphasized. General von Hoen of the O.H.L. staff, for example, deprecated the alteration to be made in the dispositions of the front divisions and would have retained for them a modified form of the rigid-defence system in a less dispersed area, relying more entirely on the reserve divisions for the immediate counter-attack (*Gegenstoss aus der Tiefe*). General von Gallwitz, an ardent partisan for bringing the offensive spirit into the defence on all possible occasions, comments in his diary on the *Hoen'sche Theorie*, that it must be expected that this counter-attack 'out of the deep' would often arrive too late to be immediate and would therefore lose its value for General von Hoen's purpose, and he expresses surprise that such a theory should come from an 'otherwise very intelligent man'.[1] It is noticeable, too, that Colonel von Lossberg, in his Somme memorandum, gives considerably more space to the methodical than to the immediate counter-attack by the reserve divisions, as if in belief that more often than not they would arrive too late for the immediate counter-attack.

In order that the text-book doctrine might be thoroughly examined in the light of practical experience, Colonel von Lossberg recommended to General Ludendorff that a 'school' should be set up which divisional commanders, who were now to have the full responsibility of fighting the battle, should attend and give their opinions. A school for this purpose, *Divisions Kommandeur Schule*, was started at the end of January 1917 in Solesmes, with a complete infantry division and its artillery near at hand to give practical demonstration of different methods. It was attended by a number of staff officers, and brigade and battalion as well as divisional commanders; and General Ludendorff, the Crown Prince Rupprecht of Bavaria, and Colonel von Lossberg were among its early visitors. It was so successful that a similar school was set up shortly afterwards in Sedan behind the central Group of Armies.

It may be mentioned here that, about this time, 25th February 1917, to ensure a greater unity in the issue of

[1] Von Gallwitz, *Erlebem im Westen, 1916–18* (Mittler, Berlin, 1929), pp. 108, 174.

orders and instructions, the German armies on the Western
Front were organized into three Groups of Armies, a northern group under the Crown Prince Rupprecht of Bavaria,
from the North Sea to La Fère, a central group under the
German Crown Prince William to Pont-à-Mousson, and a
southern group under Duke Albrecht of Würtemburg to
the Swiss frontier.

II

The Hindenburg Postition and its elaborate defensive
organization was only twice severely tested in battle. The
first occasion was the offensive against it by massed British
tanks on the 20th November 1917. Surprise was gained,
and it was only garrisoned by a comparatively skeleton
force, skinned for the Passchendaele battles, especially its
artillery. This British offensive, inadequately supported by
infantry, was checked in front of or about the Hindenburg
II Line, at the back of the rearward battlezone, and nine
days later fresh divisions, hurriedly collected, made a
methodical counter-attack (*Gegenangriff*) and recaptured a
great part of the lost ground. When the Hindenburg
Position was again attacked during the summer of 1918
the German Army had lost its inner strength, its foundations were fast crumbling. The fact that the position was
overrun in such circumstances was no test of a defensive
organization. It may be said, therefore, with some truth
that the Hindenburg Position and its text-book organization can only be regarded as an academic exhibit, untested
by battle.

For this reason its chief value and interest does not lie
in itself, but as a point of departure. It was to give to the
remaining German defensive battles of the war their shape
(for example, the Wotan Position in the Arras battles and
the Flandern Position in the Passchendaele campaign),
and, if nations continue to fight with armies backed by all
the resources of science and mass-production, it probably

shows the way to the defensive battle of the future. Its importance is its place in the general development of the defensive battle in military history. In that great compilation of experience it has become another corner-stone.

Chapter VIII

BATTLE OF ARRAS—VIMY RIDGE: 9th April 1917

The Hindenburg Position was the German answer to the great strides made by the British and French Governments in the mass-production of munitions in 1915 and 1916. Those strides can be best appreciated by figures. At Festubert, for example, in May 1915, only 26,000 shells were available to prepare the British assault on a frontage of three miles. At Loos, five months later, 233,000 shells prepared the assault on a frontage of six miles, but even that quantity did not suffice to flatten out the German front-trench system; only where it was supplemented by cylinder gas did the infantry succeed in breaking into the position, and where it failed the German garrison mostly held the line. By the following summer the munition production had so greatly increased that the British artillery was able to batter the German front defence system on the Somme uplands with 1,508,000 shells on a fourteen-mile front preparatory to the infantry assault on the 1st July 1916, over twelve times the weight of metal per mile of frontage used at Festubert. This succeeded in demolishing wide sectors of the German trench lines except for the deepest mined dug-outs; but, sheltered in these deep caverns, a large percentage of the garrison survived to meet and check the assault.

Before the conclusion of the Somme battles General Ludendorff realized, however, that the *Materialschlacht* was about to enter a new phase. He foresaw that in the immediate future the mass-production of munitions would enable his opponents on the Western Front to batter or to neutralize not only a trench system 400 to 600 yards in depth but an entire zone back to effective range of the field batteries, a depth averaging 1,500 to 2,000 yards. His new text-book, issued on the 1st December 1916, made provision to hold that zone, doomed to become a wilderness of shell-holes, only lightly and to concentrate the bulk of the defence forces close behind it, ready to make an immediate counter-attack.

But in the first two tests by battle of this new German doctrine, at Verdun on the 15th December 1916 and at Arras on the 9th April 1917, its fundamental requirement, the presence of the bulk of the defence forces close behind the Second Line, was neglected, and the whole machinery of the doctrine broke down accordingly.

I

The French offensive on a six-mile (11,000 yards) front near Verdun on the 15th December 1916, to recover ground lost in the previous German attacks, was delivered under the direction of General Nivelle by four fresh divisions, with the four divisions in position following as a second line of attack,[1] supported by 827 guns. More than ever it was a case of 'l'artillerie conquiert, l'infanterie occupe'. The artillery preparation lasted for six days before the assault, and had been worked out in minutest detail during the four previous weeks. The final preparatory bombardment, directed by aeroplanes, battered the German trenches, dug-out entrances, and observation posts and the battery positions behind it. The infantry assault at 10.30 a.m. was preceded by a double creeping barrage, one of shrapnel seventy yards in front and one of high

[1] In all fifty-six battalions with ten of the forty-eight battalions in position took part in the assault, the remainder being in the second line of attack.

explosive 150 yards in front, and simultaneously a barrage of shrapnel was laid along the German Second Line at the back of the battle-zone, to cut off the retreat of the front garrison survivors and to stop reinforcements. In addition, every known dug-out entrance was kept under shell-fire until the infantry was close upon it. To cover the assault in this manner and for the preparatory bombardment over a million (1,169,000) shells had been allotted, approximately double the proportionate quantity used to prepare and cover the opening British assault on the Somme six months before (1st July 1916). The period, already foreseen by General Ludendorff, had arrived when the mass production of munitions enabled the neutralization not only of a trench system but of a deep defended area.

The five German front divisions, supported by 533 guns of all calibres, garrisoning this defended area, 2,500 yards in depth, had two-thirds of their strength in the battlezone and one-third back in rest billets six to ten miles away.[1] But the deep dug-outs in which the front garrison was sheltering proved to be man-traps out of which only a few of the defenders escaped before either the entrances were blown in or the French infantry had reached them. Out of a total strength of 21,000 these five front divisions lost 13,500 in casualties during the battle (15th–16th), of which about 9,000 were prisoners.

The reserve battalions of the front regiments (i.e. the third part of the front divisions in rest billets) did not reach the battlefield till the evening. The two counter-attack divisions, although ordered forward the previous evening in anticipation of the attack, were at midday still fourteen miles from the battlefield, and their leading regiments did not reach it till early the following morning. Both they and the reserve battalions were too late to make an immediate

---

[1] Two of these divisions were already weak, about 3,000 each strong instead of the normal 7,000. There were in all twenty-nine battalions, approximately two-thirds of the infantry, in or near the battlezone.

counter-attack, the French having already consolidated for defence the captured positions. The entire battlezone and most of its garrison were therefore lost. The necessity, expressly laid down by General Ludendorff in his text-book, issued a fortnight previously, for bringing up the reserve formations close behind the battlezone had been neglected, and the two commanders responsible, of the Fifth Army (General von Lochow) and of the XIV Reserve Corps (General von Zwehl), were dismissed the following day.

2

Although the two outstanding reasons for the collapse of the German defence on this occasion, the deep dug-outs in the front-trench system and the absence of reserves for the immediate counter-attack, were stressed in a pamphlet issued by O.H.L. shortly afterwards (25th December 1916), both mistakes were repeated almost identically on a larger scale at the battle of Arras-Vimy, four months later.

The Arras battlefield extended for nearly eleven miles astride the Scarpe (see Sketch 12). The seven-mile sector north of the river, to Givenchy, comprised mainly the Vimy Ridge position, which lay on a long forward slope with a steep escarpment behind it. This position, con-structed during 1915 on rigid defence principles, had accommodation for the bulk of the front garrison in deep-mined dug-outs in the front-trench system and only few dug-outs in the rearward lines. The four-mile sector south of the Scarpe, to beyond Neuville-Vitasse, consisted mainly of the new Hindenburg Line, to which the front garrison had swung back in the middle of February. That, too, had deep-mined, and only a few concrete, dug-outs in the front-trench system, although, being sited near the top of a long reverse slope, it lent itself to be built up in depth behind. The lie of the ground in this Tilloy–Neuville–Vitasse sector did not favour building up a defence-in-depth in front of the existing line, as had been done in the First Army sector

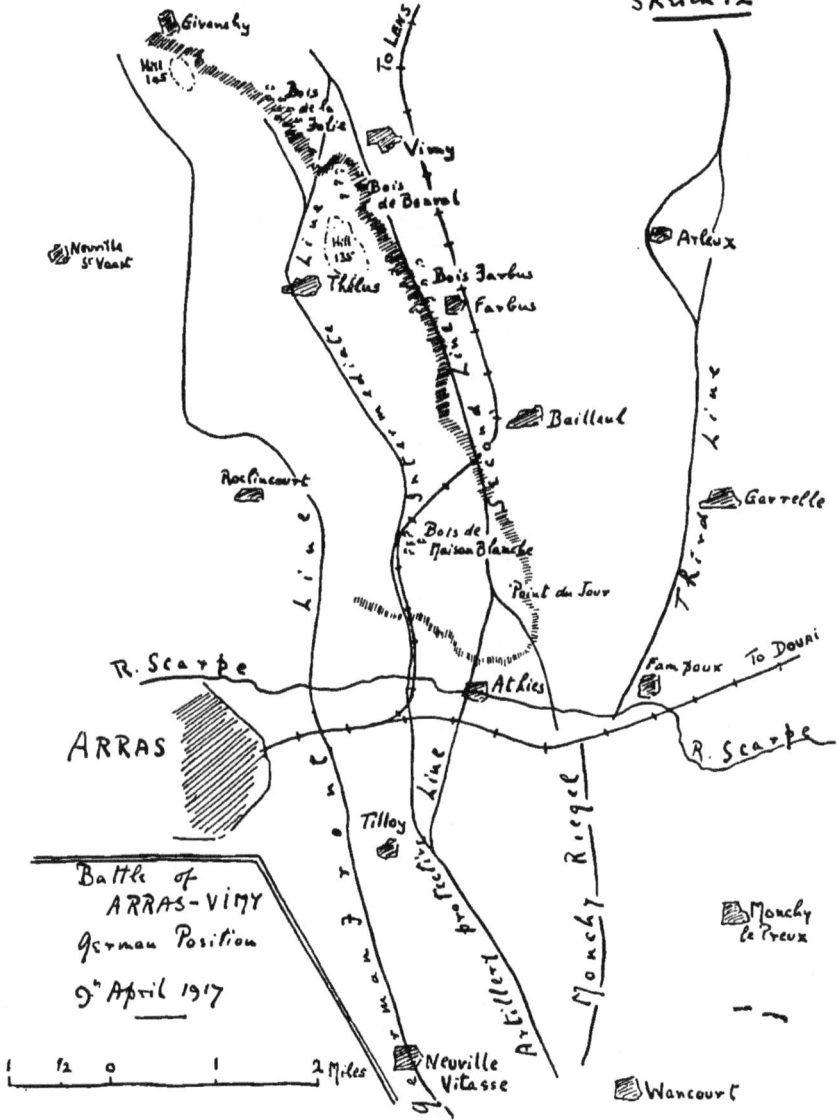

Sketch 12

Givenchy

Hill
145

Bois
de la
Folie

To Lens

Vimy

Bois
de Bonval

Hill
135

Neuville
St Vaast

Thélus

Bois Farbus

Arleux

Farbus

Bois de
Maison Blanche

Bailleul

Roclincourt

Gavrelle

Point du Jour

Third Line

R. Scarpe

Fampoux

To Douai

ARRAS

Athies

R. Scarpe

Tilloy

Monchy Riegel

Monchy
le Preux

Battle of
ARRAS-VIMY
German Position
9th April 1917

Neuville
Vitasse

Wancourt

1   ½   0   1   2 Miles

south of Quéant, neither would it have been practicable owing to the nearness of the enemy. But if Sixth Army headquarters had been as far-seeing as the First Army, on its left, where Colonel von Lossberg, already in February, was reshaping his sector of the Hindenburg Line into a Hindenburg Position, the main line of resistance would have been brought back from the front-trench system to the Intermediate Line, north of the Scarpe, and to the artillery protective line, south of the river (see Sketch 12). There is, however, no indication of any such suggestion in the Sixth Army sector.

During December and January a programme of reconstruction and training had been drawn up for the garrison on the principles laid down in General Ludendorff's new text-book: the creation of a deep fortified zone which was to be defended by a mobile defence, instead of the former rigid defence of a front-trench system. The programme was also influenced by the supplementary pamphlet issued by General Ludendorff nearly a month later, 25th December 1916, on the 'Experience of the Recent Fighting at Verdun (15th December 1916)',[1] which gave as one of the first lessons of that 'serious and regrettable reverse' that the front part of the new fortified zone was to be held lightly, like an outpost zone. 'The front trench cannot be held too thinly', it said, and suggested as a suitable garrison 'one man to every six yards, or one shallow dug-out (of concrete and steel girders) to accommodate a group (one non-commissioned officer and eleven men) every fifty-five yards, or double group every 110 yards', which was equivalent to making the front trench into a line of strong sentry posts; it also insisted that as 'deep-mined dug-outs in the front-trench system are man-traps' they were only to be

---

[1] A captured copy of this pamphlet was printed (2,000 copies) by British G.H.Q. on the 28th of February 1917. A copy of General Ludendorff's text-book was not captured until April 1917, but this Verdun pamphlet showed the tendency of the new defensive battle, the defence of a deep zone rather than of a trench line.

used in the rearward lines. It emphasized that 'depth is essential', and, for that reason, 'the rearward portion of the fortified zone will consist of a system of strong points and machine-gun nests'. On that network of machine-gun nests the mobile defence of the zone by counter-attacks was to be based.

The programme of reconstruction, therefore, demanded primarily the construction of concrete shelters (*Mannschafts-Eisen-Beton-Unterstände*), easy of exit, in the front-trench system to replace the deep-mined dug-outs, the excavation of an extra number of deep dug-outs in the back (intermediate and second) lines for distributing the garrison in depth, and the building of a number of fortified localities and concrete machine-gun emplacements between those back lines (see Sketch 13).

Although the Arras offensive was foreseen as early as mid-February,[1] this programme remained, in its essentials, a paper one, and various reasons are given. The Crown Prince Rupprecht of Bavaria, commanding the Northern Group of Armies, writes in his diary that it was 'due to shortage of labour that the position, built on obsolete principles, was not reconstructed in time'. Some of the regimental histories say that it was owing to the very wintry conditions of that early spring, which prevented the concrete setting, others that it was feared to thin the front garrison, as British raiding parties might notice the change and alter their plan of attack accordingly, and another reason given is that the careful watch kept by the British aeroplanes enabled all new work in this chalk-covered district to be easily spotted by photograph and to be shelled to destruction immediately. Probably all these reasons contributed to the result that, when the British and Cana-

---

[1] On the 13th February Crown Prince Rupprecht informed Sixth Army headquarters that the British would probably attack the left wing of the Sixth Army (from the Scarpe to Croisilles) and attempt to capture the Vimy Ridge as soon as the German withdrawal to the Hindenburg Line began.

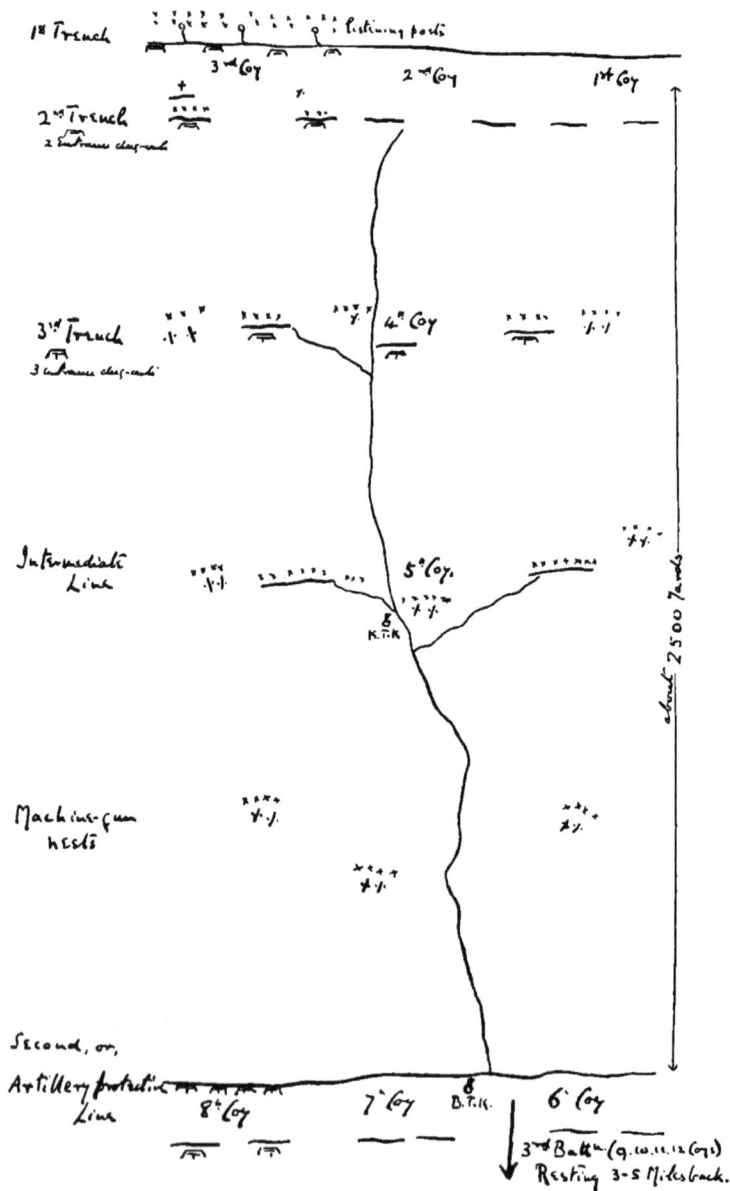

Construction programme: Defence Diagram used for guidance of a German Regiment at ARRAS: March 1917
(1st Battⁿ in front line, 2nd Battⁿ in Support, 3rd Battⁿ Resting).

Sketch 13

dian artillery bombardment opened in the latter part of March,[1] defence in depth by the German garrison had not been achieved, either of men or of machine guns or of fortified localities. Of the five or six fortified localities in each battalion sector, few were in fact where most required —in the rearward part of the battlezone; most were in the forward part of the battlezone, often extemporized out of existing dug-outs. It was emphasized, nevertheless, in the defence plan, 'that these strong points were to be the main centres of resistance (*feste Punkte*) of the new defence system and that they were to be held at all costs, even though surrounded by the enemy, to make easier the counter-attack by the troops from the back of the battlezone' (*aus der Tiefe*).[2] The reconstruction of the artillery positions was equally backward. The batteries were still grouped in lines, easy to see from the air and easy to gas, instead of being spread out in depth according to the new instructions.

During the preparatory bombardment the British and Canadian artillery fired 2,687,000 shells on to the German position on a frontage of eleven miles. On the Vimy Ridge sector alone nearly a million shells were hurled across no-man's-land on a frontage of four miles, compared with the one and a half million on a fourteen-mile frontage to prepare the Somme assault on the 1st July 1916. The casualties of the German garrison during this week of suffering (*Leidenswoche*), as they aptly name it, were not heavy, but from all accounts the men became exhausted both by the endless task of keeping open the dug-out entrances and by the difficulty of obtaining food owing to the condition of the ways of communication and to the shelling of the ration-carrying parties; numbers of men had no meal at all for two or three consecutive days. Although the six-day inter-battalion reliefs were maintained throughout, with

---

[1] The Canadian Corps and First Army bombardment began on 21st March, that of the Third Army on the 4th April.

[2] *Osterschlacht bei Arras, 1917* (Reichsarchiv monograph), VOL. I, p. 96.

great difficulty, the resting battalions in the villages several miles behind the position were so constantly shelled by the British heavy batteries that they had to move out into the open and had little sleep during this period. By the eve of the infantry assault the front-trench system had become lines of mud-filled shell-holes and the wire entanglement had been blown into shreds. One regimental history (2nd Bavarian Reserve, south of Thelus) describes the position as 'consisting no longer of lines of trenches but of advanced nests of men scattered about where formerly lay the first and second trenches (front-trench system), with a line of island positions along the site of the third trench (about 500 yards behind the first)'. Another (262nd Reserve) describes its front-trench system as 'lost in a crater field' and, taking the battlefront as a whole, the three companies which normally garrisoned the front-trench system along the 1,000 yards of each regimental sector consisted of a number of isolated defence groups, with sentry posts in shell-holes in front. On an average, one-third of the front divisions was in the deep dug-outs of the front-trench system at the mercy of the full weight of the British bombardment, another third was in support within 1,000 to 2,500 yards of the front-trench system, and the other third was resting in villages four to six miles behind.

3

The British and Canadian infantry assaulted at 5.30 a.m. on the 9th of April. The assault was preceded by a five-minute hurricane bombardment after a comparatively quiet night. This unusual bombardment procedure came as a surprise to the German garrison;[1] and the majority of

[1] Several of the German sentries had heard the arrival of infantry in the assault assembly trenches a couple of hours previously, but messengers were the only remaining means of communication and their reports reached battalion headquarters too late for artillery action to be taken (rocket signals were only to be used when an attack had actually begun).

those in the deep dug-outs of the first and second trenches, cramped twenty-five to forty men in each, had not time to clamber up the twenty or more steep steps to daylight before the entrances were in the enemy's hands. Many, when taken prisoner, were still half-dressed, and of those who tried to escape back a great number were without boots or else stuck in the knee-deep mud of the communication trenches, and were subsequently captured.

At the moment of assault it was still dark. A westerly wind was blowing a squall of sleet and snow into the faces of the Germans, and the dawn light was delayed by the heavy clouds. These weather conditions favoured the assault, for it affected the aim of a number of machine-gunners in the front-trench system and in the fortified localities thereabouts. It was these few men who caused most of the casualties in the opening stage of the assault, but thanks to the darkness they were in most cases quickly outflanked, surrounded, and bombed. In places a stronger resistance was offered, especially in the Hindenburg Line sector, south of the Scarpe. Here, as also immediately north of the river, where the battlefield had been less churned up by a shorter artillery bombardment, tanks, according to the German evidence, greatly assisted the British success both in the earlier and later stages of the attack; but the few in the Vimy Ridge sector were unable to master the mud of the German front-trench system and stuck thereabouts.

Simultaneously with the start of the assault, the British and Canadian counter-batteries had shelled and gassed all the German battery positions between Givenchy and Wancourt, putting out of action a large proportion of the guns, exploding shell dumps, completely disorganizing the ammunition supply, and gassing the horses of the batteries and supply columns. In addition the artillery observation posts, chiefly along the crest of the Vimy Ridge and in the Monchy Riegel, were mostly either destroyed by shell or smothered by a smoke-screen. Seldom during the war can counter-battery work have been so effective. At best, the Germans had in position less than a third of the artillery opposed to them, and there was, as a result of this crippling counter-battery bombardment, only a feeble answer when the coloured rocket signals went up from the German front garrison asking for artillery support.

On wide frontages the assaulting infantry was able to press on as fast as the mud allowed. Ankle-deep in it, the men dripped with perspiration, in spite of the temperature and snow falling, as they plodded across the puddled wilderness towards their first objective, about 600 yards beyond the front-trench system. There was now a glimmer of daylight, but so dim that the isolated nests of Germans in the third trench, with sleet still blowing in their faces, were unable to see, till close upon them, whether the mass of men approaching were their own front garrison retiring elastically, as was to be expected, or the enemy. At the start the proportion of assaulting troops to the defending garrison (front and support battalions) was about four to one, but as the front battalions had been eliminated in wide sectors, the scattered companies of the support battalions were now faced by nearly double that proportion of attackers. Some of them were surrounded before they could appreciate the situation, but a great proportion were able to take advantage of the new text-book's permission to yield, and fell back hurriedly to the intermediate and second lines. It was their wisest course in the circumstances. Within an hour, or less, the forward part of the battlezone had been overrun on the greater part of the assault frontage, and consequently nearly a third of the front divisions captured or killed. The assault, pressing through these great gaps, caused the resistance in intervening sectors to collapse. By about 8 a.m., with few exceptions, such as on Hill 145 at the northern extremity of the battlefront, there remained in the battlezone only the surviving companies of the support battalions, with a few remnants of the front battalions. The reserve battalions, the remaining third of the front divisions, though alarmed about 6.15 a.m., were still far from the scene of action.

Generally speaking, the support battalion commanders spread out their companies along some defined line which made a rallying position for men and machine-gunners streaming back from the front. There was to be no more 'yielding by detachments' except at their orders, and the force at their disposal was too weak to make local counter-attacks. There were exceptions, but this course seems to have been taken instinctively by most of the battalion commanders concerned. In the Vimy Ridge sector, where the intermediate line had been overrun on both sides of Thelus, the Ridge itself was abandoned and the companies were rallied along the Second Line or along the railway embankment at the foot of the escarpment. Farther south, however, to the Scarpe, the intermediate line was held and the corresponding, artillery protective, line south of the river.[1]

To these rallying positions withdrew also a number of survivors with machine-guns from the forward fortified localities, for the course of the battle showed that, in a long-prepared assault such as this, only in rare instances will a small isolated garrison 'hold on at all costs' for any length of time with an overwhelming attack passing both its flanks. Of the fifty or more forward fortified localities on the Arras battlefront the number that long resisted can be counted on one hand.[2] Although these, and a few less

---

[1] In greater detail, these rallying lines lay roughly, from right to left, along the Second Line at the foot of or on the escarpment of the Vimy Ridge (79th Reserve Division), along the intermediate line between the Farbus–Arras and Bailleul–Roclincourt roads (1st Bavarian Reserve Division), in the Railway Position (intermediate line) south of Maison Blanche Wood (14th Bavarian Division), along the railway embankment astride the Scarpe (11th Division) and in the 3rd trench of the Hindenburg Line (about 600 yards behind the first trench), south of Tilloy (17th Reserve Division).

[2] For example, the most gallant defence put up in the strong point on Hill 145 (261st Reserve Regiment) on Vimy Ridge, that in the strong point known as 'Prinz Franz Hutte' (2nd Bavarian Reserve

notable, hampered considerably the advance before they were overcome, it seems that those garrisons of the forward fortified localities, in this case the majority, who adopted a mobile attitude and assisted in forming a line of defence were more effective in temporarily stemming the assault and had a better chance of survival.

After a pause for nearly an hour fresh British and Canadian battalions began to advance on their next objective, 600 yards or more ahead. The sleet had turned to a heavy fall of snow, which covered their approach. On the Vimy Ridge the Canadian Corps reached the objective, the intermediate line, but elsewhere, although the majority of the fortified localities in the intervening ground were forced either to surrender or fall back, the scattered companies in the rallying positions along the intermediate line or artillery protective line south of the Scarpe held fast; in a few places where forced back they retook the line by local counter-attacks. Crown Prince Rupprecht in his diary gives his opinion that these companies would have delivered counter-attacks all along the line at this period of the battle, as they had been trained, if local commanders had known that strong reserves were behind them. But there was no sign or news of reinforcements and, in addition, there was a shortage of machine-gun ammunition and no artillery support, which made it impossible to demoralize by fire the advancing masses of British infantry, an essential preliminary to the immediate counter-attack.[1] These surviving companies of the front divisions therefore remained for the most part on the defensive and continued to resist for some hours, waiting expectantly for the promised reinforcements.

Regiment) on the Arras–Farbus road, and in the Chalk Pit (162nd Regiment) north of Wancourt, all of which held out till well on into the morning, and, on Hill 145, till the afternoon.

[1] A full train-load of machine-gun ammunition belts destined for the Arras front had in fact gone astray a few days before and was held up till too late.

About 10.30 a.m. the day changed its colouring. The browns and greys of mud, smoke, and sleet were transformed as the sun broke through on the battlefield from a blue sky. To quote the history of the 1st Bavarian Reserve Regiment, 'the squalls of sleet and snow, which till now had hidden the landscape, ceased, and the air suddenly became clean and clear, filled with spring sunshine.' From the Vimy and Tilloy high ground the German survivors could now see back for some miles, looking over the open country behind them, but there was no sign of reinforcements, and their supporting artillery was practically silent. By 11 a.m., and in places sooner, the British infantry began to penetrate unopposed the large gaps between the isolated German rallying positions. There were but few previously sited machine-gun nests in the rearward part of the battle-zone to cover these intervening stretches of ground, and, as the attack passed on behind the flanks, the last lines of resistance broke. The Canadian divisions reached the crest of the Vimy Ridge and the vast panorama of the plain of Douai was suddenly unfolded to them; they could even see the spires of that town, eleven miles away, glistening in the sun. Their advance was limited to the capture of the Ridge, and the Germans continued to hold the Second Line along its foot, but on the remainder of the battlefront the Germans fell back during the early afternoon across the open towards the Third Line and its equivalent, the Monchy Riegel, 3,000 to 5,000 yards behind.

The defending infantry had been defeated in detail. The front battalions had mostly been overrun in their deep dug-outs; and the support battalions, ordered not to reinforce the front battalions but to wait to deliver local counter-attacks, had found themselves faced by an overwhelming superiority. Being without artillery support most of the support battalion commanders had decided to wait on the defensive until the arrival of the reserve battalions; before reinforcements arrived, however, they were either surrounded or forced to retire.

4

The absence of any German reserves immediately behind the Arras–Vimy battlefront is one of the dramatic tactical failures of the war.

The Sixth Army commander, General von Falkenhausen, in his appreciation of the situation shortly before the battle, considered that 'parts of the front position may be lost but the whole of it cannot be overrun, and it will suffice if the five counter-attack [*Ablösung*] divisions are brought forward so as to be able to relieve the front divisions on the evening of the second day of the battle'. His chief of staff, General von Nagel, stated at a conference in Douai on the 6th, three days before the assault, that the relief of some of the front divisions might have to be carried out on the evening of the first day of the battle, but he believed that although parts of the front position (*I Stellung*, that is, back to the Second Line) might be overrun, these break-ins would be checked and held by local immediate counter-attacks of the front divisions. Further, the opinion of Sixth Army headquarters on the 7th was that, after all, the British attack which was imminent would probably be confined to the capture of the Vimy Ridge, which would be used as a springboard (*Sprungbrett*) for a big offensive later; possibly to coincide with the big French offensive in Champagne, which French prisoners had stated would not be delivered for another week about the 14th–16th April.

These, briefly, are the reasons given in the *German Official History* (vol. xii) why Sixth Army headquarters failed to comply either with the request of General Ludendorff, who 'on the 6th April had no doubt that a great British offensive at Arras was imminent and begged [*bat*] that the reserve divisions be brought near to the battlefield in the Sixth Army area', or with the request of the Crown Prince Rupprecht commanding the Northern Group of Armies, who wrote in his diary on the evening of the battle-day:

'We now have to suffer for the fact that Sixth Army head-quarters, despite my expressed wishes (on the evening of the 6th), did not send its reserves up closer to the front line divisions. I cannot but feel myself to blame for not having ordered Sixth Army headquarters to move its reserves up nearer the front.' To these requests the Sixth Army commander had replied that he wished 'to avoid overcrowding the villages near the front', and as a result the five reserve, or counter-attack, divisions were on a line east of Douai, and fifteen miles from the battlefield, when the British offensive was launched on the morning of the 9th. Moreover, on hearing the news, he did not send these divisions forward, but ordered all available resting battalions from flank divisions, and three battalions in Sixth Army reserve at Lille, to block the flanks of the British advance, retaining the reserve divisions intact to relieve the front divisions according to his original intention.

The distance of the reserve divisions from the battlefield had caused the front divisional commanders to hold back some or all of their reserve battalions, which were consequently put in too late. For example, the reserve battalions of the 14th Bavarian Division, north of the Scarpe, were still back resting in Douai on the morning of the 9th and did not reach the battlefront until the early afternoon. Of the resting battalions of the other front divisions, few were able to reach the rallying lines of the support battalions before the withdrawal of the latter had begun, and of those of the 17th Reserve Division, south of the Scarpe, two were held back, by orders of the division, all day behind Monchy, 6,000 yards away, 'as no other reserves were in rear'. Like the counter-attack divisions, the resting battalions, which formed a third part of the front divisions, were too far away to give timely assistance.

The confusion as to the purpose of the reserve divisions is confirmed by the fact that although they had for some weeks, according to their own histories, been 'trained in open warfare on the assumption that the task immediately ahead of them was to deliver a counter-attack from behind the Arras–Vimy battlefront, according to the new O.H.L. instructions', the Sixth Army order of the 3rd April said that they were to be 'ready to relieve the front divisions during the course of a protracted defensive battle'.

The divisional history of one of the counter-attack divisions concerned (4th Guard Division) sums up the matter in a few words: 'The British preparations for the Arras offensive were noticed long beforehand, but Sixth Army headquarters had not yet taken sufficiently into consideration the lessons learnt by experience in the Somme battles, which had been summarized by O.H.L. in its new textbook.'[1] General von Falkenhausen was seventy-three years of age, which might account for a disinclination to accept a new doctrine, but in his defence it must be said that his immediate superior, the Crown Prince Rupprecht of Bavaria, a man twenty years younger, seems to have been equally surprised at the course of events. 'No one', he wrote in his diary the following day (10th April), 'could have foreseen that the expected offensive would gain ground so quickly.' On the other hand, the Crown Prince Rupprecht's chief of staff, General von Kuhl, states in his *Weltkrieg* (vol. II, pp. 84–5), that 'the mobile defence in depth [*bewegliche Verteidigung aus der Tiefe*] was not practicable on the Vimy Ridge, which lent itself to be captured in one blow [*schlagartig*]', and adds, 'that he would have preferred to abandon many sectors of the Arras front before the battle as being unsuitable for defence'. If this was his belief, he had failed to convince either his own Chief or Sixth Army headquarters.

The story of the German defeat at Verdun on the 15th December 1916 had been repeated. The Vimy Ridge and the Arras battlefront had been lost and, with it, a great part of the garrison of seven divisions, the losses of which

---

[1] Kurt Gabriel, *Die 4 Garde Infanterie Division*, p. 85.

during the day's battle (9th April) are given as 474 officers
and 15,174 other ranks and 230 guns.[1]

5

On hearing the result of the Arras battle General Ludendorff was, he writes in his *Memoirs* (vol. II, p. 421), 'very
depressed; had our principles of defensive tactics proved
false, and if so, what was to be done?' Actually the defeat
had confirmed the principles given in his new text-book,
but Sixth Army headquarters had tried to fight the battle
after the manner of the early battles of 1915, such as Neuve
Chapelle, Aubers Ridge, and Loos, before the British and
French munition production had begun to take effect, and
had not yet realized the need for an échelon of reserves,
such as had been introduced during the Champagne
battles in the autumn of 1915 and become the outstanding
feature of the later battles of the Somme campaign.

If those five reserve divisions had been close behind, or
even within an hour's march of, the Second Line on the
morning of the 9th, as General Ludendorff had 'begged'
and as the Crown Prince Rupprecht realized, too late, he
should have ordered, the battle must have taken a very
different course. Four of them were north of the Scarpe,
as the main weight of the British offensive was expected
against the Vimy Ridge. Covered by the low clouds, which
had prevented air reconnaissance throughout the first half
of the morning, their leading regiments should have reached

[1] Kronprinz Rupprecht von Bayern, *Mein Kriegstagebuch*, VOL. III,
p. 161 (entry for 19th April 1917).
The British casualties on the Arras-Vimy battlefront during the
period 9th–11th of April were about 14,000 all ranks, but that figure
should not be taken as a comparison with the German. The British
total includes every wounded man who attended a dressing station,
whereas the German casualties were reckoned from divisional returns
every ten days, and the figure given above for one battle-day is probably very approximate and would not include the lightly wounded
who had returned to duty.

the crest-line of the Vimy Ridge within three or four hours after alarm.

The British and Canadian infantry, advancing by a deliberate time-table, did not reach the greater, southern, part of the crest-line until six hours after the opening of the assault, and the inflexibility of this time-table method did not allow advantage to be taken of the collapse of the German defence which had occurred. It gave time for the German support battalions of the front-line regiments to rally along intermediate lines, and the reserve battalions, which would not have been held back, would have reinforced them there. Behind that screen the leading regiments of the reserve divisions would have had two or three hours in which to consolidate a new line of defence.

The battle would have been joined about the steep wooded slopes on the eastern face of the Ridge, about the Bois de la Folie, Bois de Bonval, Bois Farbus, and Bois de Maison Blanche. Those woods would have become famous in military history, but happily they have avoided that distinction and still grow in quiet obscurity with their wild daffodils and blue periwinkles. That final act of the battle of Arras was never played; the tale stopped short of its intended end, and only the white beacon of the Canadian Vimy Memorial remains as a reminder of it, as well as being the symbol of a great victory.

6

Twice the new German defensive battle doctrine had failed because it had not been properly applied. General Ludendorff now made certain that the experience of Verdun and of Arras should not recur in the defence against the French offensive near Rheims known to be imminent, and delivered a week later (16th April). To avoid further confusion as to the purpose of the reserve divisions they were from now onwards to drop the name of *Ablösungs-divisionen*, which merely meant relief-divisions, and to be called *Eingreif-divisionen*. The verb *eingreifen* means 'to inter-lock' or 'to dovetail into', and, as a military term, 'to intervene' or 'to take part in a battle (come into action)', so that the English translation 'counter-attack division' does not cover the full meaning. But the German expression did convey unmistakably the sense that the *Eingreif* divisions were to be regarded as part and parcel of the defensive battle, and not merely lookers-on from a distance, waiting to relieve the front divisions when required. In addition, General Ludendorff gave his personal attention to the preparations, and, to quote General von Kuhl's *Weltkrieg* (vol. II, p. 88), 'the correct application of the principles laid down in the new text-book for the conduct of the defensive battle was ensured by frequent discussions and exercised by the troops in training schools and prac-tice areas.' There was no element of surprise; and in the sector to be assaulted, known from captured French docu-ments, 'the foremost lines were to be held thinly, and as many divisions taken out of the line as possible to act as *Eingreif* divisions; these, too, were carefully trained in their special task.' Behind twenty-one front divisions were placed ten *Eingreif* divisions at about 10,000 yards' distance from the foremost line; and about 10,000 yards behind again were the heads of a second line of five *Eingreif* divisions (Group of Armies reserve) ready to take the place of any of those of the first line which went forward. In this man-ner there was arrayed on a frontage of about forty-five miles and to a depth of nearly twenty miles about 300,000 infantry—nearly half a million men, including artillery and supply services—for the defensive battle.

The French offensive was made under the direction of General Nivelle, who had succeeded Marshal Joffre as French Commander-in-Chief at the end of 1916. Despite many warnings he clung to the belief that the method of attack which he had employed at Verdun on the 15th December 1916 was the key to the German fortress on the Western Front; even the capture on the 16th February

1917 of the German document 'Experience of the Fighting at Verdun', which disclosed the new defence-in-depth, and the fact that the Verdun defeat was chiefly due to a failure to apply it, did not alter his opinion, nor did the known capture by the Germans in a raid at Sapigneul (4th April) of the plans for his offensive, twelve days before it was to be launched. The author of *Kritik des Weltkrieges* comments that there is 'a borderline between determination in a commander, following undeterred a prearranged plan, and obstinacy, in the sense of refusal to bow before the obvious; General Nivelle had reached and crossed that borderline.'

The main French assault was made on the 16th April on a front of twenty-five miles against the German position along the Chemin des Dames, a battleground not unlike a large-scale Vimy Ridge. It was to be delivered by approximately 400,000 men against half the German concentration, about 150,000 infantry dispersed in great depth. It was to be 'brutal et continu', capturing in one bound ('un seul élan') the enemy's organized position and his battery positions. This first bound was to carry the assault through the entire German battlezone, to cross the Chemin des Dames Ridge and to reach the north bank of the Ailette beyond the steep northern slope of the Ridge, an average advance of 3,000 yards. Three hours were allotted for this movement and for consolidation, when the second bound was to begin to objectives 3,000 yards beyond again, for which another three hours were allotted. It was to be followed by a third bound of about 2,000 yards, so that within about eight hours the infantry were to break through to a depth of 8,000 yards and open the way for the cavalry to exploit the victory.

It will be seen at once that the farthest depth of the infantry advance, when the cavalry were to pass through, would scarcely have reached the first line of the German *Eingreif* divisions, nor was the artillery preparation by 5,350 guns and howitzers lasting ten days either as accurate or as intense as that of the Canadian Corps on Vimy Ridge.[1] But quite apart from that, it is interesting to consider what would have happened if the principles of General Ludendorff's text-book, or rather the ideas of those junior members of the O.H.L. Operations Section who were its authors, had in fact been faithfully carried out on this occasion; if, that is to say, the German front divisions had withdrawn from the Chemin des Dames Ridge across the Ailette stream at its foot, followed closely by those 400,000 French infantry, who would definitely have accepted this invitation-to-walk-right-in. Once across the Chemin des Dames Ridge they would have been out of sight of their artillery observers and in full view of the German batteries, and after crossing the Ailette they would have been at the mercy of the machine-gun nests on the northern side of the valley, backed by the *Eingreif* divisions in the woods behind and with observed artillery support. The retreat of the French survivors would have been cut off by a barrage of shell on the northern slope of the ridge.

That remains another of the unfought battles of history, but it was the battle for which General Nivelle's plan laid itself open. His infantry assault, *brutal et continu*, without first establishing artillery observation posts along the Ridge overlooking the Ailette valley, exactly suited the German dispositions. Many German authorities, at the time and since, have regretted that fuller use was not made of this opportunity for testing the elastic defence-in-depth; the French plan was known and the eighteen-mile Chemin des Dames Ridge was a perfect stage for such an operation.

Actually, however, the German defence along the Ridge itself was very strong. It had a number of tunnelled caves in the battlezone from which exit was easy, and the back of the battlezone, along or just behind the crest of the

[1] Roughly six million shells were used by the French Fifth and Sixth Armies during the whole of April on a twenty-five mile battle-front, compared with one million on the four-mile Vimy Ridge front for the bombardment alone.

Ridge, had been strengthened by a network of machine-gun nests. The front divisional commanders therefore decided to fight the battle on the lines of the new *Manual of Infantry Training*, which, it will be remembered, was Colonel von Lossberg's 'Somme' memorandum, instead of on the lines of the new defensive battle text-book. They gave no invitation to enter, with the result that the French attack failed even to cross the crest of the Ridge; the assistance of the *Eingreif* divisions was needed only in a few places for local counter-attacks and to relieve front divisions.[1]

The entire French offensive was defeated with a loss of 117,000 casualties (including 32,000 killed) in a few days, but the moral effect on the French army and nation was more important than the casualty list. They had been promised a victory which would drive the Germans out of France and end the war but, instead, not even the Chemin des Dames Ridge had been captured. Mutinies broke out, and a defeatism and weakness set in throughout the French army which lasted for several months. Fortunately the Russians continued to hold nearly half the German army on the Eastern Front, and the British army by fighting the battles of the Scarpe, Messines, and the Passchendaele campaign kept German attention away from the French battlefront during that critical period.

[1] A good account of the German defence is given in *Chemin des Dames*, by Gustav Goes (Hamburg, 1938).

Part III
THE ELASTIC DEFENCE

Chapter IX

THE WOTAN POSITION

When darkness began to cover the Arras battlefield on the evening of the 9th April 1917, the German front line lay roughly along the lower slopes of the Vimy Ridge and behind the railway embankment at its foot as far as Farbus, from where it fell back by Bailleul to the original German Third Line at Gavrelle (see Sketch 14). South of that village this Third Line had been crossed by the British advance, and the line along which the Germans finally held ran due south from Gavrelle close in front of the Gavrelle–Rœux road, and astride the Scarpe west of Rœux village. From the south bank of the river the new line turned westward again to join the Monchy Riegel, near the Arras–Cambrai highway, and then along that trench, held very lightly, to the original front-trench system, the Hindenburg Line in front of Wancourt.

The Vimy Ridge and the entire Arras position had been lost in the day's battle, and this new front was held by the survivors of the German front divisions, who had been belatedly reinforced by their resting battalions in the course of the afternoon. During the night and early hours of the 10th the five counter-attack divisions (1st Guard Reserve, 4th Guard, 17th, 18th, and 26th), together with a sixth (the 11th), diverted from Douai on its way north, began to arrive astride and north of the Scarpe. These six fresh divisions supported the survivors of the original seven front divisions behind or in the broken battleline between Givenchy and Wancourt.

191

The WOTAN Position
13 April 1917

—·—· = German front line 9th April.
— — = " " 10th
——— = " Position 13th

10,000 0   10,000 Yards

I

The orders of General von Falkenhausen, the Sixth Army commander,[1] on the evening of the battle-day (9th) were that the original Second Line, north of the Scarpe, and the Monchy Riegel, south of the river, were to be held at all costs as the new front line, and where lost to be recaptured; the former Third Line was now to become the Second, and the Wotan Line would be the new Third Line. Counter-attacks were ordered accordingly.

Early the following morning (10th), hearing that part of the Monchy Riegel had been evacuated in error, he visited his Group (Corps) commanders. General von Fasbender, commanding Group Vimy, north of the Scarpe, made a counter-proposal that the battlefront be withdrawn from the foot of the Vimy Ridge back to the original Third Line, Méricourt–Gavrelle; the line northwards to be continued around the west of Lens by the already prepared Avion Riegel joining the front line again at the Double Crassier, near Loos. This would mean the abandonment of an area 4,000 to 6,000 yards in depth, but the Méricourt–Gavrelle line, although sited on obsolete principles on a slightly forward slope, was a completed trench well-wired in front, whereas he maintained that the Second Line along the foot of the Vimy Ridge, overlooked by British observers immediately above it, was untenable in the circumstances. South of the Scarpe, too, the Monchy Riegel lay half-way down the long forward Monchy slope in full view of the British observers on the Tilloy high ground (Telegraph Hill), but by abandoning all that 4,000 yards of the forward Monchy slope a reverse-slope position offered itself from Rœux lake across the Monchy high ground to Guemappe; farther south, the Wancourt Tower Ridge offered a continuation of this reverse-slope position

[1] On the 10th of April the sector of the Sixth Army was from five miles south of Armentières to Mœuvres, a distance of forty-five miles; the entire Arras battlefield was within it.

to join the Hindenburg Line north of Croisilles, and would cut off the difficult Wancourt salient created by the British advance on the 9th.

General von Falkenhausen turned down this proposal, although it was justified by the new text-book instruction that a defensive battle should only be fought on favourable ground, and, if necessary, ground of no tactical value should be abandoned; also that 'in all counter-attacks the ground to be recaptured must be proportional to the anticipated losses'; for, as a position for defence, the Second Line and the Monchy Riegel were now not worth the cost of a single life. These persuasive arguments were, however, of no avail, and, instead, he placed the Group Arras, south of the Scarpe, at the disposal of General Fasbender and ordered him to prepare and carry out a big counter-offensive on both sides of the river to recapture the whole of the original Second Line and of the Monchy Riegel.

Crown Prince Rupprecht of Bavaria, commanding the Northern Group of Armies, when he heard of this plan was not satisfied, and early in the afternoon his chief of staff, General von Kuhl, telephoned to General von Falkenhausen to convince him of the necessity to withdraw to a line such as General von Fasbender had proposed. It was arranged to carry out a withdrawal as suggested during the night of the 12th–13th.

In the meantime the general uncertainty as to where and how to dispose the six fresh divisions arriving in the battle-area had led to inevitable confusion. This is exemplified in the conflicting orders for holding the Monchy Riegel, and also in the report of the Group Vimy commander to the effect that, after the Arras experience, he recommended an almost unresisting withdrawal from position to position until the unrestricted submarine warfare, then in progress, had had its expected decisive effect. Fortunately for the Germans, the British pursuit failed to take advantage of this lack of decision and confusion of ideas.

2

The Germans were puzzled as to why the British Third and First Armies tarried so long in the puddled wilderness of the Arras–Vimy battlefield when only a few scattered remnants of the seven defeated German front divisions lay between them and important artillery observation areas such as Greenland Hill and the Monchy high ground. Their histories attribute this delay to bad generalship (*mangelnde Führung*), and too rigid methods. The British Commander-in-Chief, Sir Douglas Haig, in his instructions for the battle, had asked the Third Army to exploit success south of the Scarpe by pushing through divisions of cavalry across the Wotan Line to Cambrai, while the First Army was to cover its left flank, north of the river, by holding the Vimy Ridge and sending a cavalry division through towards Douai. He was so optimistic that he even asked the Fifth Army, on the right of the Third, to break a passage through the German position at Bullecourt and send another cavalry division through at about the same time to make a converging advance on Cambrai. Two years of bitter experience of the fire-power of machine guns and quick-firing artillery had failed either to modify his contempt for the German power of resistance, or to kill his idea of employing infantry as a battering-ram to force a passage for cavalry. The corps commanders, on the other hand, closer to realities, knew that the German reserve divisions, some at least of the fourteen estimated to have been released by the withdrawal to the shorter Hindenburg Line, had not yet been engaged; and they expected that every trace of a German trench and strong point, marked on their maps from air-photographs, would be defended as stubbornly as during the Somme battles.

On the evening of the 9th, the evening of the Arras battle, there was therefore this marked contrast in outlook in the British direction of the operations. Sir Douglas Haig, back at G.H.Q., having heard the glad news of the collapse of the German defences on the whole eleven-mile front of attack, was picturing his cavalry divisions about to canter steadily on towards Cambrai with the German Sixth Army scattered ahead, eyes and feet firmly set towards the Rhine; the corps commanders, on the other hand, were writing orders for the morrow (10th) for their infantry to attack strips of trench a few hundred yards ahead, on the farther fringe of the day's battlefield, and which they considered would block any further advance. They appear to have regarded the Commander-in-Chief's cavalry instructions as purely romantic, and did not believe the Germans would vanish away.

Thanks to the chain system of command from corps headquarters downward, about 90,000 British infantry waited through the night for the respective Corps orders to permeate to battalions and companies, and they spent the greater part of the following day attacking and enveloping, according to those orders written the previous evening, positions which the Germans had evacuated overnight except for a few rearguard patrols. During the morning (10th) Sir Douglas Haig, hearing of the extent of the German defeat and that the cavalry had not yet gone forward, was exasperated at the delay and urged General Allenby, the Third Army commander, to send forward cavalry in pursuit at once through the waiting mass of infantry. At Neuve Chapelle, two years before, his request under similar circumstances had not been complied with; unfortunately General Allenby now approved and it was carried out. Even junior British infantry subalterns, watching the cavalry going through ahead of them, thought that the war must be over to justify such an order, and were not surprised when, later, they found that hundreds of dead horses littered the battlefield south of the Scarpe and blocked the streets of Monchy.

The German survivors on the Monchy high ground and in the Wancourt salient watched throughout the day the mass of British infantry marching and counter-marching in the distance. To men whose training was based on the Clausewitz doctrine of speed in the attack, 'every moment of halt, voluntary or enforced' being considered 'a precious moment wasted', this parade-ground entertainment was incomprehensible. They had expected, as early as the previous evening, to see a great fan of widely extended infantry patrols, strongly supported in depth, advancing towards them, with a few tanks and field artillery sections to settle local arguments; but, instead, after a whole night and half a day of waiting, they now 'rubbed their eyes in amazement' when about midday they 'saw clearly against the snow-covered ground a mass of cavalry advancing north of Neuville Vitasse, 3,000 yards away'.[1] The cavalry made little progress, but towards evening the British infantry at last arrived and prepared to attack the thinly held Monchy sector. They were, however, too late. The 3rd Bavarian Division, which had been hurried down from Lille, was arriving simultaneously behind this last weakly held gap in the new German battleline. The German official monograph gives a vivid description of the scene. 'At this critical moment the few German survivors looked back for reinforcements and saw a magnificent and unforgettable battle-picture lit up by the golden rays of the evening sun. Batteries of field guns seemed to come out of the ground in the middle distance and, galloping forward across the open, took up position in a great inverted crescent shaped formation on a wide front and opened fire at once. Help had come at last. What no one till this moment had thought possible, happened; Monchy was held.'

Once again, as at Neuve Chapelle, at Loos, and during the Somme battles, obsolete British methods had frustrated the efforts of the infantry to advance, and had given the Germans time to rally along a new line of defence. Marshal von Hindenburg, referring to the Arras battle in his book of reminiscences, writes that 'the English did not seem to

[1] Klahn, *Das Reserve Infanterie Regiment 86* (Berlin, 1920), p. 207.

know how to exploit the success they had gained: it was a
piece of luck, as so often before.'[1]

3

The discovery made by General Allenby, during the
afternoon of the 10th, that the Germans had indeed vanished from a deep and wide area of ground led him to
believe that the Commander-in-Chief's picture of a great
German retreat was not so romantic as it had seemed. It
lent colour to the idea, previously suspected, that the Germans might fall back to the Drocourt–Quéant (Wotan)
Line, and he decided to hurry after them with all speed.
In his Third Army operation order for the 11th, written
during the late evening of the 10th, he stated that the
Army was 'now pursuing a defeated enemy', and he gave
the Wotan Line as the objective for the day's advance. It
was to be directed, in continuation of the instructions for
the original offensive, chiefly south of the Scarpe; and the
Arras-Cambrai highway, leading up to and beyond the
southern side of the Monchy high ground, was to give the
general direction.

German regimental histories give flashes of insight into
what happened. The history of the 125th Regiment,[2] south
of the Scarpe, relates that, 'early on the 11th we could
scarcely believe our eyes when English squadrons rode
towards us in widely extended formation from the Arras–
Cambrai road. We stood up as on a rifle range and, laugh-
ing, greeted this rare target with a hail of bullets. The
survivors turned and galloped back with many empty
saddles.' The German official monograph (II, p. 83) adds
that 'never, in their two and a half years of campaigning,
had these men seen such a scarcely credible picture of
attacking cavalry squadrons, and only a few riderless
horses reached the front line. It was an easy victory for

[1] Von Hindenburg, *Out of My Life* (Cassell, 1920), p. 135.
[2] Stühmke, *Das Infanterie Regiment 125* (Stuttgart, 1923).

disciplined troops.' Later, about 2 p.m., the history of the 86th Reserve Regiment states that 'a few batteries fired into a mass of cavalry and our machine guns completed their destruction. Countless riderless horses galloped over the battlefield and we captured many.' On the other hand, British infantry, supported by a few tanks, captured Monchy village at daybreak (11th), a success which made the situation of the garrison in the Wancourt salient precarious.

The belated arrival of the leading regiments of the German reserve (*Eingreif*) divisions during the previous day and night, though too late to act as counter-attack divisions for the defensive battle on the 9th, had reinforced the survivors of the original front divisions, and sufficed to check the British 'pursuit' at the outset, with the exception of the loss of Monchy village.

4

General Allenby's order to 'pursue a defeated enemy' was given twenty-four hours too late. More important still, within a few hours of the writing of that order a new chief of staff was appointed to German Sixth Army headquarters who, within two days, was to convert the new German battleline into a defensive position as strong in organization as any yet seen.

Already, at the end of March, German O.H.L. had realized that the British preparations at Arras and about Rheims foreshadowed two big offensives against the flanks of the Hindenburg Line to which the Germans had withdrawn earlier in the month. To strengthen the Rheims front it was decided to move there the bulk of the First Army and its headquarters. About 10 a.m. on the morning of the 11th General von Below, the First Army commander, and his chief of staff, Colonel von Lossberg, were about to start from Solesmes[1] for Rethel, their new head-

---

[1] German First Army H.Q. had moved from Bourlon to Solesmes during March, with the withdrawal to the Hindenburg Line.

quarters, when an orderly ran out to the car and told Colonel von Lossberg that General Ludendorff wished to speak to him on the telephone. General Ludendorff then told Colonel von Lossberg that the Kaiser William had appointed him chief of staff of the Sixth Army and asked him to take over at once.

Colonel von Lossberg writes in his book that he already knew the chief cause of the Arras defeat, a wrong handling of the reserve divisions, and as the Sixth Army was next door to him (on the right of the First Army) he fully appreciated its difficult position at that moment. In order to master it, he demanded from General Ludendorff, there and then on the telephone, 'full powers' (*Vollmachten*), and he defined those two words by explaining that he wished to be free to take any measures he considered fit after personally examining the situation. In order to ensure this, he asked General Ludendorff to inform his new Army commander, General von Falkenhausen, and also the commander of the Northern Group of Armies, Crown Prince Rupprecht of Bavaria, and its chief of staff, General von Kuhl, that O.H.L. had given to him those full powers to decide how the defence was to be conducted. To these requests General Ludendorff agreed. Such precautions were undoubtedly due to the strong divergence of opinion then current throughout the German Army on the subject of the defensive battle, but they seem to have been unnecessary on this occasion. He evidently did not know that a ready welcome awaited him. Crown Prince Rupprecht in his diary entry for that day (11th) writes that General von Kuhl, usually very reserved in his comments, remarked on hearing of Colonel von Lossberg's appointment: 'If anyone can straighten out this tangle, he will.'

Having obtained full powers, Colonel von Lossberg made a final request to General Ludendorff before putting down the telephone receiver; he asked for permission to visit at once the Sixth Army front, and he asked General Ludendorff to tell General von Falkenhausen not to expect his arrival at Sixth Army headquarters in Tournai till the evening. Instead of going south-eastwards to Rethel with General von Below, he therefore set off alone in another car north-westwards.

There can be little doubt that when he started off on this new adventure he was quite decided to fight the defensive battle in the same way as he had fought it in Champagne and on the Somme, that is, by giving up no foot of ground and fighting the battle in the foremost line. He had paid little attention to the new text-book, knowing its authors, and the care he had taken to ensure his 'full powers' was probably to enable him to disregard it in practice.

His first visit was to the headquarters at Marquette close at hand, of the southernmost corps, Group Quéant (XIV Corps), of his new army. He found that Corps heavily engaged in a defence against an onslaught by the British Fifth Army delivered that morning at Bullecourt, threatening the important junction of the Wotan Line with the Hindenburg Position. The German defences at Bullecourt had been in his own (First Army) sector until the dissolution of the First Army the previous day and, unlike those on the Arras–Vimy front, had been built up in depth behind the Hindenburg Line. General von Moser, who had been appointed to command this corps three weeks earlier (18th March) after being the first director of the new *Divisionskommandeur-Schule* at Solesmes, had ensured that defence-in-depth was put into practice, and he writes that Colonel von Lossberg was satisfied that 'whatever the British superiority in men and material they would not break through there for the time being.'[1] His forecast was correct. The offensive of the British Fifth Army, intended to break a passage through the German position for a cavalry division to ride through to Cambrai, failed, and by 4 p.m. the Germans were again in possession of their

[1] General von Moser, *Feldzugsaufzeichnungen 1914–18* (Stuttgart, 920), p. 266.

foremost line; the 4th Australian Division, principally concerned, had lost 3,300 casualties, and the seven tanks engaged had been put out of action. Later attacks on the Bullecourt sector in 1917 were almost equally unsuccessful.

Continuing his journey northward soon after midday, Colonel von Lossberg visited the other Group headquarters (Group Arras and Group Vimy) and then several divisional headquarters nearer the battlefront. At these places he learnt the situation of the German front line and of the British advance, and also the orders already given by Sixth Army headquarters to withdraw from the Vimy Ridge and the Wancourt salient. He then went to various commanding artillery observation points, and saw for himself that the decision to withdraw, caused by the dominating position gained by the British on the Vimy–Point du Jour Ridge, was the only possible one. Walking forward to the foremost units in places to see the actual battle-conditions, he also realized that he would have to give up the stubbornly held principle upon which he had fought his previous defensive battles, and which he had so strongly advocated in his 'Somme experiences' memorandum. 'I saw', he writes, 'that in such a situation it was no longer possible to hold the foremost line and every foot of ground to the last man, and that such a principle would have to be abandoned' (*'ich gab malso eine bisherige scharfe Einstellung auf'*). North of the Scarpe the British, with their artillery observation posts along the Vimy Ridge, would be able to precede an infantry assault with an observed barrage of shell up to the depth of the effective range of their field batteries. He decided that the best method of defence in such circumstances was to regard the zone within that range as a lightly held battlezone, and that although the weak garrison might be able to resist minor attacks, in the event of a big offensive it would have to be allowed to fall back (*sprungweise auszuweichen*) through the battlezone. The bulk of the defence force would be held in readiness behind the battlezone, and when the attackers were reaching the back of it they would be met by an immediate counter-attack by these reserves which, supported by the mass of the artillery, would then advance through the battlezone and recapture the foremost line. He admitted that there was a considerable risk in this procedure, carried out under the eyes of the British observers, but he counted on the British infantry following close on the artillery barrage, and on the heels of the retiring German garrison, through the battlezone, and that they would be so intermingled with the German counter-attack troops on the return journey that their artillery would have the greatest difficulty in either supporting them effectively or of checking the counter-attack. He calculated that it would be late in the day by the time the German counter-attacks could recapture the foremost line and that the garrison of the battlezone could be redistributed in depth under cover of darkness.

While making this tour he heard, and could see, that the high-lying Monchy village had been captured by the British early that morning, and he considered that the observation facilities they had thereby gained would make a similar elastic defence necessary in places south of the Scarpe. He could also see from the back of the Monchy Ridge that a further small British advance there would make untenable the proposed Guemappe Riegel, on the reverse slope of the Wancourt Tower Ridge, a barren expanse which would then be overlooked for some thousand yards and more back, so that a further withdrawal to the Sensée river south of Vis-en-Artois was a probability in the near future.

He calculated that the British artillery would require at least three more days, till the 14th or 15th, to cross the puddled crater-field of their own creation on the old Arras–Vimy battlefield and to make a fresh deployment, so that at least that period of time would be available to organize a new position. In all that nine-mile area between Gavrelle and Croisilles there was no trench worthy of the name, and he considered that by the time the next big British offensive was delivered the existing front line would probably be a crater-field. He therefore set about to find a back position close behind it, similar to the back positions he had organized behind the foremost crater-fields during the Somme campaign. The southern part of such a position would also have to take into account the probable withdrawal from the Wancourt Tower Ridge to the Sensée river.

He writes that he pencilled a rough line on his map to mark the probable limit to which an effective British artillery barrage could reach. That line was to be the artillery protective line, later called the Boiry–Fresnes Riegel, and marked the back of the new battlezone. About it were a number of possible artillery observation points, such as the hill of Bois Bernard, the eastern end of the Gavrelle spur about Mauville Farm (1,000 yards north of Fresnes), and the important ridge between the Scarpe, at Biache, and Boiry. These commanding foothills would be the eyes for the mass of artillery which would have to support the counter-attack by the bulk of the defence force from behind the battlezone; and the artillery protective line, the Boiry–Fresnes Riegel, would have to lie a few hundred yards in front of them; from in front of Bois Bernard in the north, past the front of Fresnes, Biache, Boiry, and Remy to l'Espérance Farm, on the Cambrai–Arras highway, in the south. As a foremost line he intended to use the original Third Line in the Méricourt–Oppy sector, but from Oppy southwards he planned a new line to which the existing front line would probably be shortly compelled to withdraw. This was to lie close behind Gavrelle village, in front of the windmill, and thence along the reverse slopes of Greenland Hill and Balloon Hill to Plouvain and the Scarpe, this sector to be called the Gavrelle Riegel; south of the river it was to pass through Pelves and across the reverse slope of Infantry Hill, in front of the Bois du Sart and Bois du Vert, and thence by Saint-Rohart and across the back of the hill south of Vis to join the foremost line of the Hindenburg Position at the Moulin-sans-Souci, north of Quéant.[1] This line, the Vis–Gavrelle Riegel, gave a battlezone of about 2,500 yards, mostly on a reverse slope out of sight of the British artillery observers. The Wotan Line, already partially constructed, was about 3,000 yards behind the Boiry–Fresnes Riegel, and this back area was to be the rearward battlezone in which the bulk of the defence force would be arrayed for the immediate counter-attack.

5

I shall not forget the interest with which I followed the tracks of this great Position on my first visit to it about three years ago; for it soon became evident that in this most unlikely stretch of country Colonel von Lossberg had discovered, with the flair of an artist, an almost continuous battleground ten to twelve miles in length which had all the tactical advantages of the Py brook valley position. Once more, as for the forward shift of the Hindenburg Line, it was to serve as his model. From the back slopes of Greenland Hill, in the north, across those of the Monchy and Vis hills to the Moulin-sans-Souci, in the south, his new foremost line could be sited about 200 yards behind some sort of crest-line, with back artillery observation over the ground immediately in front of it, and a deep battle-zone was provided out of sight of the enemy's ground observers. It would be difficult enough to grasp the essential tactical values of these foothills in a single afternoon in perfect peace, with the roads in good motoring condition. But on that afternoon of the 11th April battles for the Wancourt salient and Monchy village were raging and British infantry were pressing hard against the new German line between Rœux and Gavrelle. All the roads behind this great Arras battlefield, between Souchez and the Sensée rivers, were crowded with reinforcements hurry-

[1] To avoid confusion of detail this line has unfortunately had to be omitted in Sketch 14.

ing forward to strengthen the German resistance and with ammunition lorries to supply the urgent demands of the forward battery positions. That Colonel von Lossberg was able to accomplish what he did, with the noise of battle and all the excitement of crowded roads on every side, justifies the Crown Prince Rupprecht's comment upon him, at this time, that he was 'almost superhumanly imperturbable' (*'der unverwüstliche Hüne'*).

6

It was dark when he left the battlefield and motored on to Sixth Army headquarters in Tournai. At a conference which he held on arrival with General von Falkenhausen, his new Army commander, and with General von Kuhl, who had come over from Cambrai to meet him, he agreed to the orders which had been given the previous evening, except that owing to the loss of Monchy village he wished to evacuate the Wancourt salient at once instead of waiting till the night of the 12th–13th, and this was ordered accordingly. That same evening he telephoned to General Ludendorff to tell him that he had organized a new Wotan Position to a depth of 6,000 yards in front of the Wotan Line, and that within this three-mile-deep position he intended to fight an elastic defence. General Ludendorff agreed, and must have been not a little surprised to hear that this man, who at the Cambrai conference only six months before had so strongly protested at the very mention of the words 'elastic defence', was to be the first to put the doctrine into actual practice. Although it was the exceptional circumstances of the Vimy Ridge which had primarily caused Colonel von Lossberg to adopt this method of defensive battle, it was almost certainly the discussions with those junior members of his Operations Section across the dinner table in Mézières during the summer of 1915 which had put the idea into his head; and it was the training given during the previous months to the

German infantry in the principles of the new defensive
battle text-book which those junior members, whom he
had once so criticized, had written which was to enable
the elastic defence to be put into practice at a few days'
notice.

That same night Colonel von Lossberg wrote out the
necessary orders and instructions for the preparation of the
new Wotan Position and for the elastic defensive battle
within it. The general idea underlying these orders and
instructions was, except for the elastic procedure, much
the same as that upon which he had based his plan of
defence on the evening of the 26th September 1915 to
meet the expected resumption of the French offensive in
Champagne in rather similar circumstances. But the increased material strength in artillery and machine guns
now enabled that plan to be intensified. The artillery, by
an annihilating barrage (*Vernichtungsfeuer*) on the enemy's
front-trench system immediately an assault began, was to
be the first line of defence to bear and break the initial
impetus of an offensive. The second line of defence was to
be the machine-gun organization, which would continue
to harass and check the lines of attack by direct and in-
direct fire as they entered and passed through the battlezone. The final and decisive factor in the battle was, however, still the infantryman; it was the local reserves, or the
Eingreif reserves as the case might be, who were to exploit
the fire-effect of the artillery and machine guns by immediate counter-attack and to recapture the original position.

In the event of the British changing their method of
attack and making effective use of the great advantages
given to them by the Vimy Ridge observation area,
Colonel von Lossberg requested the Crown Prince Rupprecht that same night to order the construction as soon
as possible of a Wotan II Line, which was to lie approximately from the western edge of Douai southwards in
front of Goeulzin and along the eastern bank of the Agache
where, about Sains-les-Marquion, it would meet the cor-

responding Hindenburg II Line. The Wotan Line now became the Wotan I Line, and the fact that most of these lines of the Wotan Position were not even begun was immaterial. Their trace on a map marked the limits of the various zones, and it was in the disposition of the troops in depth within those zones that lay the strength of the defence.

7

Colonel von Lossberg writes that he spent most of the next few days in and about the battlezone to see that the defence was organized according to his instructions. During the 11th–13th, nine, mostly fresh, divisions occupied the eighteen miles of battlezone between Loos and the Hindenburg Line; nine miles of the foremost line of which, from Gavrelle astride the Scarpe to the Hindenburg Line north of Croisilles, was as yet only a line of hastily dug shelter-pits.[1]

Whenever possible this foremost line lay behind some sort of crest-line; and, for example, even the slight rise of ground alongside the Gavrelle–Rœux road sufficed to give its garrison a certain concealment. By night sentry posts were placed a few hundred yards in front, and by day a few observers were left in forward shelter-pits.

In the battlezone, that is, the area between the existing front line and the Boiry–Fresnes Riegel, he ordered that there was to be as little digging as possible. The system of 'the invisible garrison' (*die Leere des Gefechtfeldes*), applied

---

[1] See Sketch 14. The nine divisions were the following: the 80th Reserve and 50th, to be withdrawn from the Lens sector, unattacked on the 9th April, were to remain as front divisions in the Avion–Loos Riegel; four of the Sixth Army reserve (counter-attack) divisions (4th Guard, 17th, 18th, and 26th) and one passenger division (111th), on its way north diverted from Douai to the battlefield, were to occupy the original Third Line from Méricourt to Gavrelle and thence astride the Scarpe along the new defence-line to north of Monchy-le-Preux; the two divisions (3rd Bavarian and 35th) from O.H.L. reserve were to hold the Monchy sector and thence astride the Cojeul stream and along the Guemappe Riegel to the Hindenburg Line, north of Croisilles.

on the Somme to the shell-hole garrison of the foremost line, was now to be applied to the entire 2,000 yards depth of the battlezone. The front and support battalions, disposed within it as thinly as in the Hindenburg Position which was considered the minimum consistent with security against raids and minor attacks, were to be sheltered in dug-outs in the occasional woods or grouped in shell-hole areas in folds of the ground; and those in the latter were to change position frequently so as to mislead enemy air observers for artillery fire. The reserve battalions of these front divisions were to remain in villages two or three miles back.

An important innovation was in the siting of the machine guns. Those of the front battalions were in shell-craters a few hundred yards behind the foremost line. Those of the support and reserve battalions were in dug-outs or shelters sited chequerwise in the intermediate part of the battlezone, ready to take up position in the open where required. The system of placing them in defended localities to be held at all costs and spread about the battlezone, which had been a special feature of the Hindenburg Position, was discarded; instead, their purpose was now to be not so much to break up an assault as to provide the essential fire-support preparatory to the immediate counter-attacks. They were, therefore, to be able to change position as the situation demanded. The disposition of the marksmen (*Scharf-Schützen*) machine-gun brigades, one of which (consisting of fifteen to twenty guns) was allotted to each front-line division, was also reorganized. In the Hindenburg Position they had been placed in the more important defended localities within the battlezone, but by an O.H.L. order at the end of March 1917 they were to be used 'to protect the artillery' and the position of these divisional machine guns was, therefore, to be about the artillery protective line.[1] For the first time these S.S. machine-gun

[1] This order was too late to be applied to the Arras–Vimy position before the battle on the 9th April. For example, the guns of the 20th

brigades, formed in the autumn of 1916 and specially trained at their own school established at Rozoy, were now arrayed about the back of the battlezone, 1,500 to 2,000 yards from the front line, where they were to act as rallying points (*Anklammerungspunkte*) for its garrison, and also to be ready to provide the essential fire-support for the immediate counter-attack by the *Eingreif* regiments.[1]

Similar methods were adopted for concealing the field artillery batteries. They, too, took up position mostly in folds of ground, and frequently changed position, so that the reports of British aeroplane observers were nullified; during an attack the guns were to be man-handled up to a position from which they could fire at, or barrage, the British advance and support the German counter-attacks.

8

By the morning of the 13th the nine front divisions were disposed accordingly, and by that time also the advanced troops holding below the Vimy Ridge and those in the Wancourt salient had been brought back, and all the scattered elements of the original front divisions had moved away to rest areas. By that same morning, too, six divisions from O.H.L. reserve had arrived behind the front divisions as the new *Eingreif* divisions. They were billeted in villages behind the Wotan I Line, behind the corps (Groups of divisions) they were to support.

That Colonel von Lossberg expected the British to exploit their Arras–Vimy victory by an advance north of the Scarpe, where the outlying spurs offered a succession of artillery observation positions over a continually falling

S.S. Machine-Gun Brigade attached to the 79th Reserve Division on Vimy Ridge were sited about the middle of the battlezone, 800–1,200 yards from the front line, and were destroyed early in the battle.

[1] A good account of the formation of the S.S. Machine-Gun Brigades may be read in the history by Brauns, *Maschinen-Gewehr-Scharfschützen-Abteilung No. 22* (Berlin, 1923).

slope, is shown by the fact that he placed four reserve (*Eingreif*) divisions (15th Reserve, 1st Guard Reserve, 185th, and 208th) north of the river, and only two (221st and 3rd Guard) on an equal frontage south of the river, where the conditions for the defensive battle were incomparably more favourable.[1]

As these reserve (*Eingreif*) divisions were now to be used in the manner proposed by General Ludendorff's textbook, that is for a form of elastic defence, and their counter-attack action was to be, as it had said, of 'decisive importance', Colonel von Lossberg prepared a more detailed organization for them than ever before. So far the arrangements for their intervention in the defensive battle had been only tentative. They may be said to have originated during the Somme battles, when, at the end of September 1916, Colonel von Lossberg had organized two battle-reserve groups (*Kampfreserve-Gruppen*) of infantry and artillery of his reserve divisions, close behind the more threatened sectors of the Somme battlefront; they did not have to be employed as such, but the idea was a further development of the principle of the échelon of reserves he had prepared behind the Champagne battlefront in the autumn of 1915. In both these instances, however, their intention was to be that of exerting a constant forward pressure against an invader by immediate counter-attacks, each échelon taking the place of the one in front as it went forward, until the foremost line was recaptured. General Ludendorff's text-book of the 1st December 1916 had asked that 'as many intact [*geschlossene*] divisions as possible be held in readiness behind the front either for immediate counter-attack or to relieve the exhausted front divisions', but both at Verdun on the 15th December 1916

---

[1] North of the Scarpe the 15th Reserve Division arrived in the Libercourt area on the 11th of April, the 1st Guard Reserve Division in the Ostricourt area on the 10th April, the 185th Division in the Pont de la Deule area on the 12th April; south of the Scarpe, the 221st Division arrived in the Bellone area and the 3rd Guard Division in the Ecourt Saint Quentin area on the 12th April (see Sketch 14).

and at Arras–Vimy on the 9th April 1917 the reserve
(*Ablösung*) divisions had been too far back to take any part
in the battle. The experience of those two battles was not
to be repeated, and the preparations to meet the French
offensive about Rheims, described in the previous chapter
but which had not yet been delivered (16th April), and
the British offensive astride the Scarpe, believed to be
imminent, took it into full account.

Behind the Chemin des Dames battlefront one *Eingreif*
division was placed behind every two front divisions; one
of its regiments with a complement of artillery was in a
support assembly position close to the Second Line, and
its other two regiments were back behind the Third Line.
For example, behind the Vailly–Beaulne sector (Group
Vailly) the forward regiment of the 45th Reserve Division
(*Eingreif* division) was about Trucy near the Ailette, 5,000
yards behind the foremost line, and the other two regiments were about Chivy, 6,000 yards behind again. Simultaneously, Colonel von Lossberg was making similar preparations for support and reserve assembly areas in the
rearward battlezone behind the Scarpe battlefront, but he
placed those two back *Eingreif* regiments closer; for example, the support assembly area behind the Monchy
sector, which was a normal one, was 5,000 yards behind
the foremost line, and the reserve assembly area was only
about 3,000 yards farther back (see Sketch 15).

In both the Rheims and the Scarpe battle-areas the time
and place for the intervention of the *Eingreif* divisions
remained in the hands of the Army commander concerned,
but in the Scarpe area a more detailed organization was
arranged to avoid delay in their forward movement. As
soon as an *Eingreif* division had been handed over by the
Army headquarters to a Group commander, one word sent
by the latter to the *Eingreif* division was to suffice for its
orders to move. For example, the 221st Division was *Eingreif* division to the 26th and 3rd Bavarian Divisions, and
the word 'Hamblain' signified the immediate movement

of its *Eingreif* regiments to their respective support and reserve assembly areas behind the 26th Division, and the word 'Boiry' to those behind the 3rd Bavarian Division. On arrival, the leading *Eingreif* regiment came automatically under the orders of the front divisional commander. In this way there were arranged a succession of lines, or échelons, of reserves back to ten thousand yards; and, as in the Hindenburg Position, the bulk of the defence forces was arrayed behind the battlezone. Normally, of each front-line division the six front battalions were about the foremost line, the six support battalions were in the back part of the battlezone, and the six reserve battalions were resting in the rearward battlezone, while behind each two front divisions was one *Eingreif* division (nine battalions); making fifteen battalions behind the battlezone to twelve within it.

9

Already, by the morning of the 13th, the great gap made by the British offensive on the 9th had been barred and bolted. Within forty-eight hours Colonel von Lossberg had created and completed a new defence organization on a frontage of eighteen miles and to a depth of ten with fifteen divisions—about 150,000 men including artillery and engineers—and with every unit in a position of readiness; probably a record for rapid and efficient staff work. It was an achievement which fully justifies the tribute paid in a brief account of the Scarpe battles, issued by the German General Staff in January 1918, 'to the prodigious creative mental energy [*unglaubichen geistigen Spannkraft und fabelhaften Willensnatur*] of this exceptional man'. To him, the account adds, 'is due the credit for having given practical shape to the organization of the new defensive battle in all its details'.

It was evident that the British artillery were taking longer to come forward to new positions than the expected three or four days. April showers of snow and rain had continued, and made movement across the shell-torn battle-area of the 9th very difficult. Colonel von Lossberg therefore decided to continue to hold the existing front line as a foremost line and not to withdraw to the proposed foremost line of the Wotan Position until compelled. Owing to the probable weakness of the artillery support for any British attacks in the immediate future he also modified his original intentions. He ordered that the elastic defence be put into effect only in sectors where the ground was favourable for the local immediate counter-attack, and that elsewhere the existing foremost line was to be held as long as possible. This was in effect a compromise between his previous principles and those of the elastic defence. The general invitation-to-walk-right-in (*An-sich-herankommen-lassen*) of the Hindenburg Position was now to be limited to a few narrow and widely separated doorways.

On the 14th this Wotan organization was to be put to its first test.

10

After the check, on the 11th, to the advance of General Allenby's Third Army, the original far-reaching objectives given to it by British G.H.Q. were abandoned and replaced by the more modest one of reaching the Drocourt–Quéant (Wotan I) Line, the site of which had long been known from air photographs. As a preliminary the VII and VI Corps were ordered to carry out attacks on the 14th April with the object of capturing two commanding areas of observation, Hill 92 on the Wancourt Tower Ridge, south of the Cojeul, and Infantry Hill, 1,200 yards east of Monchy village. The exploitation of the two salients thus created and the observation points obtained would, it was believed, enable the general advance of the Third Army to be continued.

The two comparatively minor battles which resulted

from a clash with the new Wotan organization are worth
describing in some detail as they show the practical application, one of the rigid and the other of the elastic method
of defending the foremost line.

II

The main attack of the VII Corps on the Hill 92 (Wancourt Tower Ridge) sector was delivered by the 56th
Division at daybreak (5.30 a.m.) with the Queen Victoria's
Rifles (1st–9th London Regiment) and Queen's Westminster Rifles (1st–16th London Regiment) leading, and
the histories of those two regiments tell of its course.[1] The
battalions were to advance in two waves, each of two lines
200 yards apart, and with 300 yards between the waves;
the men of each line to keep six paces apart. The objective
was Chérisy and the line of the Sensée stream, and the
divisions on either flank were to conform. The short preliminary bombardment and subsequent barrage by the
British supporting artillery are described as 'merely groping, in the sense that there was no information as to where
the Germans had made a stand. Consequently it only had
the effect of warning the Germans that an attack was on
foot.' It was a fine, clear morning with the remains of a
moon to help the dawning day, and the record of the
Westminster Rifles adds that 'as soon as the leading waves
of infantry had gone over the Tower Ridge and started
down the further slope they were met by a murderous
machine-gun fire. Practically no messages got back and
there were hardly any survivors from the leading waves.'
According to the history of the Queen Victoria's Rifles,
'within a few seconds, or so it seemed, of the beginning of
the attack the German batteries opened a counter-barrage
on the advancing lines and played havoc with them, check-

[1] Major S. A. Keeson, *Queen Victoria's Rifles: 1792–1922* (Constable,
1923), p. 234; Major J. Q. Henriques, *Queen's Westminster Rifles:
1914–18* (Medici Society, 1923), pp. 149–53.

ing the pace so that our own barrage, firing according to a time-table, gradually crept further and further away, with the result that our men, when they continued the advance, were at the mercy of the German infantry and machine guns, who were able to come up from cover and open a devastating fire'. The two battalions lost in casualties about two-thirds of their strength (Q.V.R., 11 officers and 350 other ranks; and Q.W.R., 12 officers out of 15, and 256 out of 482 other ranks), and by 8 a.m. the survivors were back to the line from which the attack had started.

Those few quotations justify the German dispositions, which, as mentioned above, were based on the assumption that the British artillery had not had time to discover the whereabouts of the German front line and machine-gun nests, sited on a reverse slope, nor of the German batteries in the woods and depressions of the Cojeul and Sensée valleys. It was for that same reason, complete ignorance of what lay on the other side of the hill, that, to quote the history of the Queen Victoria's Rifles again, 'to most of us the enterprise appeared to be over-rash' when the orders arrived for it the previous evening.

The German garrison was to hold the foremost line here as long as possible; for the ground, sloping away behind, was bare of cover or undulation for several hundred yards; and therefore unsuitable for elastic defence. The sector attacked was defended by three companies of the 61st Regiment, the four companies of its front battalion being spread out along a frontage of 2,300 yards from Wancourt Tower to the Hindenburg Line, with the support battalion 1,200 to 1,500 yards behind, west of Chérisy. The German account[1] states that in the sector attacked, between Wancourt Tower and the Heninel–Fontaine track, the front companies lay in 'man-made rabbit-holes and shelter pits behind the crest of the ridge, varying from 100 yards behind it on the right by the tower-ruins, to 600 yards by the Fontaine track, with listening posts on the crest-line'.

[1] Von Kaiser, *Das Infanterie Regiment 61* (Berlin, 1928).

It adds that after the drum-fire bombardment at 5.15 a.m. the British assault was expected, and that 'the advancing lines, after suffering heavy loss from the German barrage, were mown down by machine-gun fire as they came over the crest-line and down the reverse slope with no fire-support'. In these circumstances it had only needed a few machine guns in the hands of cool-headed, efficient gunners, firing 500 bullets a minute, to stop an attack by two battalions within the space of a few hundred yards. The ground in front, the account adds, 'was soon strewn with dead and wounded, and on the left (where some Q.V.R broke in temporarily) twenty-five unwounded English were taken prisoner and the line retaken'. The German casualties in the action are given as thirteen killed (including one officer) and thirty-six wounded.

12

Within sight, 2,000 yards to the north across the Cojeul valley, another tragedy was being enacted simultaneously, for the offensive by the British VI Corps, north of the Arras–Cambrai highway, had a similar fate, though in a different manner. The key operation was the attack by the 29th Division along the Monchy Ridge, a west-to-east feature saddle-shaped between Monchy village and the rise of ground 1,200 yards to eastward, known as Infantry Hill (see Sketch 15). The intention was to occupy Infantry Hill as a preliminary to the advance on Boiry, but here again the method employed was disastrous. It would have sufficed to gain the excellent observation points on the flanks of Infantry Hill, keeping the centre of the line back behind the crest-line, where it would have been in a good position for defence and well supported by observers in Monchy. Instead, however, the attack was ordered to press on to a line out of sight on the farther, reverse, slope, and to send patrols on to the Bois du Vert and Bois du Sart.

The attack was to be carried out on a frontage of 1,000

Sketch 15

Wotan I Line

R. Scarpe

Pelves

26 Div.

Hamblain

Reserve assembly area

II Batt⁷/18

II Batt⁷/17

Etaing

Reserve assembly area

R. Sensée

Support assembly area

I Batt⁷/23

3 Bav. Div.

Support assembly area

R. Sensée

Support assembly area

I Batt⁷/18

I Batt⁷/17

Boiry

R. Cojeul

35 Div.

I Batt⁷/23

9/23

10/23

Riegel

Bois des Aubépines

11/23

Bois du Sart

12/23

6/23

Infantry Hill

Bois du Vert

Bois du Sart

Bois le Vert

M.E Wood

9/17

13/5

19/5

9/5

3/5

11/5

Arrow Head

Park Copse

Twin Copses

7/23

Windmill

6/23

5/23

12/17

10/17

11/17

ARRAS

CAMBRAI

Monchy le Preux

Monchy le Preux : 5 a.m. 14 April 1917

500   0   1000 Yards

yards by the Newfoundland and 1st Essex Regiments, the leading waves of which assembled in a trench dug overnight 100 yards east of the village. The preparatory bombardment, which began at 4.30 a.m., was not so 'groping' as that on Tower Ridge, for the German front line, though on the reverse slope of a slight undulation in front of Infantry Hill, was only about 500 yards from the higher-lying Monchy village and had been roughly located by observers there. A black, brown, and green cloud of smoke from the bursting shells soon covered it, but before the conclusion of the bombardment the German garrison was seen, in the dim dawnlight, hurrying away from the trench. Shortly afterwards, at 5.30 a.m., the bombardment lifted forward and the British infantry advanced. They crossed the first trench and halted at the scrapings of a second trench, 200 yards beyond, finding both practically deserted, and then waited, according to time-table, while the support waves came forward from Monchy village. The advance then continued, both battalions moving on in high spirits and meeting little opposition.

On the right the flank guards of the Newfoundland battalion passed the Windmill and occupied Machine-Gun Wood, 500 yards beyond, where, by light of some burning wooden huts, its battalion headquarters in Monchy saw the men digging in, but that is the last that is known of them; they never returned. The centre of the Newfoundland battalion halted before reaching Infantry Hill and a second wave went on over the crest-line, but here again no report and no survivor ever came back. Two machine guns were sent forward to cover the second wave while it dug in beyond Infantry Hill, but they too were seen no more, though the guns were heard firing at intervals. It is, however, known from a message sent back by the Essex battalion that the Newfoundland battalion reached its objective and that its patrols advanced into the Bois du Vert as ordered, but beyond that message there is no further evidence.

Meanwhile, on the left, the left flank of the Essex battalion had captured Arrow Head Copse, taking two German machine guns, and then pressed on to the northern side of Twin Copses, where a chain of strong points overlooking the slope northward down to the Scarpe was sited. This was intended to protect the northern flank of the main body of the Essex battalion which had also reached its objective, the northern part of Infantry Hill, and sent forward patrols to see whether the Bois des Aubepines and Bois du Sart were still in German occupation. Messages which reached the Essex battalion headquarters in Monchy soon after 7.30 a.m. stated that large numbers of Germans were in those woods, 'already preparing for a counter-attack', but unfortunately the German barrage which opened on Monchy and all around at this time broke the telephone cables back to the British batteries and killed two messengers sent to them, so that they were not informed in sufficient time to break up this concentration.

So far as is known the two battalions reached their objective about 7 a.m. They may have seen the panorama of fresh country which the capture of Infantry Hill laid at their feet, all the ground eastward to and beyond the valleys of the Cojeul and the Sensée as far as the Wotan I (Drocourt–Quéant) Line, and north-eastward to and beyond the Scarpe, overlooking the German battery positions in Jigsaw Valley and the important Boiry–Biache spur along which lay the Boiry–Fresnes Riegel. But they would at best have had no care for such things, for no sooner had they begun to dig in along the new line than their situation rapidly became critical. Being on the reverse slope of Infantry Hill they and their further actions were lost to the sight of the observers in Monchy, but were in full view of the German machine-gunners in the woods ahead and of the German artillery observers.

Shortly before 7.30 a.m. the German artillery began a heavy bombardment both on the British supporting batteries along the Feuchy Chapel–Feuchy road and on the original British front position on either side of and in Monchy village. The village itself, until then not too badly damaged, collapsed 'like a pack of cards', and the German barrage prevented any immediate further support of the troops in the salient. At 7.30 a.m. a message from the Essex front line reported the enemy to be concentrating on its left flank, but, after that, there was silence, nor did any more wounded report at the first-aid post. About an hour later large numbers of Germans were seen through the mist closing in on Infantry Hill from the north while a smaller party, estimated at 200, was seen closing in from the south. About 10.5 a.m. a man of the Essex limped into Newfoundland headquarters and said that all the Essex had been killed or captured, and, at 10.30 a.m., another message stated that no unwounded men of the Newfoundland battalion were east of Monchy village. The Newfoundland Regiment and the 1st Essex had in fact vanished, except for the two battalion headquarters in Monchy who had hastily gathered a few stragglers together and taken up a position in front of the village. Early in the afternoon the other two battalions of the brigade, the 4th Worcestershire and 2nd Hampshire, took over the original front line. The Germans had meanwhile reoccupied their former trenches.[1]

The British 29th Division history states that the German counter-attack was believed to be a previously planned attack by the 3rd Bavarian Division to recapture Monchy village, which the Essex and Newfoundland attack had forestalled and upset. Sir Douglas Haig's dispatches refer to the 'exceedingly fierce struggle on the morning of the 14th April', and the 'enemy's most violent counter-attacks, which were completely repulsed with great loss'. General

[1] This brief version of the British side of the Monchy affair is a summary of the accounts given in the following histories: Captain Stair Gillon, *The Story of the 29th Division* (Nelson, 1925); Richard Cramm, *The First Five Hundred (Royal Newfoundland Regiment)* (Williams, New York); J. W. Burrows, *Essex Units in the War, 1914–19* (Southend-on-Sea, 1923).

Allenby, the Third Army commander, called in person that same evening on General de Lisle, commanding the 29th Division, to congratulate him on the result of the day's fighting. So easily can truth be twisted to suit individual requirements.

13

The German account of this affair at Monchy is of special interest because it was the first occasion on which the elastic defence was deliberately staged on a modern battlefield.[1] Unlike the barren reverse slope of Tower Ridge the ground behind the German front line here provided a succession of small woods and undulations which exactly fulfilled the text-book ideal that 'the deeper the attack penetrates into the defender's position, the more it will find itself faced by surprise and unforeseen conditions .

The assault came up against the three companies (5th, 6th, and 7th) of the 23rd Bavarian Regiment in the centre of the 3rd Division's sector (see Sketch 15). These held the front line, with the other (8th) of its front battalion in support behind the northern end of Infantry Hill; the inner company of the regiments on either flank, the 11th of the 18th Bavarian Regiment, on the right, and 12th of the 17th Bavarian Regiment, on the left, were also affected. In face of the British assault the three centre companies gave way elastically; in other words, the 7th–23rd and the 6th–23rd moved back to the north-east beyond the woods and the 5th–23rd to the south-east, back behind the slope between Machine-Gun Wood and Bois du Vert. The two flank companies (11th–18th and 12th–17th) swung back to avoid being outflanked, to form a flank protection. In this way a passage was left open for the British advance,

---

[1] The following account summarizes that given in the German official monograph *Osterschlacht bei Arras, 1917*, as also accounts in *Das 17 K.B. Infanterie Regiment, Kriegsarchiv* (Munich, 1927), and *Das 18 K.B. Infanterie Regiment, Kriegsarchiv* (Munich, 1926). Sketch 15 is adapted from a sketch-map in the latter regimental history.

which, about 7 a.m., was seen to be halted and digging in across the open summit of Infantry Hill facing east and along the edge of the northern woods facing north, forming a deep salient into the German defence.

The turning-point of the action had now been reached. German batteries, at about 7.30 a.m., began to lay a barrage across the back of this salient, about Monchy village, to prevent reinforcements entering it, and counter-batteries shelled the British supporting artillery. Meanwhile the machine guns of the companies (11th and 12th) of the support battalion of the 23rd Regiment in the Bois du Sart and of the 17th Regiment (9th) in the Bois du Vert held down by fire the British on Infantry Hill, while the counter-attacks were prepared. Owing to careful training the procedure was mutually understood, but it was assisted by the company commander of 11th–18th, the northern flank company which had swung back together with 6th–23rd, to a favourably situated fold of ground. From here, about 7.30 a.m., this party of about 200 rifles advanced under cover of the bombardment, retook their sector of the front trench and occupied a low ridge in front of the eastern side of the village. British machine-gun fire from Monchy Park caused heavy losses to this detachment, but the survivors held their ground and successfully barred the line of retreat from the salient, about sixty men facing east for the purpose. The left of this movement was reinforced by a support company (10th) of the 18th Regiment, which overran Arrow Head Copse, capturing fifty of the Essex, and about 150 others ran back towards Monchy, but few reached it. Another support company (12th) of the 18th Regiment had also moved south and came up on the left of the 10th, but its advance was checked with heavy loss by machine-gun fire of the Essex from Twin Copses.

Meanwhile the British infantry on the open summit of Infantry Hill were gradually being overpowered by machine-gun fire from the front and from their right flank, from the wood-edges in this back part of the battlezone.

Demoralization began, the men running hither and thither (*planlos hin und her*) in their search for cover, while casualties were fast thinning the line. The time for the counter-attack had now arrived. Seeing the check to the 12th–18th facing the northern side of Twin copses, the two leading support companies (11th and 12th) of the 23rd Regiment directed their attack against the north-eastern face of the British salient, advancing from Bois du Sart on either side of the Bois des Aubepines; they were closely supported by the other two companies (9th and 10th) of the support battalion. At the same time the 9th–17th from the Bois du Vert, with the 8th–23rd on its right and the 5th–23rd on its left, closed in on the eastern and south-eastern faces of the salient, while, on the extreme left, elements of the 17th Regiment overran Machine-Gun Wood. The support (1st) battalion of the 17th Regiment in Boiry had also been ordered forward to assist, but only small detachments were in time to take part in the counter-attack.

The British survivors in the Infantry Hill salient were now being attacked from three sides, and panic set in among them. About 150 raised their arms in surrender and the others ran back towards Monchy, most of the latter being killed or wounded by fire from both flanks or from the party barring their way near the eastern side of the village. The counter-attack passed over them and by 10 a.m. the 3rd Bavarian Division was again in occupation of its original foremost line.

In all, the Germans claimed to have captured 300 prisoners and twenty machine guns.[1] In total casualties the Newfoundland Regiment lost 487 out of a total of 591 all ranks, the Essex battalion 661 out of 923 all ranks who went into action. The Newfoundland memorial in the centre of Monchy remains as a constant reminder.

The German losses are difficult to calculate, but, as on Tower Ridge, they appear from the known figures to have

[1] The British published accounts state that 203 of the Essex battalion and 100 of the Newfoundlanders were taken prisoners.

been only a fraction of the British total.[1] To oppose the opening assault there were four and a half German companies, but for the immediate counter-attack there were over ten companies (including the four and a half original front-line companies but excluding the small parties of the support battalion of the 17th Regiment that arrived late on the scene from Boiry). The deeper the attack advanced into the position the greater became the resistance applied by the system of elastic defence.

Both on the Monchy and Tower Ridges the front and support battalions of the front-line regiments had been able to regain their foremost line with their own resources. The reserve battalions of these regiments, resting at Sailly and east of Boiry (see Sketch 15), had been ready but had not been engaged, and the regiments of the reserve (*Eingreif*) division, the 221st, which had arrived on the 12th in the Bellone area behind the Wotan I Line in this sector, had not even stood to arms.

14

These two actions justified the new Wotan organization, especially the compromise which had been made between the rigid and the elastic methods of defending the foremost line, and also the new machine-gun dispositions. Unfortunately, neither British G.H.Q. nor army commanders paid attention to the lessons which might have been gathered from them, so that their course was to be characteristic of the fighting about to take place in the battles of the Scarpe.

[1] The German official monograph gives the losses of the 18th Bavarian Regiment as two officers and thirty-one other ranks killed, and over 100 all ranks wounded, but the 18th Bavarian history says that many others of the regiment (in addition apparently to this total) 'remained on the field of honour'. The official monograph gives only the casualties in officers of the 23rd Bavarian Regiment, namely three killed and seven wounded. The 17th Bavarian history does not mention its casualties in the action. It is therefore as yet not possible to arrive at even an approximate figure.

Chapter X

THE WOTAN POSITION *(continued)*:
Battles of the Scarpe: 23rd April–9th May 1917

The capture of the Vimy Ridge may be said to have opened a gateway into the Wotan Position north of the Scarpe River.

Stand at the southern end of the Ridge, anywhere between Farbus Wood and Point du Jour, and look eastwards over the panorama of open ground falling away from its foot to the plain of Douai. Heavy batteries on the Ridge could shell effectively the whole of the eight-mile sector of the new German line between Méricourt and the Scarpe with observed fire, while the undulations at the foot of the Ridge, east of Vimy, Willerval, and Bailleul, gave positions for field batteries. German counter-attacks, on which their new defensive battle was based, could be swept by observed artillery fire from the outset, whether delivered by the front divisions in the battlezone or by the *Eingreif* divisions from the rearward battlezone, and would necessarily suffer very heavy losses, with small chance of success. For the attack itself, the British infantry, with observed artillery support throughout, would have every advantage on the low eastward-sloping spurs, and each forward move would capture artillery observation areas for close and more detailed observation for the next.

Cross, now, to the Tilloy–Wancourt observation line on the south side of the Scarpe and it will be seen that the entire eastern horizon is bounded by two great blocks of upland, the Monchy and Wancourt Tower Ridges, which lay immediately ahead of the British infantry on the whole eight-mile front from the Scarpe southwards to Croisilles. With the failure to capture Infantry Hill and Hill 92 on those two Ridges on the 14th April their supporting artillery had few observation facilities, and for the most part German counter-attacks would be able to reach near to the German front line unseen by the British artillery observers. In an attack on this frontage the British infantry would be lost to sight almost from the start, and would have to fight their battle single-handed against a defence fighting with both hands, with observed artillery fire supporting the infantry. Beyond too, between those two blocks of upland and the Wotan I Line, lay difficult country in the wooded valleys of the Cojeul and the Sensée, easier to defend than to attack (see Sketch 16).

I

Faced by this situation it is not surprising that the Germans believed that the British would use the Vimy Ridge as a 'spring-board' for their next advance. And yet the whole weight of the renewed British offensive on the 23rd April by General Allenby's Third Army was put in on a frontage of 11,000 yards south of the Scarpe, while north of the river a simultaneous attack on a frontage of 4,000 yards was only intended to round off and protect the northern flank of the main assault. Further, the objectives given were about three miles distant so that not only would the assaulting infantry have to overcome the German front garrison on a reverse slope unaided but, should that giant task be accomplished, they would then have to defeat the German counter-attack divisions at the back of the battle-zone, in the wooded valleys of the Cojeul and Sensée streams, also without observed fire-support from their artillery.

The battle was consequently to take a lop-sided course.

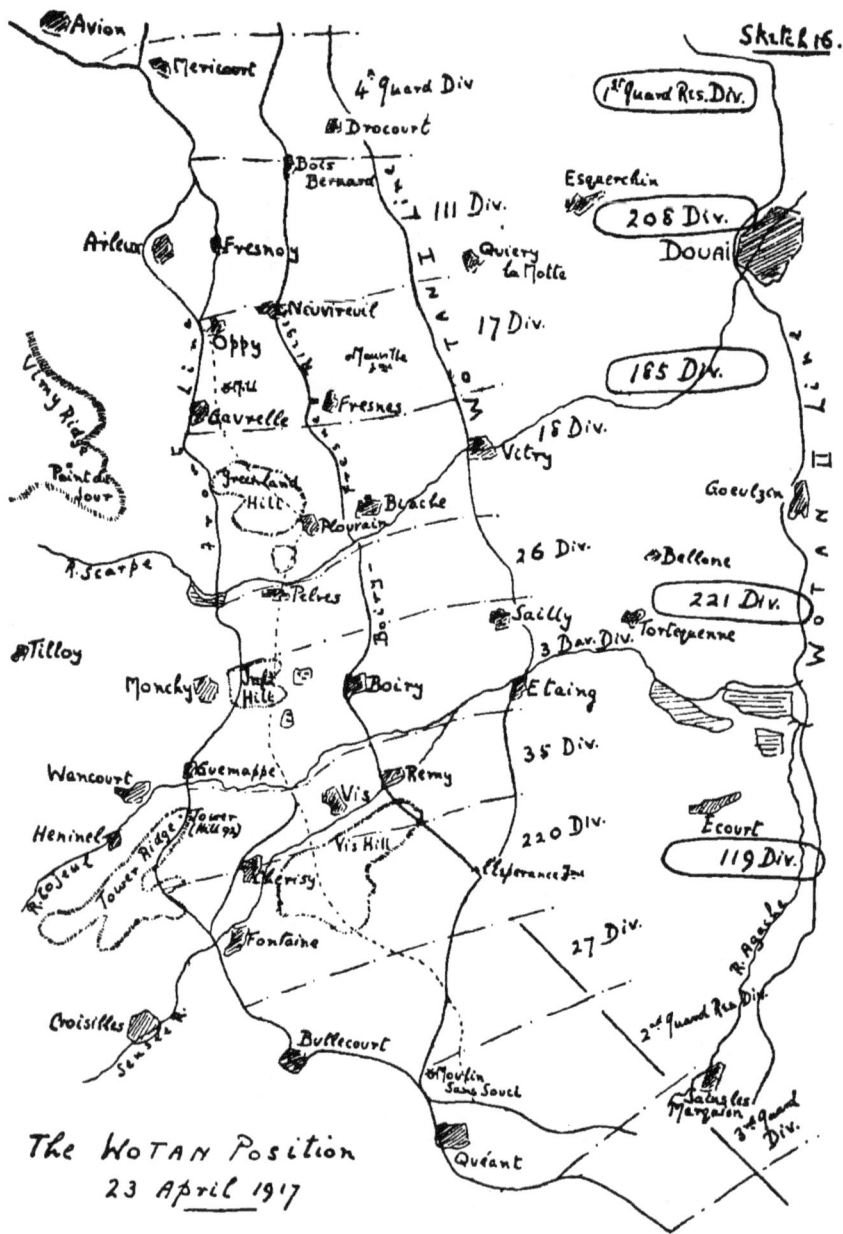

Sketch 16.

The WOTAN Position
23 April 1917

Trace of the Vis-Gavrelle Riegel.
Divisional Boundaries.

This is reflected in the German official monograph, whose author, still apparently unable to fathom the British plan, devotes fifty pages to the fighting in the 4,000 yards front north of the Scarpe, and only twenty pages to the 11,000 yards front of the intended main battle south of the river. While six British divisions, about 50,000 infantry, were to make a great frontal assault south of the Scarpe against the most difficult sector to attack of the entire Wotan Position, Colonel von Lossberg had arrayed most of his *Eingreif* divisions north of the river. Owing to the small damage the German artillery had suffered during the preceding days, he hoped to be able to avoid the 'risky' elastic battle he had at first visualized there, on the 11th, and had therefore ordered the front divisions to continue to hold the foremost line of shell-holes as long as possible, except where the ground suited a local elastic defence. But the *Eingreif* divisions were ready, if required, for the immediate counter-attack from behind the battlezone (i.e. from behind the Boiry–Fresnes Riegel); also the Wotan II Line was already taking shape as a further insurance in the event of the capture by the British of the Gavrelle Mill and Greenland Hill observation areas north of the Scarpe, which would make a wide sector of the existing Wotan Position untenable.

2

Generally speaking, on the main assault-frontage south of the Scarpe, the German front line was about 200 yards behind some sort of crest line, whether of ridge or undulation, and during the nine days since the British failure to capture Hill 92 and Infantry Hill, the German infantry had further improved their position, as also had the German batteries, hidden in the wooded Cojeul and Sensée valleys and in the deep undulations behind the Monchy Ridge. Neither these infantry dispositions on the reverse slopes nor those of the artillery had been effectively discovered by the British observers, ground or captive balloon, and British aeroplanes had been so harried by the temporarily faster machines and more efficient tactics of the famous Richthofen squadron, which had now appeared on the Arras battlefront, that observation by air-photography had become extremely hazardous and inadequate.

Despite the preliminary bombardment of the German position by 2,685 guns of all calibres (which fired over half a million shells on to the German position during the three battle-days 22nd–24th April) the Crown Prince Rupprecht writes in his diary (23rd April 1917) that the German batteries behind the attack-frontage (1,329 of all calibres) were almost untouched (*so gut wie intakt*) when the assault was delivered, and that the artillery observers were able to function almost undisturbed (*ohne wesentliche Störung*) throughout the day.

The preparation and circumstances therefore gave the assaulting infantry of General Allenby's Third Army little chance. After crossing the crest-line of the Wancourt Tower and Monchy Ridges, soon after leaving their assembly trenches, they would have to advance to the Fresnes–Boiry Riegel without observed or effective artillery support.

3

A ground mist covered the opening of the assault at 5.45 a.m., thanks to which the leading battalions were able to cross the crest-line and reach close to the German front line on the reverse slope, but they were then mown down by machine-gun fire in hundreds and made no further progress: it was a tragic repetition on a grand scale of the gallant but hopeless assault of the Queen Victoria Rifles and Queen's Westminster Rifles over the crest-line of Wancourt Tower[1] Ridge nine days before, on the 14th. In

[1] Wancourt Tower was a windmill on Hill 92, converted by the Germans into a watch-tower, but levelled during the 14th–19th April fighting.

places, however, the mist and their own courage enabled the men to penetrate into the position, but, as soon as the sun cleared away the mist, they fell an easy prey, killed and captured, to the German immediate counter-attacks by the support battalions (*Gegenstoss in der Stellung*); the Germans then reoccupied their foremost line on the reverse slope. In this manner the 2nd Argyll and Sutherland vanished north of Fontaine-les-Croisilles[1] at the southern end of the Tower Ridge, and so did a great part of the York and Durham battalions of the 150th Brigade on Hill 92,[2] at the northern end of the same Ridge. Similarly the 1st–7th Argyll suffered severely in the sector immediately north of the Scarpe, between the river and Rœux railway station, where the German front line lay on the reverse slope of a long elevation, behind which Rœux village and a wide depression formed a regular death-trap.[3]

In sectors where the ground suited, the elastic defence was applied in the same manner as at Monchy le Preux on the 14th. Such a sector, for example, was the sunken part of the Fontaine–Heninel track, 600 yards behind the front line. To this German companies fell back 'elastically', and within a couple of hours the greater part of the 2nd Royal Scots and 17th Manchester had vanished.[4] Against a renewed British assault in the evening the same elastic operation was repeated, and the 18th Manchester disappeared. Two considerable British cemeteries a few hundred yards apart mark the spot as a perpetual warning how not to attack a reverse-slope position.

Throughout the main battle-area, south of the Scarpe, the German front-line regiments were able to check the assault with their own man-power, and only in one sector, where early in the afternoon the left of the 3rd Bavarian

[1] See Preusser, *Das Infanterie Regiment No. 176* (Berlin, 1931).
[2] See Schilemann, *Das Infanterie Regiment 141* (Berlin, 1936).
[3] See the *Reichsarchiv* monograph: *Die Osterschlacht bei Arras 1917*, II, pp. 139–49.
[4] See von Kaiser, *Geschichte des Infanterie Regiments No. 61* (Berlin, 1928).

Division began to weaken south of Monchy and at Guemappe, was the leading (*Stoss*) regiment of an *Eingreif*
division sent forward to assist. How difficult was the task of
British artillery observers here is shown by the fact that the
battalions of this regiment, advancing in widely extended
lines of companies, were able to reach to within 400 yards
of the foremost German line, north of Hubertus Farm on
the Arras–Cambrai highway, before they came under artillery fire.[1]

That slight British advance south of Monchy had, however, altered the entire prospects of the German position
on Tower Ridge. Stand at the southern entrance to
Monchy village, where the British artillery observers could
now be firmly established, and look back over the Cojeul
valley. On the barren reverse slopes of the Tower Ridge,
beyond the stream, every German machine-gun nest,
every shell-hole garrison was overlooked and every German counter-attack movement could be followed with
observed fire. In position warfare, with concrete machine-
gun emplacements and shell-proof shelters, such commanding observation might not have been so vital, but in the
existing conditions of open warfare, with no such shelter
available, it was of dominant importance. Translated into
British terms it meant that an infantry advance across the
Tower Ridge could now be supported by observed artillery fire; it also meant that a concentrated British effort to
capture that observation area on the Monchy southern
slope, prior to the big offensive, would have given every
chance of a bloodless advance as far as the Sensée in this
southern part of the battlefield.

As Colonel von Lossberg had foreseen, when he first
visited the area on the 11th, that observation from the

---

[1] From its billets at Tortequenne this regiment reached the reserve
assembly zone at Étaing at 10.30 a.m., where it was placed at the
disposal of the 3rd Bavarian Division. By order of the latter it moved
on to the support assembly zone at Moulin Lannoy, north of Remy,
and at 1.30 p.m. received orders for the counter-attack. See Hansch,
Das Grenadier Regiment No. 9 (Berlin, 1929).

Monchy southern slope was the great weakness of the
Tower Ridge position, and as the British now held the key
to it he ordered its evacuation overnight to a new line, the
Chérisy Riegel, west of the Sensée stream, about 2,000
yards back, which was a protective line while his proposed
foremost line of the Wotan Position across the hill south of
Vis, east of the Sensée, was being prepared. A local success
of the British 150th Brigade on Hill 92 in the evening
assault assisted, but did not cause, this decision.

4

Most of the eight thousand British casualties during this
second battle of the Scarpe occurred on the reverse slopes
astride and south of the river, where conditions favoured
the new defensive battle. The corresponding German
casualties were less than half;[1] but north of the river, from
Rœux station to Gavrelle, this proportion was reversed.
Here the ground lay bare and open behind the German
front line and in full view of the British artillery observers
on the Point du Jour–Vimy Ridge. Foothills, such as
Greenland Hill and the Mauville Farm spur, made a forward slope for a thousand and more yards behind it, a
condition fatal to the delivery of immediate counter-
attacks unless, as Colonel von Lossberg had hoped might
be possible, they followed close on the heels of a British
attack.

The British objectives north of the Scarpe, limited to a
flank protection of the advance south of the river, were
mostly gained and with little loss. The western and northern slopes of Greenland Hill were reached after a suc-

---

[1] The casualties of the two hardest-hit German divisions, south of
the Scarpe, the 3rd Bavarian on the Monchy Ridge and the 35th
on the Wancourt Ridge, are mentioned in the Crown Prince Rupprecht's diary (entries for 26th and 30th April) as 2,200 and 3,000
respectively; but these figures refer to the whole ten-day period of
13th–23rd April, including the battle on the 14th April. See German
regimental histories concerned.

233

cessful advance of 1,000–1,500 yards, and, farther north, Gavrelle village was captured. Here the British infantry could be supported effectively by its artillery, and, as the German accounts lament, 'a heavy British artillery barrage prevented successful local counter-attacks'; these efforts, made as soon as the mist cleared, being seen at once by British artillery observers. Unfortunately, owing to the failure of the main attack south of the river, the advance was not pressed.

By 8 a.m. the messages that reached Group (Corps) Vimy headquarters in Douai, says the German official monograph, showed all the signs of a possible break-through north of the Scarpe. The particular sector, including Gavrelle Mill and Greenland Hill, which reports led to believe was threatened, if not already overrun, was regarded as the key to the Wotan Position astride the Scarpe. From Greenland Hill the long, bare northern slope of the Monchy Ridge back to the Boiry Riegel lay exposed in every detail, so as to be untenable in its existing unprepared state, and the whole of what the Crown Prince Rupprecht calls the *fatale* (awkward) *Monchy Höhe* must have quickly fallen into British hands; the ill-fated frontal attack by the Essex and Newfoundland battalions nine days previously would have been revenged by the simpler method of exploiting the flank observation from Greenland Hill. The loss of the Gavrelle Mill observation area promised to have almost equally disastrous effects on the Wotan Position organization at and north of Fresnes.

To German Sixth Army headquarters the importance of preventing the British acquiring these two areas of observation could not be overestimated, and it was naturally assumed that the whole efforts of the British leaders would be exerted to that end. The two *Eingreif* divisions (185th and 208th) behind the sector were placed by Sixth Army headquarters at the disposal of Group Vimy, and they were ordered to send forward their leading regiments to the reserve assembly positions behind the threatened sector, ready to stem the expected flood. As soon as it was known that the offensive had not extended northward, beyond Gavrelle, the more northern *Eingreif* division (1st Guard Reserve) was also ordered to send a regiment south to assist in the Gavrelle sector.

So began a series of desperate German counter-attacks both on Gavrelle and against Greenland Hill, intended to prevent a break-through which might well have been possible but of which the British had no intention. These counter-attacks, delivered under the most unfavourable conditions, show the machinery in action and also the weakness of the new German defensive battle, and are therefore worth a detailed description.

5

Gavrelle village was captured by the British 63rd (Naval) Division at 7.30 a.m. Immediate local counter-attacks by the support battalion failed, and at 8.10 a.m. the German regimental commander concerned (90th) ordered his reserve battalion, behind Fresnes, to retake it, the counter-attack to start at 10 a.m. Two companies were deployed in three widely extended lines for the purpose, one west of Fresnes and the other north of the Fresnes–Gavrelle road, to converge on the objective. The front battalion commander near to Gavrelle, seeing the hopelessness of such an attack in the bright morning sun in full view of British observers on the Point du Jour, sent back a messenger, who was in time to stop the northern company but too late to reach the other already advancing from Fresnes; watched by British artillery observers, this latter was forced to halt by an artillery barrage, combined with heavy machine-gun fire from Gavrelle.

The loss of Gavrelle village was important not so much for itself as for the rising ground immediately north-east of it where stood Gavrelle Mill. For the Germans the village, with its deep, shell-proof cellars, had been a stronghold intended to deny the commanding area of observation about the Mill to the enemy. The capture of that area, which now seemed imminent, would enable British machine guns to sweep the length of the spur for 1,000 yards eastwards to the Fresnes Riegel, in front of Mauville Farm, and allow British artillery observers to overlook all the ground behind Greenland Hill back to the Fresnes Riegel north of Biache. In the circumstances of comparative open warfare still prevailing in this sector, where no deep dug-outs yet existed, such predominance would have necessitated the abandonment of the forward zone of the Wotan Position between Gavrelle and the Scarpe.

A knee-deep trench, the Gavrelle Riegel, to which the German survivors had retired, lay about 300 yards east of the village; and, according to the German official monograph, was untenable (*unhaltbar*) against a determined attack. The German Group (Corps) commander therefore considered it essential to recapture the village, if possible, before nightfall.

Meanwhile at 9 a.m. the leading regiment of the *Eingreif* division (28th Reserve Regiment of the 185th Division) behind this sector had been moved forward from its rest area about Esquerchin to the reserve assembly area in the wooded valley east of Quiery-la-Motte and behind the curve of the railway embankment south of the village (see Sketch 17). Here at 11 a.m., after the failure of the local counter-attacks, it received orders to make a further attempt to capture Gavrelle, another regiment (89th) of the front-line division counter-attacking simultaneously on the left across Greenland Hill. The 28th Reserve Regiment thereupon moved forward to the support assembly area in the depression west of Izel and in the Wotan I Line behind that place. From here, at 1.30 a.m., it moved on to Fresnes, covered by the head of the Mauville Farm spur, and then advanced with one battalion in extended lines of companies on either side of the Gavrelle road, its third battalion remaining at Fresnes in reserve. It was a sunny afternoon

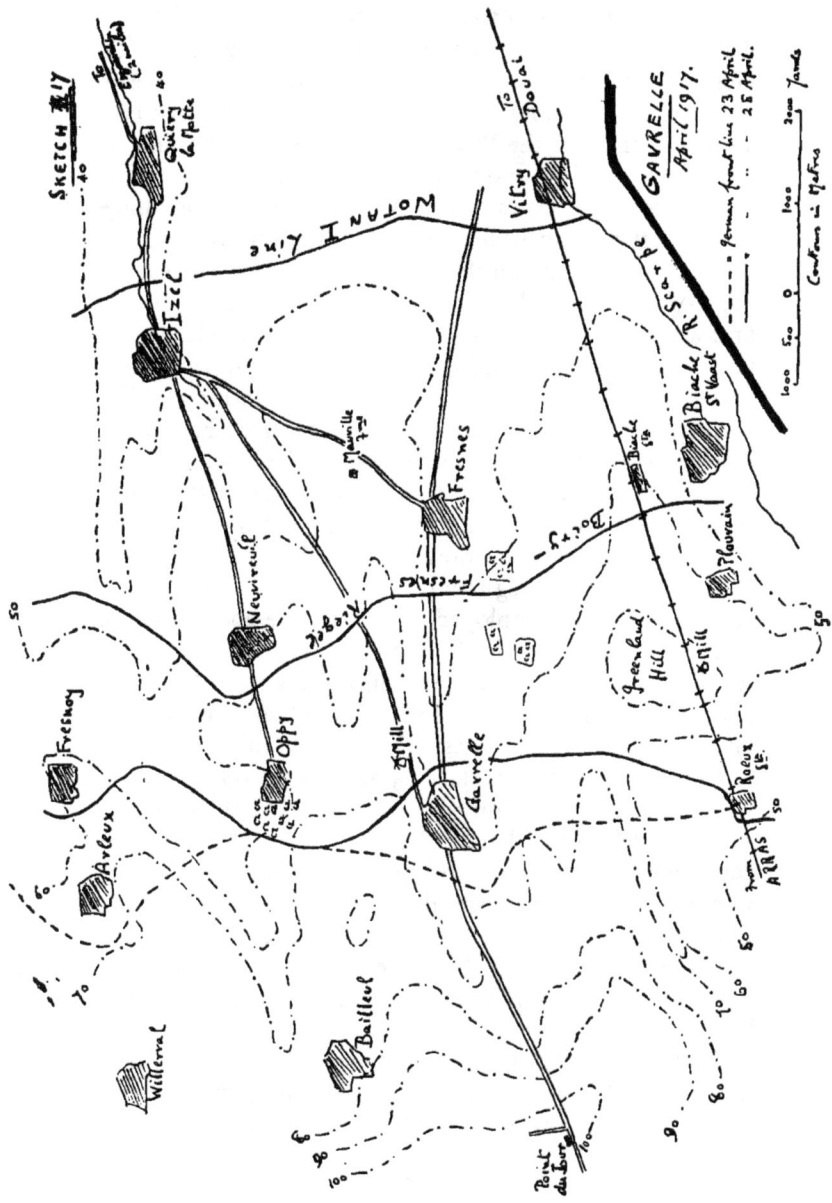

GAVRELLE
April 1917.

and this advance up the shallow depression along which the road runs straight westwards from Fresnes to Gavrelle was fully exposed to the British artillery observers; also the German artillery preparation had affected only the centre of the village, and left almost untouched the eastern edge along which were the British machine guns. Running the gauntlet of artillery and machine-gun fire, both sides of the road almost to Fresnes being visible from Gavrelle village, small parties of the attack, which in the circumstances was carried out most gallantly, did actually reach the eastern edge of the village but could make no further headway, and withdrew to the Gavrelle Riegel, a few hundred yards back. The regiment had lost 500 casualties in this effort, and the survivors, in the words of the German official monograph, 'waited yearningly for nightfall'. For similar reasons, good British artillery observation and the difficulty for German observers to direct their fire on the British position, an effort to recapture the lost ground on Greenland Hill during the evening also failed.

As the other two regiments of the 185th (*Eingreif*) Division were already employed elsewhere, the 208th Division was moved up from the Brebières area, and at 8.45 p.m. it was ordered forward by Group Vimy to the support assembly position between Fresnes and Biache behind the Greenland Hill (18th Division) sector. At midnight it was ordered to counter-attack, at 5 a.m., from the line Mauville Farm–Fresnes–Plouvain, with objective the line Gavrelle–Gavrelle road–Rœux. In other words, it was to recapture Greenland Hill, and the units in front of Gavrelle were to co-operate by a simultaneous attack on that village. On Greenland Hill this counter-attack was only partially successful, but against Gavrelle village it again failed, being seen and stopped by a 'very heavy British artillery barrage'.

Another *Eingreif* division (1st Guard Reserve) had been sent overnight to replace the 185th behind the Gavrelle sector, and on hearing of the failure of the early morning attack Group Vimy ordered its leading regiment (64th Reserve) to move forward from Esquerchin to the reserve assembly area at Quiery-la-Motte. Here, at 10 a.m., it was placed at the disposal of the front (17th) Divisional commander, who ordered it to prepare to recapture Gavrelle, as the original Group Vimy order had not been cancelled. Marching to the support assembly area about Izel, it was, at 1.15 p.m., given attack-orders by its regimental commander, who meanwhile had looked at the ground from Mauville Farm. He had decided to approach the village astride the Izel–Gavrelle road, across the Mauville spur, instead of astride the Fresnes–Gavrelle road, so as to avoid the machine-gun fire which had been the primary cause of the previous failures. Again it was a bright sunny afternoon, and, although the preparatory shelling of the village had already begun, the regimental commander asked divisional headquarters if the attack might be postponed to a later hour, but his request was refused. The assault assembly trenches were therefore ordered to be reached by 4.15 p.m., and the assault to be delivered at 4.30 p.m., the village to be attacked simultaneously from north and north-east, east and south-east. Moving off at 2 p.m. the battalions were deployed by 3.20 p.m. on the general line Neuvireuil–Mauville Farm, the 3rd north of the Izel–Gavrelle road and the 1st south of it, with the outer company of each écheloned behind the outer wing. The 2nd Battalion followed later in reserve in two waves behind the left wing of the 1st Battalion. After 700 yards the lines advancing across the Mauville spur came into full view of the British observers about Point du Jour, and when still 1,300 yards from the Gavrelle Riegel, a heavy artillery barrage showered down on them and moved level with their advance. The two leading battalions were, however, out of sight of the machine guns in Gavrelle village, and despite losses from the artillery barrage reached the assault assembly trenches. Carrying forward the medley of companies of two different regiments already in the front line, they moved on at 4.30 p.m. to assault the village. The 3rd Battalion, on the right, was now taken in flank by about six British machine guns, and was checked after 150 yards. The 1st Battalion succeeded in entering the village, large parties reaching the centre square, but they were there assailed by fire from concealed shelters on all sides, and eventually, by 7 p.m. had to abandon the ground gained, withdrawing to the Gavrelle Riegel. This regiment alone had lost over 430 casualties in the counter-attack, and the German official monograph stresses the great confusion of units in front of the village at this period. Companies of three different regiments were thoroughly intermingled and in an exhausted and demoralized state, but no move was made by the British to exploit the local victory they had gained and capture the important Gavrelle Mill observation area.

The difficulty of deciding the border-line between an immediate and a deliberate counter-attack, between *Gegenstoss* and *Gegenangriff*, had been faced eighteen months before, during the Champagne battles in the autumn of 1915, but this immediate counter-attack (*Gegenstoss*) by the 64th Reserve Regiment on Gavrelle was delivered more than thirty hours after the village had been taken. It was made without any special preparation and over ground unknown to the regiment, but was ordered by the front divisional commander in accordance with the Group (Corps) Vimy order that the village was to be re-captured. Under the new system of command the front divisional commander had the fullest powers and he could have justified his action by saying that a regiment fresh to the ground was more likely to capture the village by daylight than in the dark. Nevertheless, as proof of disapproval, an amendment was added in the next edition of the Defensive Battle text-book to the effect that 'immediate counter-attacks [*Gegenstösse*] launched too late differ in no wise from premature deliberate counter-attacks [*Gegenangriffe*]; they serve no good end and are prohibited.'

By Group Vimy order at 9.45 p.m. the two original front-line divisions, 17th and 18th, were withdrawn during the night, as also the 28th Reserve Regiment; the two *Eingreif* divisions, 1st Guard Reserve and 208th, relieved them as front-line divisions. The Group Vimy order to recapture Gavrelle was repeated, but no further counter-attacks were made. So long as the observation area about Gavrelle Mill was held, local commanders considered the village itself of little importance and its recapture not worth the loss of more lives.

<h2 style="text-align:center">6</h2>

The affair of Gavrelle shows how difficult a situation might have arisen for the Germans if the weight of the British offensive had been pressed north, instead of south, of the river.

The casualties of the Nelson and Hood, supported by the Hawke, battalions of the 63rd (Naval) Division which had captured and held Gavrelle from the 23rd to 25th, and of the Howe battalion, which had relieved Hood early on the 24th, were about 600 in all for the battle, whereas the losses of the battalion of the German 90th Regiment, which had garrisoned the village defences, and of the two *Eingreif* regiments, which had counter-attacked against the village, were well over double that figure. At that rate the *Eingreif* divisions, in their efforts to recapture successive artillery observation positions, would have been rapidly consumed, and the proclaimed British purpose of attrition would have been on the credit instead of on the debit side.

Crown Prince Rupprecht in his diary (19th April 1917) writes that he knew that during the Arras battle the British had captured O.H.L. documents which disclosed the new German defensive battle doctrine and that he expected the fairly obvious counter-measures; that they would organize a series of attacks, supported by observed artillery fire, concentrated against the four principal observation areas, or 'keystones' as they were called, of their defence system astride the Scarpe, i.e. Fresnoy village, Gavrelle Mill, and Greenland Hill, and the Monchy Ridge; the capture of any of these would give observation on to the Wotan I Line and the battery positions about it, and therefore compel counter-attacks, either immediate or deliberate, to be delivered in most unfavourable conditions; and that the British would meet these counter-attacks, when spent, by fresh attacks spaced in time or regulated by observers. In a later entry in his diary (30th April) he adds that 'the crowding together of men of considerably mixed units necessitated by counter-attacks forms a moment of weakness which the British commanders have not yet succeeded in exploiting by fresh, rapidly organized attacks'. The only alternative to these costly counter-attacks across forward slopes, and the consequent rapid consumption of the limited number of reserve (*Eingreif*) divisions, would have been a local withdrawal, the dislocation of a wide stretch of the Wotan Position on both sides of the Scarpe, and thereby the bloodless surrender to the British of another 'springboard' for a further advance into the plain of Douai.

This was the risk which Colonel von Lossberg had foreseen, but he calculated on the British continuing the same unskilled methods of attack which they had used on the Somme, trusting to their artillery to smother all resistance in the defence. The course of the Scarpe battles proved his calculation to be correct. No notice was taken either by British G.H.Q. or army commanders of the importance of artillery observation positions, although they provided the key not only for making a great success of the battles of the Scarpe but also for the capture of the Passchendaele Ridge a few months later. Instead they continued to attempt to overrun the German line on wide frontages regardless of ground conditions.

From Colonel von Lossberg's point of view, however, the defensive battle on the 23rd had been completely successful. The losses in front of Greenland Hill and Gavrelle were due to the fact that the British offensive had made less progress than he anticipated, so that the counter-attack regiments instead of advancing through the battle-zone on the heels of the attackers, and thereby confusing the British artillery observers, had had to cross it alone exposed to the full blast of British artillery and machine-gun fire. The battle had shown, what he had feared, that counter-attacks to recapture the foremost line delivered in such conditions were of doubtful value, and as a result of this experience no further immediate counter-attacks from behind the battlezone were delivered in this sector, from Greenland Hill northwards to Méricourt. Where the British made important gains in this area in the subsequent battles only deliberate counter-attacks (*Gegenangriffe*), after some days of preparation and with adequate covering fire, were allowed to be made to eject them.

7

The great opportunity to exploit the capture of the Vimy ridge began to diminish, after the failure of the 23rd April. The so-called battle of Arleux five days later, on the 28th, opened in circumstances considerably less favourable. The accounts in Crown Prince Rupprecht's diary of his con-versations with Colonel von Lossberg show that the latter was guided in his appreciation of the situation primarily by the condition of his artillery. During the battle on the 23rd the batteries had been little damaged, and so long as that condition remained he evidently saw no need to alter the existing disposition, nor to withdraw to the proposed foremost line of the Wotan Position. So long as the mass of the batteries were ready for action and undiscovered, he continued to hold the forward zone as a battlezone, but in order to make living conditions for the garrison more tolerable he ordered a second trench (*Wohngraben*) to be dug about 200 yards behind the foremost line of shell-holes, and on a reverse slope wherever possible. By the 28th this had been roughly completed, and dug-outs deepened in the chalk. The bulk of the front garrison occupied this second trench, leaving only sentry posts in the much battered front line. In addition, a number of shell-proof and mutually supporting machine-gun nests (*Anklammerungs-punkte*) for the divisional S.S. machine-gun detachments had by now been constructed about the Boiry–Fresnes Riegel, at the back of the battlezone. Improvements were also made in the machine-gun and artillery organization. For example, the machine-gun companies of front divisions were ordered to remain in position for two days after their infantry units had been relieved, to give time for the incoming machine-gun companies to accustom themselves to the surroundings. For the same reason, after the battle of the 23rd April, Sixth Army headquarters asked for permission to keep front divisional artillery commanders in the line for a few days after relief of their batteries, so as to ensure continuity of fire-control. With the exception of one or two batteries which accompanied the leading (*Stoss*) regiment of the *Eingreif* division, the *Eingreif* divisional artillery was held back to enable a complete relief of the front divisional artillery when needed, so that normally a counter-attack by an *Eingreif* division depended on the batteries of the front divisions for artillery support. Colonel von Lossberg also recommended the establishment of mobile field artillery reserves, both for divisions and Groups, to support counter-attacks on a large front or to reinforce the front-line artillery when needed; and he asked that special attention be paid to field artillery training in mobile warfare, for 'the British fire-control has repeatedly shown itself to be not flexible enough to be able to engage rapidly and successfully an opponent appearing unexpectedly'. The organization of command of the heavy artillery, developed during the Somme battles, divisional commanders having control of the heavy artillery in their sectors as far as possible, with a Group heavy artillery

representative at their headquarters, had continued to
work satisfactorily.

When the British offensive was launched on the 28th
many features of position warfare had therefore begun to
appear. The objective was less distant. The assault divisions were to reach a line about 1,500 yards ahead, which
included Arleux and Oppy villages, Gavrelle Mill, Greenland Hill, and Rœux, combined with an advance south of
the river to straighten the northern face of the Monchy
salient. It was an offensive with just such objectives as
these which the Crown Prince Rupprecht had feared five
days earlier on the 23rd, but he expected the attacks to be
concentrated against the observation areas, where they
could be supported throughout by observed artillery fire;
whereas the British army commanders dissipated their
strength over the whole sector, directing the assault towards continuous blue, green, and brown lines drawn
across the map 500 yards apart, regardless of reverse slopes
and death-traps.

This offensive was stated to be only preparatory to a
renewed offensive on a big scale a week later to capture
first the entire Boiry–Fresnes Riegel and, later, the Wotan
I Line. It was forever these most expensive large-scale
offensives which were ordered by British G.H.Q. and army
commanders. The presence of the German counter-attack
divisions was known from the G.H.Q. Intelligence Sum-
maries, but there was no thought-out scheme to compel the
bulk of the German defence forces to come forward into
exposed sectors of the battlezone. It was a pity that there
was no British *Divisionskommandeur-Schule* for senior commanders; there were plenty of instructional courses for
junior officers, but it was of little use to teach them the
importance, for example, of co-operation between infantry
and artillery so long as their Corps and Army commanders
continued to select positions to attack where that co-operation was impracticable and occasions when success was
most difficult. Once again the British plan foredoomed its

infantry to the maximum losses and gave them the minimum chance of success.

The British preparatory bombardment was directed mainly at the front line of shell-holes in which were only a few sentry posts, and left the greater part of the new second trench untouched. This was especially the case south of the Scarpe, where both lay on a reverse slope and the existence of the second trench had not been fully appreciated. Here the infantry assault was checked at once with heavy losses and no ground gained.

Immediately north of the river the 15th Royal Scots and 10th Lincolns walked into the Rœux death-trap. The reverse slope, on which lay the German front line and Rœux village, as well as the wide depression behind it, was out of sight of British observers, but was overlooked in every detail by German observers on Balloon Hill (see Sketch 18). Part of the front-line garrison (65th Regiment) fell back to the northern end of the village and the British lines of assault passed through into the depression, east of the village. Here they were demoralized by machine-gun fire, particularly from Balloon Hill, and then counter-attacked by the German support battalion. By this method were captured '350 English and Scottish prisoners and 26 light machine guns, and in addition hundreds of British dead lay in and about the village'.[1]

In the Greenland Hill and Gavrelle sectors good progress was made and the farthest objectives, including the northern slope of Greenland Hill and a line 600 yards beyond Gavrelle Mill, were reached, but the great importance of the capture of these particular observation areas does not seem to have been understood, and there was certainly nothing in the original attack-orders to that effect. Although observed artillery support was available it was not adequately provided, nor were the battalions concerned (8th Somerset L.I. and 10th York and Lancaster on Greenland Hill, and 1st and 2nd Royal Marines be-

[1] See Krall, *Das Infanterie Regiment No. 65* (Berlin, 1927).

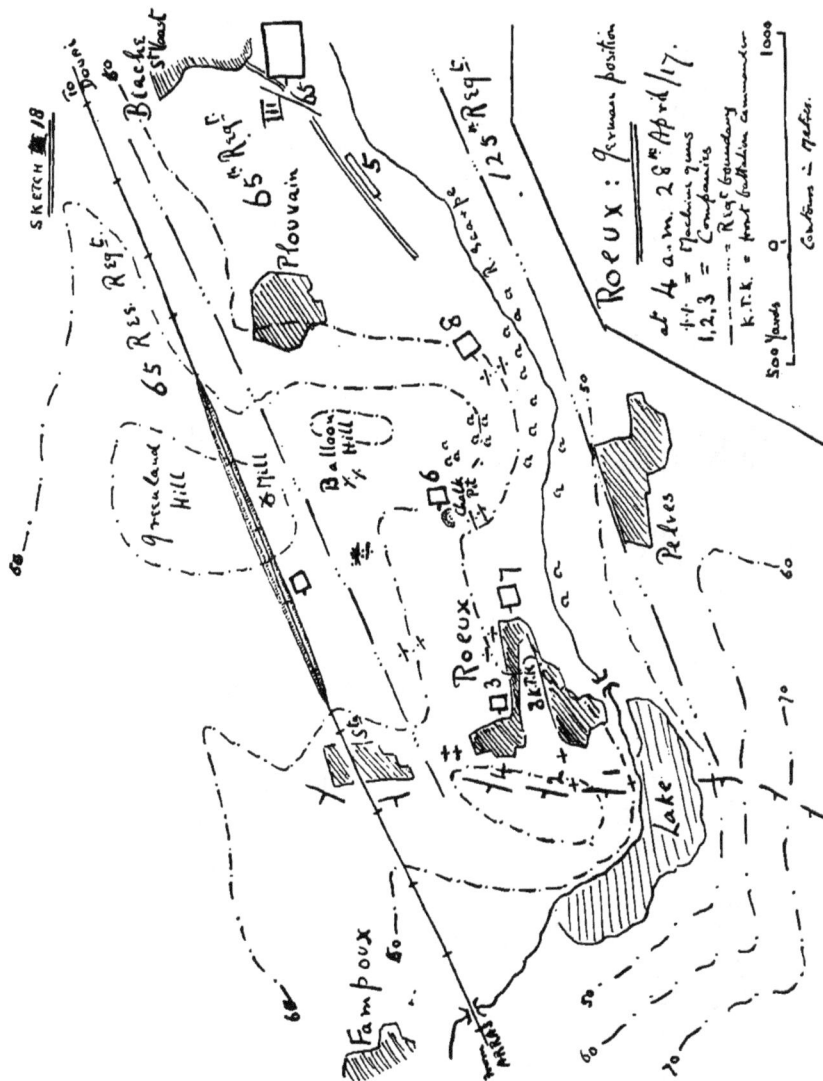

SKETCH № 18

Blache St Naast

To Douai

60

65th Res Regt.

65 Res Regt.

Greenland Hill

Plouvain

III

65

S

Ball Hill

Balloon X I Hill

Chalk Pit

6

8

R scarpe

5

125th Regt.

Roeux

3

8 R F K

L7

Pelves

60

70

S Mill

S Mill

Lake

70

Fampoux

60

60

70

60

ARRAS

Roeux : German position

at 4 a.m. 28th April /17.

++ = Machine guns
1,2,3 = Companies
---- = Regt boundary
k.T.K. = front battalion commander

500 Yards   0   1000

Contours in metres.

yond Gavrelle) sufficiently reinforced to hold their valuable gains, all of which were lost, including a great number of prisoners and casualties, to the immediate German counter-attacks. This, despite the fact that the whole of this battle-sector was under direct ground observation by British observers on Point du Jour.

Farther north, Oppy village was a most unfortunate objective to attempt to capture by a frontal attack. There was a wooded thicket, the wilderness of shattered trees called Oppy Park, close behind the German front line, and the village itself, immediately behind the park, lay in a depression of ground. Like Rœux, it was therefore one of those few places on the battlefront north of the Scarpe where an assault could not be assisted by observed artillery fire. In this instance the existence of a well-established front-trench system (the original Third Line) enabled the German garrison to employ another form of the elastic defence, the front garrison side-stepping along the trench instead of falling back from it; they allowed about 150 British to pass through and go on into the wilderness of the park, the front garrison then moving back and holding the trench against reinforcements. 'It was as if a door into a great reception-room had been opened, and then closed again as soon as sufficient guests had entered.'[1] The guests, Essex and Middlesex men, were then machine-gunned, and the survivors taken prisoner by counter-attack, by the German support companies in the park. North of the park, too, British troops broke in and reached the centre of the village, but, without observed artillery support, were unable to resist the counter-attacks by the support battalion which recaptured the lost ground and the original front line.

In the northernmost sector of the battle line, however, Canadian battalions overran Arleux village and reached their objective east of it. As the ground here was exposed to the British artillery observers no counter-attack was

[1] See Leuwer, *Das Infanterie Regiment 'Bremen'* (Bremen, 1919).

made, the Germans deciding to abandon the Arleux 'nose', or salient, and make the already constructed trench line in front of Fresnoy the new front line (see Sketch 16).

8

The third battle of the Scarpe is the official name given to the renewed British offensive astride that river a week later, on the 3rd May. The ten British assaulting divisions were told the previous evening that it was to be the biggest battle in which the British armies had yet taken part,[1] but unfortunately its success was not destined to be in proportion. The circumstances of the 23rd April, or even of the 28th, no longer existed. Position warfare had set in, and dug-outs now existed for the bulk of the front garrison. Moreover, the senior British commanders concentrated on the capture of trench lines, seen from air-photographs, in the belief that all the defenders must be in them, although General Ludendorff's new text-book (edition of 1st March 1917), which had been captured on the 9th April 1917, exposed the entire machinery of the new defensive battle.[2] The fact that the ground between the German trench lines would be honeycombed with machine-gun nests and support detachments of infantry was not taken into account in the British orders for the attack and artillery preparation, though already fully appreciated by the front-line units.

The German garrison was not seriously affected by the artillery preparation, nor were the German batteries, par-

[1] Ewing, *History of the 9th Dvision* (London, 1921), p. 206.
[2] Printed translation of both General Ludendorff's text-book and Colonel von Lossberg's *Experiences of the First Army in the Somme Battles* were issued by the British Army Printing Service, 1,250 copies of the former and 2,800 of the latter, on the 3rd May 1917. The German document, 'Experience of the Recent Fighting at Verdun (15th December 1915)', captured in February, and of which 2,000 printed copies of the English translation were issued on the 28th February 1917, also stated clearly the basis of the new German defensive battle, the defence of a deep zone rather than a trench line.

ticularly those in the wooded valleys south of the Scarpe. Up to the last moment before the British assault, between 80 per cent and 90 per cent of the German guns were still in action; and the effective barrages placed by them in no-man's-land at the beginning of the assault, to prevent the advance of the supporting lines of attack, Colonel von Lossberg considers to have had a large share in the British defeats in these Scarpe battles.[1] Nevertheless, the orders for the British infantry were the same as before. They, about 80,000 men, were asked to take a cross-country walk to the Boiry–Fresnes Riegel, 2,500 yards away, on the whole thirteen-mile frontage of the new battleline, from Fontaine les Croisilles to Acheville. Once again, blue, red, and brown lines were drawn straight across the map as successive objectives, regardless of the fact that the Germans were no longer defending trench-lines but zones of defence, and regardless also of tactical considerations such as reverse slopes and the probable action of the counter-attack divisions.

The British infantry assaulted at 3.45 a.m.; it was dark but clear, and a setting moon gave visibility for about fifty yards. On wide sectors of the battlefront, especially where the German double front trench system lay on a reverse slope, they were mown down by machine-gun and rifle fire, combined with a barrage of shrapnel by the German batteries, before they reached the first or second trench. On the extreme right, near Fontaine-les-Croisilles, about 200 men of Leicester battalions crossed the Chérisy Riegel, the protective line for the proposed foremost line of the Wotan Position, but at daylight they were all killed or taken prisoners by immediate counter-attack by German support companies.[2] So too, farther north the 7th Buffs and 8th East Surrey crossed the Chérisy Riegel and went on beyond Chérisy village; there, however, they too suc-

[1] See Kronprinz Rupprecht von Bayern, *Mein Kriegstagebuch*, II, p. 105 (diary-entry for 13th May 1917).
[2] See Rohkohl, *Das Reserve Infanterie Regiment 226* (Berlin, 1923).

cumbed to the immediate counter-attacks by the German
support companies, which took 200 prisoners, apart from
a great number of wounded, and recaptured all the lost
sector of the Chérisy Riegel.[1] On the whole seven miles
battlefront south of the Scarpe, almost without exception,
the British assault battalions were by the evening back in
their original starting-off line. The vast majority of the
14,000 and more British casualties on this battle-day were
again in this sector south of the river.

North of the river it was the turn of the 2nd Seaforths
and 1st Somerset L.I. to be sent into the death-trap of
Rœux. The German front garrison, after an initial resistance, again swung back to the northern end of the village,
leaving a gap of seven hundred yards between them and
the river through which the British crowded, and on into
the hollow depression beyond the village out of sight of
British observers and of artillery support. The immediate
counter-attack of the 23rd and 28th April was then repeated, and the story of it may be read in the histories of
the German 25th and 185th Regiments, which took 380
prisoners as they passed over the shambles of British dead
and wounded, and recaptured their former front line. To
the German infantry, sickened by two years of passive
defence, this elastic defence system was an exhilarating
change, so long as British battalions continued to be sent
without fire-support over crest-lines against machine guns
concealed on reverse slopes.

Farther north again, on the slopes of Greenland Hill,
the British infantry were faced sooner than they expected
by rifle and machine-gun fire from the German garrison,
who, as so frequently during the Somme battles, had gone
forward into the shell-holes in no-man's-land at the beginning of the bombardment and so had escaped its effect,
and were ready to meet the unsuspecting British infantry.
The latter were also misled by the double front-trench system, and after taking the first line were unexpectedly

[1] See Delorme, *Das Infanterie Regiment 114* (Konstornz, 1922).

251

swept by fire from the second, and from machine guns concealed in shell-holes thereabouts. The decision of the two
army commanders to launch this offensive in the dark, an
hour before daylight, cancelled the advantage of observed
artillery support which the attacking infantry would
otherwise have had in this sector. Large numbers of them
were allowed to pass through and beyond the front trench
system by the Bavarian defenders, the front battalions of
the 16th and 20th Bavarian Reserve Regiments[1] repeating
the guest-chamber tactics of Oppy five days before; while
the German artillery barrage hindered the advance of the
supporting waves. In this manner the 6th K.O. Scottish
Borderers was practically annihilated and other battalions
of the British 9th Division suffered severely.[2]

Much the same story could be told of the attacks in the
Gavrelle and Oppy sectors by divisions of the First Army
under General Sir H. Horne.[3] The attack on Fresnoy,
however, at the extreme north of the battlefront, was a
brilliant exception, the village being captured and held by
the 1st Canadian Division. It was the only important
observation area occupied in the Wotan battlezone north
of the Scarpe during these battles. From the eastern edge
of Fresnoy village British artillery observers could now
overlook a wide sector of the Wotan Position back to the
Fresnes Riegel, and beyond almost to the Wotan I Line
itself about Izel; to north and north-east, in the depression
ahead and on the rising ground beyond it up to Bois Bernard, no German movement by daylight was possible
without detection, and to south-east and south all the

---

[1] The 6th Bavarian Reserve Division, which had been an *Eingreif*
division behind this sector, had begun the relief of the 208th Division
with two regiments during the previous night (1st–2nd May).

[2] The regimental history says that 'only a dribble of some 50
K.O.S.B.'s ever returned'. For a British account of this attack on
Greenland Hill, see J. Ewing, *History of the 9th Division* (London,
1921).

[3] The British First Army front was northwards from Gavrelle
(inclusive), the Third Army southwards to Croisilles.

ground behind Oppy park and village, and along the northern part of the Mauville Farm spur, was now an open book to them. It was just such a success that the Germans most feared, as a prelude to further British local offensives in this sector with all the advantages of close and distant observed artillery fire. But British First Army headquarters seemed not to realize, or at least paid no attention, to the opportunity the capture of Fresnoy offered, and took not the slightest advantage of it. The Germans, after the lesson of Gavrelle, made no immediate counter-attack, but, after a careful preparation, the *Eingreif* division (5th Bavarian) in this sector was brought forward four days later, during the night of the 7th–8th May, and made a deliberate counter-attack (*Gegenangriff*) at dawn which was completely successful and recaptured the village. The histories of the Bavarian regiments concerned state that on reaching the village the majority of the machine guns and rifles of the assault battalions were so blocked with mud as to be useless, and had to be sent back to be cleaned, but the British made no attempt to counter-attack to regain this important position.[1]

With that exception none of the five German *Eingreif* divisions were used during the 3rd May; the eight front-line divisions had held the British attacks with their own resources and reoccupied the front line wherever lost. A few of the break-in incidents, where the immediate counter-attack (*Gegenstoss in der Stellung*) was applied, have been mentioned, but for the most part the British assault had been checked and defeated about the existing foremost line. During the following two nights the *Eingreif* divisions relieved the more exhausted of the front divisions, fresh divisions from O.H.L. taking their place as *Eingreif* divisions.

[1] The Fresnoy village sector had been taken over from the 1st Canadian Division by the British 5th Division on the 5th May, so that the Canadians were not responsible for the loss of this important sector. The 2nd Canadian Division was still in the line north of the village.

Minor attacks continued on the Scarpe battlefront during the summer, but the failure of the 3rd May was the last British effort to reach the Wotan Line in 1917.

The casualties of the German Sixth Army, which included the whole Arras battlefront from north of Lens to east of Quéant, during April (1st–30th) were 51,000 compared with the British total of 78,000 in the same area and period; during May (1st–31st) the similar German casualties were approximately 34,000 compared with a British total of 64,000. The casualties for the Arras and Scarpe battles combined were therefore roughly 85,000 Germans against 142,000 British; and even after allowance for the difference between the German and British definition of the term 'lightly wounded' there can be no doubt on which side was the greater attrition.[1]

9

'Contrary to all expectations,' wrote the Crown Prince Rupprecht in his diary at this time, 'the greater part of the forward defence line, first selected on the withdrawal from the Arras–Vimy position, had been successfully held.' It had not been necessary to fall back even to the Vis-Gavrelle Riegel, the originally proposed foremost line of Colonel von Lossberg's Wotan Position. The defended area of shell-holes in front of it had sufficed to withstand three British offensives.

On the 7th May, four days after the final British effort, German Sixth Army headquarters informed the Crown Prince Rupprecht that the British artillery was not yet in a position to carry out a bombardment sufficient to neutralize the German battlezone for a successful offen-

---

[1] The British casualty lists were made out from medical returns, which included every lightly wounded man who had reported at a dressing station.

The German casualty lists were made out from returns of divisional strengths every ten days, and therefore did not include lightly wounded men who had returned to duty within that period.

sive, and it was not until the end (29th) of June that a formal request was made to turn that battlezone into an outpost zone, and to make the Fresnes–Boiry Riegel the main line of resistance. From that date the Wotan and Hindenburg Positions became a similar and continuous defence-framework over 100 miles in length from Lille southwards to Soissons on the Aisne; and the Wotan II Line became the front of a Wotan II Position, with a Wotan III Line at the back of it.

The completed Wotan Position joined the Hindenburg (Siegfried) Position west of Cambrai. To the north the Wotan organization was carried on by the Flandern Position (*Flandern-Stellung*) from Lille to the Belgian coast, while the Hunding Position (*Hunding-Stellung*) continued the southern end of the Hindenburg organization eastwards, behind the Chemin des Dames, towards Verdun. In this manner by the end of June 1917 the German Western Front consisted of a succession of zones of great depth within which a mobile defensive battle was to be fought, instead of fighting it rigidly in a succession of trench lines.

On the 28th April, when the Scarpe battles were in progress, General von Falkenhausen, who, Crown Prince Rupprecht states, had become 'apathetic after the Arras defeat' was replaced as Sixth Army commander by General Otto von Below.[1] Having been previously employed on the Macedonian front, General von Below had little knowledge of conditions on the Western Front, and had continued to allow Colonel von Lossberg a free hand.

Throughout this period Colonel von Lossberg had continued to base his work on personal observation. Scarcely a day passed during which he did not spend several hours visiting sectors of the battlezone to see the situation and condition of the front divisions and the state of the ground

[1] General von Falkenhausen was removed from active operations and appointed Governor of Belgium. General Otto von Below is not to be confused with General Fritz von Below (former commander of the German First Army on the Somme).

for himself, paying special attention to the positions of the artillery and the battery observers. He seems to have been careless of his own life, never sparing himself danger or privations; and he continued to regard four hours' sleep at night as a luxury.

The general organization of the battlefront, which had been founded on his experience during the Somme campaign, had proved adequate. The Corps boundaries, made chiefly with regard to facilities for artillery observation within them, had remained fixed. From the outset Corps had been constituted as Groups of divisions with a permanent staff, which remained in control; Group Vimy (formerly 1st Bavarian Reserve Corps) from Acheville to the Scarpe, Group Arras (formerly IX Reserve Corps) from the Scarpe southwards to the Sensée, opposite Croisilles, and Group Quéant (formerly XIV Reserve Corps) from Croisilles to Mœuvres, east of Quéant. The three to six infantry divisions which formed the establishment of each Group had continually changed, moving in and out of its control as required. This system enabled divisions to be juggled with as easily as platoons can be within a battalion. Also the precision with which *Eingreif* divisions had gone forward into the battlezone, either for the counterattack or to relieve front divisions, was due in great measure to the arrangement of the support and reserve assembly areas in the rearward battlezone of each divisional sector. The success of this organization confirmed the policy, begun in the later months of 1916, of making the infantry division the independent battle-unit of the German Army.

The rank and file had been able to appreciate and understand the new mobile or elastic method of defence in comparative open warfare, and its success had increased remarkably the confidence of the German infantry. This is made abundantly clear in the German regimental histories, and there can be little doubt that the visible superiority of German leadership was largely responsible for the continued stubborn resistance by the German armies during the remainder of 1917.

Colonel von Lossberg's fame in his own country rests on his achievements during the Passchendaele campaign, which was still ahead of him, but the rapid formation of the Wotan Position and the conduct of the Scarpe defensive battles are together an outstanding example of his creative and organizing genius.

Part IV

MATERIALIZATION OF THE
DEFENCE IN DEPTH

Chapter XI

THE FLANDERN POSITION:
Messines: 7th June 1917

On the 30th April, while the battles of the Scarpe were still in progress, increased activity about the Messines Ridge, south of Ypres, led Crown Prince Rupprecht of Bavaria, commanding the Northern Group of Armies, to believe that a British offensive against it was being prepared for the near future.

The Flanders campaign which was now to begin brings us back to the waterlogged country of the first chapter. Owing to the high water-level, breastworks had to take the place of trenches, as at Neuve Chapelle, and the deep German dug-outs were replaced by large concrete shelters, called pill-boxes, which may still be seen dotted about the landscape. These pill-boxes were proof against ordinary shell-fire, but a direct hit by a heavy howitzer might split them open. With the water-level only three or four feet below the ground, they had to be built up to several feet above the surface, and although covered with turf and soil they were easily visible to British observers. They varied in size from a machine-gun nest for two guns to large low rooms with accommodation for twenty-five to forty men.

For two years the British front line had rested on the forward slope of a fourteen-mile semicircle of rising ground around Ypres, the famous Ypres salient, with the Germans on the crest above and overlooking the whole Ypres district. The Menin Ridge was the central block of this upland, with the Pilckem spur to the north-west and the Messines Ridge to the south-west forming the two arms of the semicircle (see Sketch 20). The dominant observation area of this high ground was the four-mile Messines Ridge, from the knee of the Ypres-Comines canal to the Douve valley, and from it the Germans could watch every detail of any preparations the British might make for an offensive eastwards between Ypres and the Belgian coast. The capture of the Messines Ridge would consequently have to precede any British offensive in Flanders.

Fortunately for the British it was the weakest sector of the German position. Whereas elsewhere along the semicircle, in both the Menin Ridge and Pilckem spur sectors, the Germans held the crest-line beyond which the British had no observation, in the Messines Ridge sector the entire German position back to 2,000 yards lay on the forward slope. From the hill of Kemmel, 5,000 yards east of Wytschaete, British observers could overlook every detail of this position, assisted by others on Haubourdin Hill (63), immediately south of the Douve valley, who could keep watch over its southern part. A further weakness of the Messines Ridge as a defensive position was that its reverse slope down to the River Lys was slightly convex, and only in a few places could it be overlooked from the valley behind; for this reason a mobile defence would have to be conducted without observed artillery support.

It was because of these weaknesses that the first sector of the Flandern Line to be constructed, earlier in the spring, had been a rallying line six miles behind the Messines sector, from Linselles astride the Lys through Werwicq to Becelaere, along which line were the first available artillery observation areas.

I

When, at the end of April 1917, Crown Prince Rupprecht foresaw the forthcoming British offensive against the Messines Ridge; he agreed with the suggestion of his chief of staff, General von Kuhl, that it would be better to forestall such an offensive by withdrawing from the forward-slope position to a line on the reverse slope shortly before it was delivered. The Third (Warneton) Line was suggested as the new front line and it was to connect up with the flanks of the original front by the Tenbrielen Riegel, north of the Comines canal, and by the Flandern Riegel, north of Lille, to north and south respectively (see Sketch 19).

At a conference a few days later, the 2nd May, at Fourth Army Headquarters at Courtrai, General von Kuhl found that his proposal was opposed by all those directly concerned. Their opposition was based on the opinion that the Third (Warneton) Line was suitable neither for holding up an offensive nor for occupation as a front line; there were no artillery observation points behind from which the ground in front of it could be overlooked, so that the infantry defence could not be supported by observed artillery fire, and, secondly, the Ypres-Comines canal and the River Lys close behind it severely limited the space for manœuvre and would make almost impossible defence-in-depth demanding immediate counter-attacks. Owing to the observation facilities the British would gain on the Messines Ridge, the only alternative to holding the existing position was considered to be a withdrawal back to the Flandern Line, six miles from the Ridge, where the conditions for defence were again favourable; the Tenbrielen Riegel and the Flandern Riegel could still connect the flanks with the original front line. But the danger of such a move was that it would expose to British observers the southern slope of the Menin Ridge, the central buttress of the Flandern Position, and give an offensive south of the Ypres–Menin road every chance of success. A withdrawal to the Flandern Line would therefore, it was considered, be a direct threat to the left flank of the Group Ypres on the Menin Ridge.

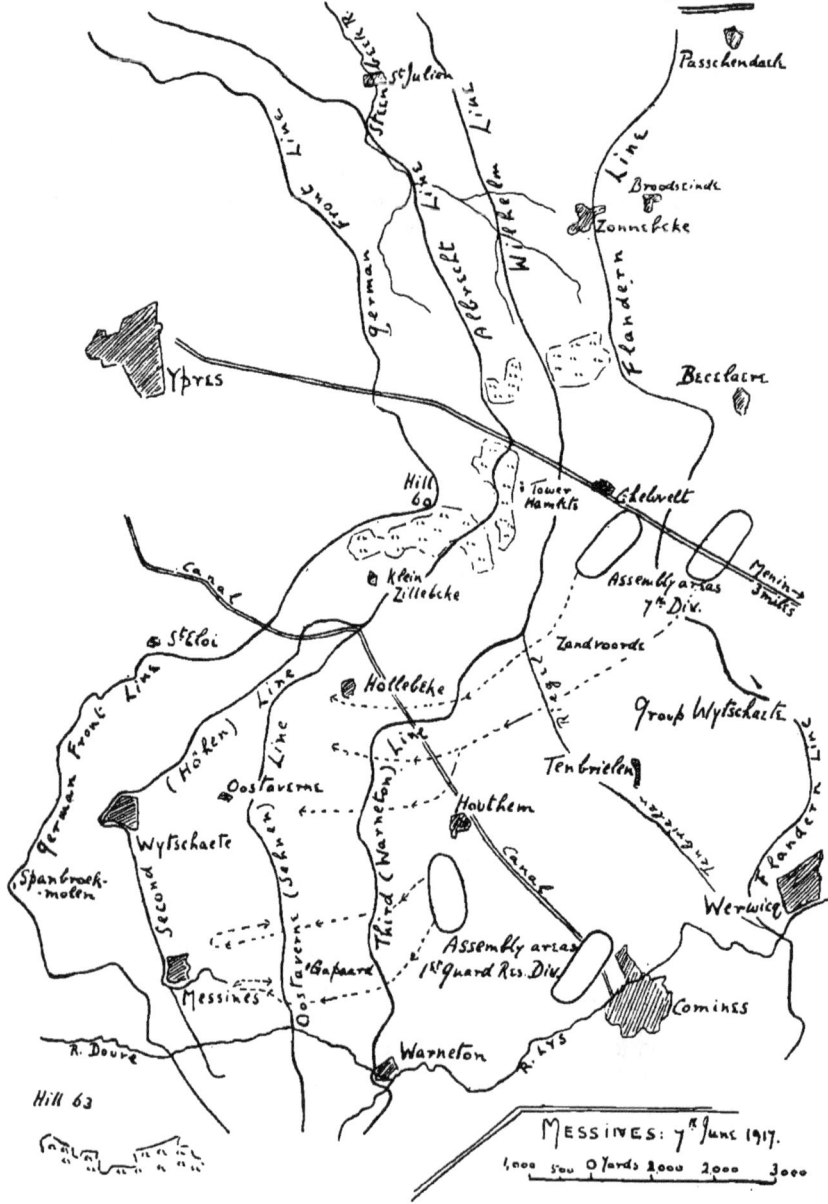

Sketch 19

Passchendaele

St Julien

Broodseinde
Zonnebeke

Ypres

Becelaere

Hill 60
Tower Hamlets
Gheluvelt
Menin Straats

Klein Zillebeke

Assembly areas 7th Div.

Zandvoorde

St Eloi

Hollebeke

Group Wytschaete

Ten Brielen

(Höker) Line

Oosttaverne

Houthem

Wytschaete

Werwick

Spanbroek-molen

Messines

Gapaard

Assembly areas 1st Guard Res. Div.

Cominss

R. Douve

Warneton
R. Lys

Hill 63

MESSINES: 7th June 1917.

1,000 500 0 Yards 1000 2000 3000

Although General von Kuhl gave his opinion that the Messines Ridge was unsuitable for defence in depth and lent itself to be overrun, after the example of the Vimy Ridge, in one rush, the other members of the conference were in fact, unanimous for holding the existing positions. The three divisional commanders concerned maintained that the defences had been brought completely up to date and could be held. They were influenced decisively by the evidence of the commander of mining operations, who allayed their only suspicion, namely that the garrison of the front-trench system might be put out of action by underground mine explosions as a preliminary to a big assault. Deep under the waterlogged surface-soil of this district was a stratum of the Ypres blue-grey clay-stone, soft but impervious, which offered little resistance to mechanical boring operations, and for months past the Germans had known of the British efforts to undermine their front-trench system. They had tried to stop it by boring down to and flooding the galleries, and according to this expert opinion these counter-mining operations (*Quetschungen*) had been so successful, especially during April, that 'a subterranean attack by mine explosions beneath the front line to precede an infantry offensive against the Messines Ridge was no longer possible'.[1]

After a further examination of the Third (Warneton) Line and also of the intermediate (Sehnen or Oostaverne) line which had been constructed between it and the Second (*Höhen*) Line on the Ridge, Crown Prince Rupprecht agreed with the objections, and the plan for a withdrawal was dropped. Accordingly it was decided to strengthen by all available means the existing position. The three divisions/forming the Group Wytschaete (XIX Corps) were reinforced by a fourth, the 24th, in the front line on the 6th May. The importance given to the northern flank where it joined the Menin Ridge is shown by the density of the divisional frontages; the 204th (Zandvoorde) Divi-

[1] Wolff, *Das Infanterie Regiment 104* (Dresden, 1927), p. 45.

sion had 2,600 yards and the 24th (Hollebeke) Division 2,800 yards, while in the left centre the 2nd (Wytschaete) Division had 4,000 yards and the 40th (Messines) Division 4,800 yards. In the following days, also, two *Eingreif* divisions were brought up behind the four front divisions, the 35th to the Menin area and the 3rd Bavarian to near Roncq, three miles south-east of Werwicq. In addition, the Group Wytschaete was reinforced with artillery, ammunition reserves, and aeroplanes.

2

From the 8th May onwards the British artillery bombardment of the entire Messines salient, from the Ypres–Menin road to the Douve valley, began to increase in intensity and so started their gigantic task of destruction to prepare the position for the infantry assault. For this purpose the Second Army under General Sir H. Plumer had assembled 2,233 guns and howitzers, as opposed to 630 German guns and howitzers in the same sector, and 300 aeroplanes, as opposed to about one-sixth that number which the German Group Wytschaete had available.

Each German front-line regiment held its sector of 700 to 1,200 yards frontage with one battalion (*Kampf*) in the front line, one in support (*Bereitschaft*) and the third in reserve, resting three or four miles back. The front battalion normally had three companies in the front system of breastworks and one back in an intermediate (*Sonne*) line which lay between the front system and the Second (*Höhen*) Line along the crest of the Ridge. The support battalion had also one company in this intermediate (*Sonne*) line which was at the tactical disposal of the front battalion commander (K.T.K.) for a local immediate counter-attack, and the other three companies were back in the shelters in the two trench-lines of the Second (*Höhen*) Line. The entire garrison was sheltered in a series of concrete shelters, those in the front system being small and sometimes only of wood, while those farther back were in the large pill-boxes holding twenty-five to forty men. Scattered about in suitable sites within the position were also a number of concrete machine-gun emplacements, about thirty-two in each regimental sector, including those for the divisional S.S. machine-gun detachments behind the Ridge.

The British artillery set about to destroy all this quantity of shelters in the German position. The shelling soon caused their covering of earth and sods to fall off, and when on those bright May afternoons and evenings the sun began to sink into the west behind the British observers on Kemmel and Haubourdin Hill the array of pill-boxes stood out in all their white nakedness as perfect targets.

From the 23rd May onwards this general bombardment became more intense. The breastworks of the front system were gradually and completely broken down by the new torpedo-mines, fired from close range, which on bursting made holes six feet deep and five yards in diameter, and the Germans counted as many as a hundred of these bursts in a day on one regimental sector alone. Not only were the concrete shelters on the forward slope systematically destroyed but also those behind the Ridge, along the Oostaverne Line and the Third (Warneton) Line, the fire being directed not very effectively by aeroplane observation. The British superiority in the air was sufficient to permit British air observers to cruise over the German lines, as many as sixty or seventy at a time, without molestation; Richthofen's famous squadron (the Circus) had been sent from the Scarpe front to cope with the situation but was unable to make any deep impression on the great numerical superiority which the British had been able to mass in the Messines sector. The British had, in fact, complete mastery over the German position, and, with a three-fold superiority of guns firing concentrically into the salient formed by the Messines position, were able almost at leisure practically to obliterate it.

From the 26th May onwards, to avoid unnecessary loss, the German foremost garrison was ordered to move fifty yards forward at dawn into no-man's-land and shelter in shell-holes, returning at nightfall to what remained of their normal residences; and as these gradually ceased to exist, the forward shell-holes were made into permanent shallow dug-out shelters. The remainder of the front companies farther back were also ordered to shelter in shell-holes throughout the day, and similarly the support battalions in and about the Second (*Höhen*) Line withdrew behind the Ridge. So it was that the pill-boxes, designed to protect the garrison, actually served their purpose not by sheltering them but by acting as targets to draw the British artillery fire. The casualties caused by a bombardment of unprecedented severity averaged, in the first period up to the 28th May, about ten a day in each regimental sector, and from then on to the day of assault it increased with the increasing intensity of the bombardment to an average of about forty a day. More serious was the nervous exhaustion; and this became so apparent that whereas early in May the front battalions had been relieved every five days, this period had to be reduced to every two days from the end of the month.

From the 1st June onwards for the next seven days, including the day of the battle, over three million shells were fired from British guns on to the six-mile frontage of the Messines Ridge position. On the forward slope, where ground observation was possible, the German breastworks, communication trenches, pill-boxes, and most of the machine-gun nests were destroyed; the 415th Regiment, holding the sector north of Saint-Eloi, estimated that about 1,000 heavy shells and 4,000 of medium calibre, as well as 600 torpedo mines 'thrown in as a bargain', were hurled on to its front system alone during a few hours of the evening of the 1st June. In the Second (*Höhen*) Line on the Ridge and the defences on the reverse slope, where observation had to be carried out by aeroplane observers, the destruction was not so great. Wytschaete village, according to the history of the German 4th Grenadier Regiment, was, however, smashed to pieces, the heavy shells 'marching through the sky towards it in columns of battalions and dropping by platoons [*gruppenweise*] on the roofs and ruins of the village'; Messines village suffered the same invasion. But the smaller objectives were less easy to hit, and the members of one regimental headquarters (104th) behind Wytschaete, watching from shell-holes a few hundred yards away, estimated that between 2 p.m. and 6 p.m. on the 4th June 2,500 to 3,000 shells burst within a 100 yard radius of their pill-box and although it rocked about on its watery foundation it remained intact. Similarly a great number of the pill-boxes in the Second (*Höhen*) Line remained undamaged, as may be seen to-day for example in the sector of it in the woods west of Hollebeke. The Oostaverne Line on the reverse slope also had a full share of attention, and whereas when first constructed the boast was that 'patent leather shoes might be worn in it in the wettest weather without compunction', it no longer existed as a line of defence after a few days' systematic treatment, and only a line of pill-boxes stood at intervals 'like small white forts' to mark the former trace of it, 'an excellent advertisement for the utility of reinforced concrete';[1] they may still be seen there, twenty-two years afterwards. Comines, Warneton, and Werwicq, and the villages, road-junctions, railways, and bridges in the German back areas also suffered severely, and heavy batteries caused a number of explosions of German ammunition dumps; the most important being the depot at Coucou, near Menin, on the evening of the 6th June, where a mass of high-explosive and gas-shell blew up, the gas drifting into Menin and killing a number of civilians not yet evacuated and who had no gas-masks.

In the last days of May the exhaustion of the front-line divisions was such that two of the four were stated to be no

---

[1] Crusius, *Das Infanterie Regiment 139* (Dresden, 1927).

longer fit to resist an assault. In view of the statement made by a British soldier (29th Division) captured on the 28th May that 'the offensive would not be delivered till the 7th June', the Group Wytschaete commander agreed that the 24th Division in the important Hollebeke sector might be relieved on the 31st May by the 35th Division which had assembled as *Eingreif* division behind that sector. Four days later, on the 3rd June, the Group Wytschaete commander also agreed to the recurrent requests of the 40th Division for relief. This division was responsible for the Messines sector, which included the greater part of the Wytschaete–Messines area of the Ridge, and, as the Group commander stated in his report of the battle, he feared it might be 'completely worn out' (*'vollends ausbrennen'*) before the British assault was launched. Here, too, the relief was ordered to be carried out by the *Eingreif* division, the 3rd Bavarian, which had been training for four weeks, since the 11th May, for its task of supporting the two southern front divisions holding the Wytschaete and Messines sectors of the salient.

To replace the 35th Division as *Eingreif* division behind the two northern front divisions the 7th Division arrived about Menin on the 31st May, and 1st Guard Reserve Division arrived in the Werwicq area on the 5th June to replace the 3rd Bavarian Division. Both these divisions were fresh to the district and unprepared for the difficult task of *Eingreif* formations. The Group Wytschaete commander is blamed for not using these fresh divisions to relieve the front divisions, by which means he might have left the practised *Eingreif* divisions undisturbed.

3

The front divisions were to fight a mobile defence, their instructions being similar to those given for the Hindenburg Position organization. In the front system the *Stosstrupps* about the third breastwork (1c) were to carry out immediate counter-attacks to recapture the two front breastworks (1*a* and 1*b*) if overrun; but 'if the front system was untenable and the companies of the front battalions had to fall back they would find those of the support battalions ready behind to make an immediate counter-attack to recapture the front system'.[1] The only exception to this mobile defence was that the Spanbroekmolen Hill, considered of vital tactical importance for the whole forward position, was to be 'held at all costs' ('*unbedingtes Halten*').

Some at least of the regiments concerned expected however, between the 1st and 5th June, an order to evacuate the front system owing to the mine danger. During that period listeners had heard and reported British miners moving about below the front-trench system and their fears were confirmed by the statement of another British soldier, captured during a raid in the early hours of the 6th June, who said that the British offensive would take place the following day after a series of mine-explosions.[2] The Crown Prince Rupprecht, too, wrote subsequently in his diary (9th June) that it would have been clearly the right course to evacuate voluntarily before the assault at least the front system, which was known to be undermined. Colonel von Lossberg, although he was chief of staff of another army and the affair did not really concern him, states in his book that he telephoned to General Ludendorff some days before the offensive took place to say that it was well known that the British would explode a number of mines immediately before the infantry assault, and begged him to order the evacuation of the forward part of the position and to direct that the defence measures be confined to counter-attacks from behind it. He adds that General Ludendorff made this proposal to the Fourth Army Headquarters who, however, declined to adopt it. General Ludendorff considered it to be a decision which

[1] Hoffmann, *Das Infanterie Regiment 44* (Berlin, 1930), p. 226.
[2] Scheer, *Das Infanterie Regiment 413* (Stuttgart, 1936), p. 38.

should be left to the local commanders; and both General Sixt von Armin, the army commander, and General von Laffert, commanding the Group Wytschaete, preferred to remain in the existing position. In spite of this evidence, which is confirmed in the *German Official History* (vol. xii), the report of the Group Wytschaete (XIX Corps) after the battle states that 'if there had been the slightest doubt of the mine danger the whole forward position would naturally have been evacuated in good time, the *Sonne* Line would have been held as the foremost line and the ground between it and the *Höhen* Line would have been the forward zone of defence'. The report adds that 'the assembly areas for the reserve divisions which would have had to fight a mobile defensive battle for the *Höhen* Line, would have been correspondingly farther back.'

It is possible that if this had been done the mine explosions would have failed in their purpose, and the British attack might have met a stubborn resistance after crossing the thousand yards of broken ground in front of the *Sonne* Line.

4

After a thunderstorm during the evening of the 6th the sky had remained overcast, but about 2.30 a.m. in the morning (7th), after a dark night, the clouds cleared as a full moon sank below the horizon. There followed half an hour of most unusual quiet. For two weeks scarcely a minute had passed, day or night, without the noise of shells bursting over the position, and the contrast was sufficiently striking for German accounts to mention that during this half-hour of peace nightingales could be heard singing in a distance where trees still bore leaves and woods gave cover. About 3 a.m., when it was still dark, a slight mist delaying the first glimmer of dawn, a white ball of light suspended from a parachute was seen to drop from an aeroplane over the position, and shortly afterwards

Crown Prince
Rupprecht of Bavaria

General
Sixt von Armin

FLANDERS 1917

came a ball of yellow light. At that moment the whole earth beneath the German front system, from Hill 60, north of the canal-knee, through Saint-Eloi to the Douve valley, south of Messines, trembled. There was a great pressure of warm air over it, like a strong hot wave, which bent shattered trees as if swept by a hurricane. Simultaneously, at wide intervals of distance, great jets of jagged crimson flame flashed up skywards followed by a mass of earth, rock, and débris. The *German Official History* describes the scene as it appeared to a German observer on the Messines Ridge: 'nineteen gigantic roses with carmine-red leaves, or enormous mushrooms, were seen to rise up slowly and majestically out of the ground, and then split into pieces with a mighty roar, sending up many-coloured columns of flame and smoke mixed with a mass of earth and splinters, high into the sky'. The shock, the account adds, was felt for twenty miles back.

The explosions were mostly about the remnants of the middle breastwork (1*b*), so that all three breastworks of the front system were affected. Apart from the actual casualties caused, the tremendous shock paralysed almost the entire garrison of the front system long enough for the assault to overrun them before resistance could be offered. The evidence of General Sir C. Harington in his book, *Plumer of Messines*, confirms the intensity of this physical shock.[1] After remarking that nineteen mines containing in all nearly a million pounds of explosives were fired along the six miles frontage of the assault, he adds that on the following morning in a concrete dug-out near Spanbroek-molen he found four German officers sitting round a table, all dead, with no mark of wound on any of them.

The German mine-experts had been deceived by the depth of the British mine-galleries. Begun over a year previously from about the line of the British third trench 600 yards down the slope, they reached to eighty feet below

---

[1] General Sir C. Harington, *Plumer of Messines* (Murray, London, 1935).

the German front system, whereas the Germans had estimated a depth of sixty feet as a maximum.

Before the deafening roar of the explosions had died away the whole artillery strength of the British Second Army was let loose; artillery and machine-gun barrages along the German front-trench system, standing barrages on important centres farther back, and the counter-batteries deluged all known German battery positions with high-explosives and gas shell. Looked at from the German side the flashes of the British guns in the darkness were so close together and continuous that the whole western horizon seemed to be ablaze (*in Flammen*). With this immense artillery support the infantry of nine British divisions, with three more divisions in support, advanced against the German front system garrisoned by the remains of eleven German battalions. According to German accounts, the majority of the garrison was panic-stricken (*eine ungeheure Panik*) and offered little resistance, although in some sectors the *Stosstrupps* in the third trench (1*c*) counter-attacked as trained, but these isolated efforts were quickly overwhelmed by greatly superior numbers. The assault now moved on towards the *Sonne* line, garrisoned normally by half (two companies) of the support battalions, reduced to roughly 100 men and about six machine guns in each regimental sector of 800 yards. A dense cloud of smoke and dust, caused by the explosions and the barrage, covered the battlefield and, as visibility was at best only 100 yards in the misty dawn-light, the defenders were unable to see whether the mass of men coming towards them were their own front companies falling back elastically, or the enemy. Before the situation was clear the barrage, followed closely by the assaulting infantry, was upon them and this intermediate line and the machine-gun nests about it were also overrun.

After the capture of the *Sonne* Line the British advance continued with little delay up the slope towards the Second (*Höhen*) Line, garrisoned by the remaining half of the support battalions and, normally, a company of each of the reserve battalions, with ten or twelve machine guns in each regimental sector. It was now daylight and observers of the German 4th Grenadier Regiment about this Line, at the Wytschaete end of the Ridge, in occasional glimpses through the cloud of dust and smoke, state that they saw 'masses of infantry advancing in a succession of lines followed by closed columns, and by cavalry farther behind'. Not only was the full weight of the British bombardment now directed along the Ridge but 'swarms of British aeroplanes cruised over it machine-gunning every sign of life', while others fired at battery detachments farther back, and gave light signals as to their position to the British counter-batteries. 'The few German aeroplanes', says the history of the 104th Regiment, 'had to give way before this great numerical superiority, being powerless against it.' Seldom can an infantry assault have had such efficient fire-support, and the German infantry admit they were demoralized by the complete failure of their own artillery and aeroplanes to counter it.

The widely scattered garrison of the Second (*Höhen*) Line succumbed by degrees. The 3rd Bavarian Division, previously the *Eingreif* division behind Messines, which had only taken over the Messines sector of the front during the night and now saw its sector by daylight for the first time, was apparently the first to be overrun. The capture of this southern end of the Ridge took place about 7 a.m., and it unsettled one after another the garrisons of the other three divisions to the north; each regiment mentions that the danger to its left flank caused its survivors finally to fall back to the Sehnen (Oostaverne) Line. Several centres of resistance, however, though surrounded, held out for a considerable time; the 104th support battalion headquarters between Messines and Wytschaete, for example, did not surrender till 8.15 a.m.; Wytschaete village itself, which had been turned into a fort, was entered from all sides, assisted by tanks, about 9.30 a.m.; and parties of the 4th

Grenadier Regiment held out near by, in the *Höhen* Line, almost as long, 'hoping to the last for the counter-attack which all the instructions had promised would certainly be delivered'. South of Saint-Eloi, too, the 44th Regiment states that up till 8.30 a.m. machine-gun fire and hand-grenades could be heard in the front system of its sector; while, farther north, fifty men and three machine guns of the 61st Regiment held out in the so-called Caterpillar (*Kofferberg*), a mound in the Second Line on the north side of the Ypres–Comines canal, for thirty-six hours until relieved. These isolated acts of gallant resistance in defended localities did not, however, influence the general course of the assault.

Within two to four hours from the start of the operation almost the entire German Second Line along the Ridge was in British possession. The sun had now risen into a cloudless sky, and British artillery observers with the leading lines of infantry had perfect ground observation over the German back areas as far as the Flandern Line and beyond. Added to this excellent ground observation, British supremacy in the air gave no chance for a German counter-attack to move very far without being seen and smashed by artillery fire. Nevertheless, according to the British plan for the battle the assault was to halt for ten hours, till 3 p.m., and consolidate along this Second Line, when fresh battalions would advance through to capture the Oostaverne (*Sehnen*) Line, which it would then consolidate as an advanced observation line.

The German accounts severely criticize the British choice of these two lines for consolidation. The Second (*Höhen*) Line lay along the back crest-line of the Ridge, and the history of the German 104th Regiment states that 'crowds of British infantry were seen to take off their coats on this warm summer morning and begin to dig in along the sky-line of the Ridge; working in their light-coloured shirts they made admirable targets for the machine guns'. In addition, both this Line and the Oostaverne Line beyond it had been specially sited along the few parts of the convex-sloping back of the Ridge which were in full view of the German artillery observers in the valley below, so as to be able to give the garrison observed artillery support. Consequently they were the worst lines which could have been selected in the entire battle-area as halting places for consolidation; but their selection was in accordance with the British practice, which persisted throughout the war, of giving German trench lines as objectives, regardless of ground conditions and also of the fact that the German batteries would know their exact range.

The British casualties during the actual capture of the Ridge were, according to British divisional histories, comparatively few; but during the ten hours of this hot summer's day, when every available man was set to work to dig a new line of defence along the skyline of the Ridge, and in the subsequent advance to, and consolidation for defence of, the equally exposed Oostaverne Line, the casualties mounted so rapidly that by nightfall they nearly equalled the German total of about 15,000. The artillery of the German Group Wytschaete, exposed to the concentric fire of the three-fold British superiority in guns, had lost 75 per cent of its material.

The German accounts give unstinted praise to the British Messines offensive as a feat of organization, but they criticize it mercilessly as a tactical operation. Owing to its obvious character as a set-piece, planned in every detail beforehand from first to last, it was dependent on the enemy remaining where he was. By chance that happened, but if he had withdrawn to an intermediate line, as many wished, leaving only a small outpost garrison in the front system, they claim that the entire organization would have broken down. Some of their accounts express amazement at the massed array of infantry employed, and consider the method of attack was as extravagant of men as had been the bombardment of guns and shells. The 44th Regiment, recently arrived from the Eastern Front, states that the tactical handling of the British infantry was even worse (*minderwertig*) than that of the Russian infantry; luckily the history of the British 19th Division, which was its opposite number in the battle, gives a suitable rejoinder, as it says that 'there was little resistance from the Germans, who either ran forward to surrender or, if they could do so, ran away; very few of them put up a fight'. Nevertheless these German criticisms are worth reflection.

6

The Group Wytschaete commander had intended that the two *Eingreif* divisions should arrive along the Second (*Höhen*) Line before the British could reach it, or at least meet and defeat them there before they could consolidate a line of defence along it. This might have happened if the two original *Eingreif* divisions, the 35th and 3rd Bavarian, had remained; but the 7th and 1st Guard Reserve Divisions which had taken their places were fresh to the district and to the task. They were alarmed in their billets at Menin and Werwicq at 3.30 a.m., and reached their reserve assembly areas east of Gheluvelt and north of Warneton about 7 a.m., when they were placed by General Sixt von Armin, the Fourth Army commander, at the disposal of the Group Wytschaete.

General von Laffert, commanding the Group Wytschaete, had on the 3rd June selected Houthem as the site of the support assembly area for the northern *Eingreif* division and a site north of Warneton for the southern. But the Fourth Army commander ordered the northern assembly area to be near Gheluvelt, which was three miles north of Houthem, as he feared a simultaneous British attack south of the Menin road, between the road and the canal-knee, which was the weakest part of his entire Ypres position; for close behind it was the Tower Hamlets spur, which gave observation along the southern edge of the

flat-topped Menin Ridge as far as the Flandern Line. From
the Gheluvelt assembly area he hoped the division would
be able to counter-attack either due west across the Tower
Hamlets spur or south-west across the Comines canal. The
front west of Tower Hamlets did not, however, seem
seriously threatened, and General von Laffert gave the
order to the 7th Division at 7.10 a.m. to march by Zad-
voorde on Hollebeke, and counter-attack against the flank
of the enemy south of the canal in the general direction of
Wytschaete, its right on Hollebeke and its left north of
Houthem. At 7.15 a.m. he ordered the 1st Guard Reserve
Division to advance to the Third (Warneton) Line, due
east of Messines, ready to advance on that place and on
the Ridge on either side of it, and thence to recapture the
former front system of breastworks and the enemy's original
assembly trenches beyond.

Being fresh to the district, battalion and company commanders had to have objectives pointed out individually,
and there were many delays. It was 1 p.m. before the 7th
Division had crossed the Comines canal at Houthem, and
as their march from Gheluvelt was seen by British observers, who had been established on the Wytschaete–Messines
Ridge since 8 a.m., they had suffered considerably from
shell-fire on the way and had found one of the canal
bridges already destroyed. The right of the division was
then diverted to assist in holding the line about Hollebeke,
and it was 4 p.m. before its left approached the Oostaverne
Line, east of Oostaverne village, and found British troops
already in possession.

The 1st Guard Reserve Division did not leave the support assembly area, immediately behind the Third (Warneton) Line, for the counter-attack on Messines till 11 a.m.
It was after 1 p.m. before it had crossed the Oostaverne
Line under a heavy British artillery fire. In spite of opposition, however, its leading units reached the eastern farms
of Messines about 3 p.m. This was the hour planned for
the British advance to the Oostaverne Line, and the 1st

Guard Reserve Division was exposed both to the barrage preceding it and to the full impetus of the renewed British attack. The regiments of the division, without observed artillery support, fell back with heavy losses to behind the Oostaverne Line, where they remained till the evening. On the remainder of the battlefront, too, the British advance met little opposition and occupied the Oostaverne Line. The two German *Eingreif* divisions, together with the resting battalions of the front divisions, most of which had arrived too late or else been unable to pass the British barrage, formed a new front a few hundred yards from the Oostaverne Line.

On this occasion the two counter-attack divisions had been placed too far back for them to intervene as desired. The échelon of reserves, each within close support of the other, which Colonel von Lossberg had planned as early as the autumn of 1915 as an essential of the defence in depth, did not exist.

7

The Group Wytschaete commander believed that the British advance would be continued down the slope to beyond, or at least to include, the Third (Warneton) Line, and so obtain the maximum of observation on to the southern side of the Menin Ridge. Since his remaining artillery in the Lys valley would be unable to give observed support to a mobile defence on the convex slopes of the existing position, he decided to order a general retirement under cover of darkness of all his infantry and artillery to behind the Ypres–Comines canal and the Lys River. This order was, however, cancelled when he saw that the British advance had stopped along the Oostaverne Line; and at 10.45 p.m. General Sixt von Armin, the Fourth Army commander, ordered that the existing position facing the Oostaverne Line was to be held.

The battle of Messines was a brilliant British success,

which lent itself to great possibilities for exploitation. But there was a tragedy behind the victory; for its only purpose was that the battles of Passchendaele might be fought.

Chapter XII

THE FLANDERN POSITION (*continued*): the Passchendaele campaign 31st July to 20th November 1917

Just as the capture of the Vimy Ridge by the British First Army on the 9th April 1917 opened a gateway into the Wotan Position, so did the capture of the Messines Ridge by the British Second Army on the 7th June 1917 open a way into the depths of the Flandern Position.

Look eastwards from the Wytschaete–Messines road, which was the approximate site of the Second (*Höhen*) Line, or from anywhere along the six miles of the Oostaverne Line, from Gapaard, Oostaverne, Hollebeke, or Klein Zillebeke, and it will be seen that the panorama for miles into the German position was as extensive as that from the Vimy Ridge. The foreground is more gently sloping and slightly convex, but from places such as the site of those two Lines the whole country to the Lys and beyond is overlooked; every German battery which fired could be located by direct ground observation, and German counter-attacks, whether local or by *Eingreif* reserves could be harassed by observed fire from the outset. This opportunity for exploiting to the full the weakness of the new German defensive battle, dependent on counter-attacks, was, however, allowed by British G.H.Q. to slip away, just as had that offered by the capture of the Vimy Ridge two months before; and the parallel is remarkable.

I

The Crown Prince Rupprecht of Bavaria states in his diary that he expected the British capture of the Messines Ridge to be exploited almost at once by another offensive against the northern end of it to capture the Tower Hamlets spur (one mile due west of Gheluvelt) south of the Menin road. It was the expectation and fear of such an attack, almost simultaneously with the Messines offensive, which had caused the Fourth Army commander to select a support assembly area about Gheluvelt for the northern *Eingreif* (7th) Division, instead of south of the Comines canal, behind the Oostaverne Line.

The capture of Tower Hamlets spur would have given observation along the entire southern edge of the flat-topped Menin Ridge. Counter-attacks would have been very costly, and so the way would have been prepared for the capture of observation points north of the Menin Road, overlooking the valley of the Steenbeek and all the German position behind the Pilckem spur. The situation was such that on the 9th June the Crown Prince Rupprecht proposed a withdrawal to the Flandern Line in the Messines sector, joining up with the original front line by the Flanders Riegel in the south, in front of Armentières, and by the Tenbrielen Riegel, north of the Comines canal; this northern flank to be further protected by a Gheluvelt Riegel, parallel to and one and a half miles north of the Tenbrielen Riegel, across the south-western corner of the Menin Ridge through Gheluvelt, to give additional strength to that key position. These constructional works were carried out; but the withdrawal was not, for on the morning of the 13th a new chief of staff arrived at the Fourth Army headquarters.

2

General Ludendorff had asked Colonel von Lossberg on

the 8th June, the day following the loss of Messines, to change places with the chief of staff of the Fourth Army. This was confirmed on the 12th, and Colonel von Lossberg left Tournai on the morning of the 13th for his new headquarters at Courtrai, where the Fourth Army commander, General Sixt von Armin, who had been with him as Group (Corps) commander in the First Army during the Somme battles, appears to have given him a free hand without question. Despite the fact that he had fought three most strenuous campaigns within two years, he arrived, according to eye-witnesses, as fresh as if it was his first. His tireless energy and his tremendous drive for getting things done were not diminished; and corps and divisional commanders who served with him state that few men could have inspired such confidence.

One of his first acts was to reject any idea of a withdrawal to the Flandern Line. Instead he ordered that the existing foremost line, behind the Oostaverne Line, was to be held at all costs and that it was to form the front line of a Flandern Position (*Flandern Stellung*) which was to be built up in depth in front of the Flandern Line. The Flandern Line was to become the Flandern I Line, and a Flandern II Line was to be constructed from one mile west of Menin northwards across the hill of Terhand to about Passchendaele, to form the back of a Flandern II Position (*Flandern II Stellung*). As a further precaution a Flandern III Line from east of Menin northwards through Moorslede was also begun (see Sketch 20).

As the days passed with no further British offensive Colonel von Lossberg's action seemed to be justified, but still the Crown Prince Rupprecht could not believe British G.H.Q. to be so blind to the opportunity offered to it by its Messines victory. The colossal preparations which could be seen by the Germans from their commanding positions on the Messines Ridge and Pilckem spur showed that a British offensive was imminent, and in his diary on the 19th June he wrote that he thought it would begin by a

Sketch: 20

Roulers

Sprict
Westroosebeke

Poelkapelle

Langemarck

Passchendaele

Pilckem

St Julien

Passchendaele Ridge

British

Attack

31st July
1917

Ypres

Menin
Ridge

Menin

Messines
Ridge

Wytschaete

Werwicq   R LYS

Messines

LYS   Comines

Waasten

Armentiéres

Flanders Switch

Lille Defences

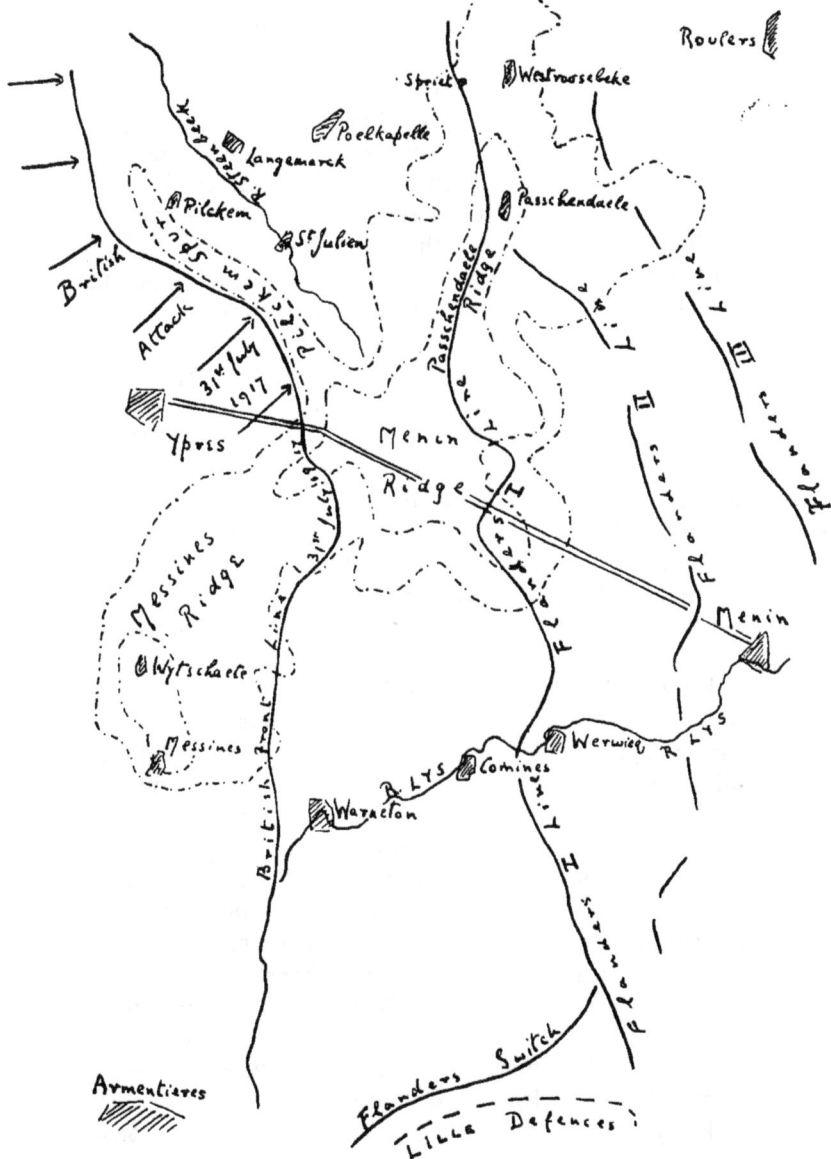

FLANDERS Position
31st July 1917

Scale of miles

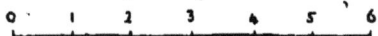

0   1   2   3   4   5   6

number of minor attacks near together in order to engage and eliminate the German reserves prior to launching the main break-through offensive (*auf breiter Basis angesetzten Durchbruchs-angriff*). This main offensive he expected to be delivered south of the Menin road, between it and the Ypres–Comines canal. With their right flank established on the Lys, at the canal junction at Comines, and on the Menin Ridge, he believed the British would then deliver another offensive north-east and north of Ypres and along the Belgian coast to capture the German submarine bases. Although he had faced the British army throughout the length of the war he still gave British G.H.Q. the credit for such a plan; and so critical did the situation of the Group Ypres along the Pilckem spur, north of the Menin road, appear to him in the event of a British advance on the Menin Ridge that at a conference on the 30th June his chief of staff, General von Kuhl, proposed a general withdrawal before the offensive to the Flandern I Line along the Passchendaele Ridge, the *Flandern Riegel* (north) would connect up with the front line again north of Langemarck, and the *Flandern Riegel* (south) rejoin it opposite Armentières. Such a withdrawal, it was claimed, would obviate an over-hasty retirement which might become necessary from the Pilckem spur, and also upset the British preparations which would take some weeks to repeat after a new deployment. This proposal followed one which General Ludendorff had made to the Crown Prince Rupprecht five days earlier, on the 25th June, that the Group Ypres should withdraw to the Third (*Wilhelm*) Line before the offensive, leaving only outposts in the Albrecht Line.

Colonel von Lossberg, on the other hand, believed that the British offensive would be delivered in the same way as those in the Somme and the Scarpe battles; a long preparatory bombardment followed by an all-out offensive on a wide front, from Bixschoote (two miles north of Pilckem) to Frélinghien (three miles south of Warneton), and therefore regardless of ground conditions. To meet such an offensive he considered the existing position a suitable one. In the south an attack from the Oostaverne Line would encounter considerable difficulties in the triangle between the Lys River and the Comines canal. In the centre, the key position between the canal-knee and the Menin Road would have to be most stubbornly defended, for which the Group Wytschaete would be well provided with *Eingreif* divisions. In the north, the six-mile long Pilckem spur position, with the valley of the Steenbeek behind it and overlooked by the Passchendaele Ridge farther back, was ideal for defence. The Pilckem spur position was, in fact, another copy of the Py brook valley position in Champagne; the Germans held the whole length of the crest of the spur so that the British had nowhere observation over its reverse slope, and German observers on the Passchendaele Ridge could enable counter-attacks in the Steenbeek valley to be supported by observed artillery fire. A British offensive against it, if delivered before a footing had been established on the Menin Ridge, would once again have to fight the battle with one arm against a defence with two.

3

The result of this conference on the 30th June was that the Germans did not withdraw either to the Flandern or the Wilhelm Line; and Colonel von Lossberg had anticipated this decision by making the fullest defensive preparations. He writes that it was the first occasion on which he had had 'sufficient time to organize a defence in all its details from the beginning'. In the previous defensive battles which he had conducted (Champagne, Somme, and Scarpe) he had arrived after the first battle had been fought and had had to extemporize with conditions as he found them, but he could now proceed as he wished.

On the 27th June, a fortnight after his arrival, he issued in a Fourth Army Order his instructions for the defence

MATERIALIZATION OF THE DEFENCE IN DEPTH
dispositions and the conduct of the battle. This Order he
has reproduced in full in eight pages of his book, and it is
of such importance for an understanding of the stage to
which the defence in depth had reached at this period that
I have given a summary of its main features in Appendix I
at the end of this book.

The front system of breastworks consisted of three lines
(1*a*, 1*b*, and 1*c*), each about 200 yards apart. Its garrison
was the four companies of the front battalions, with a line
of listening-posts in shell-holes out in no-man's-land.

About 2,000 yards behind was the Second (*Albrecht*) (or
artillery protective) Line, which marked the back of the
forward battlezone (*Kampffeld*) (see Sketch 19). The companies of the support battalions were disposed in depth at
the back of this zone with half of them sheltering in the
pill-boxes of the Albrecht Line. Sited chequerwise a few
hundred yards in front of that Line were the divisional
S.S. machine-gun nests (two or four guns to each) and this
array of strong points was called the *Stützpunkt-Linie*.

The Albrecht Line also marked the front of the greater
battlezone (*Grosskampffeld*) at the back of which, about
another 2,000 yards distant, was the Third (*Wilhelm*) Line.
In this zone were most of the field batteries supporting the
front divisions; and in the pill-boxes of the Wilhelm Line
were the reserve battalions of the front-line regiments
which were the divisional reserves.

Behind the Third (*Wilhelm*) Line back to the Flandern I
Line was the rearward battlezone (*rückwärtige Kampffeld*)
in and about which were the support and reserve assembly
areas for the *Eingreif* divisions. Added importance was now
given to these assembly areas. Experience gained in the
Verdun (December 1916) and Arras (April 1917) battles
had been that in all probability the entire forward battlezone would be overrun by the opening offensive, and that
although the front divisions might break its impetus by
machine-gun fire and local counter-attacks, most of their
battalions would have to be sacrificed; in the words of

THE FLANDERN POSITION: PASSCHENDAELE

General Balcke, in his essay in Schwarte's *Militarischen Lehren des Grossen Krieges* (p. 52), 'they will have done their duty so long as they compel the enemy to use up his supports, delay his entry into the position, and disorganize his waves of attack'. Consequently it was expected that the defensive battle proper would have to be fought by the *Eingreif* divisions in the greater battlezone (*Grosskampffeld*).

From this aspect the entire organization of front and *Eingreif* divisions came to be regarded as similar to that of the Roman legions of the third century B.C. which vanquished the Greek phalanx and withstood the onslaughts of Hannibal's armies. The front divisions were comparable to the light troops or *hastati*; the leading (*Stoss*) regiments of the *Eingreif* divisions in the support assembly areas were comparable to the *principes*, or supports of the legion; and the remaining regiments of the *Eingreif* divisions in the reserve assembly area to the *triarii*, or reserves of the legion. The Roman *principes* moved up and interlocked with the *hastati*, while the *triarii* advanced up close behind; so now, on a greatly enlarged scale, the leading regiment of an *Eingreif* (interlocking) division was to move up into the zone of the front division, while its other two regiments advanced into close support.[1] It may have been the influence of General Graf von Schlieffen, who had dominated German military teaching for many years before the out-

---

[1] The light troops, *hastati*, formed a front line in *maniples* or squares of 120 men, twelve in front and ten deep, and between each *maniple* was an interval equal to a maniple frontage. The second line, *principes*, was in similar formation 250 feet in rear, but its *maniples* were directly behind the intervals between the ten *maniples* of the *hastati*. The third line, *triarii*, composed of veterans, was in a similar formation with each maniple (of 60 men instead of 120) 250 feet behind the intervals in the *principes*.

When attacked, the *hastati* engaged and held the enemy, but if they wavered, they either fell back between the *maniples* of the *principes* or the latter moved up into the intervals between the *hastati maniples*. If further reinforcement was needed to give the knock-out blow, the *triarii*, or veterans, came up either round by the flanks or immediately in rear, throwing their spears over the heads of the *principes-hastati* line. (See Parker, *The Roman Legions* (O.U.P., 1928), pp. 10–20.)

break of war, which caused this cast-back to historical precedent. In his book, *Cannae* (p. 3), Count Schlieffen wrote that 'although weapons and methods of war have completely changed in 2,000 years [since Cannae 216 B.C.], the fundamental battle conditions [*die grosse Schlacht-bedingungen*] have meanwhile remained unaltered'. As if to give practical justification for that statement, the support and reserve assembly areas of the Flandern Position in July 1917 were named the *Fredericus Rex (principes) Raum* and the *Triarier (triarii) Raum* respectively. A comparison of the two organizations, ancient and modern, in detail will in fact show ample cause.

In peaceful periods the *Eingreif* divisions were billetted 10,000 to 12,000 yards behind the foremost line, but, on alarm, they moved up to their assembly areas on a system similar to that used in the Wotan organization.

4

The conduct of the defence within this Flandern Position was based upon Colonel von Lossberg's 'Somme Experiences' memorandum rather than on General Ludendorff's text-book and the Hindenburg Position. This is reflected in its names of a 'forward battlezone' and 'greater battlezone' instead of the corresponding 'outpost zone' (*Vorpostenfeld*) and 'battlezone' (*Hauptkampffeld*) of the Hindenburg Position. The authors of General Ludendorff's text-book had meant the outpost zone to be a zone from which the garrison could fall back elastically in the event of a big attack, so that the defensive battle might be fought in the battlezone behind it; but Colonel von Lossberg's intention was to fight the battle with the front divisions in that forward zone and he therefore called it a forward battlezone; only if the front divisions failed to check the attack did he intend to fight the defensive battle with the *Eingreif* divisions in the zone behind it, which he therefore called the greater battlezone. In the Wotan Position, while the British artillery were taking up new positions and had no time to establish a continuous ammunition supply he had compromised with the elastic defence idea to meet the needs oi open warfare in special conditions; but the Flandern Position was faced by massed artillery in permanent positions, with a system of light railways to the ammunition dumps near the batteries. In the circumstances he returned to his old principle of holding the foremost line to the last man. The order to individual regiments was that 'the front line of sentry groups [*Postengraben*] is to be fought for at all costs. It is the line to be held in all circumstances with the certain assurance that an immediate counter-attack will be delivered to recapture any lost sector of it and to relieve the defenders.'

His rejection of the elastic procedure in these conditions was not an obstinate sticking to principles. It is explained in his 'Somme Experiences' memorandum in the following words: 'If a trench garrison retires in a zone of fire it quickly becomes disorganized; all experience proves that such troops can no longer be expected to carry out a counter-attack; the result is almost invariably the loss oi the sector of the line evacuated and, as a further consequence, the creation of a very difficult situation for the troops on the flanks.' From men who had been exposed to the terrific bombardment to which he was certain the Flandern forward battlezone would be subjected he expected no more than a resistance in the position they held and he considered that a withdrawal on their part could only result in upsetting the counter-attacks moving forward to their assistance. That was the essence of his difference of opinion with the junior members of his former staff in the Operations Section at Mézières, who had written General Ludendorff's text-book. The zone names which he gave to the Flandern Position were officially adopted, being also given later to the Hindenburg Position, and have remained in the German training manuals for position warfare to this day; the names of outpost zone and battlezone being applied only to open warfare.

Although Colonel von Lossberg's instructions expected from the garrison of the forward battlezone a resistance to the last in the positions they held, he did not mean that resistance to be conducted rigidly from fixed positions. There was to be no yielding, but the garrison of each shelter could move either forwards or to a flank to escape artillery fire and to counter-attack. Above all, these groups, sections, or companies were to leave their shelters immediately the bombardment ceased, ready to meet the assault in the open. His instructions state explicitly that 'troops must not cling to their shelters. These are only man-traps. Only if the garrison is outside its shelters can it be fully in readiness to fight the defensive battle. The order for their evacuation must be strictly enforced.' That, too, was the experience of the Arras battle given in the Crown Prince Rupprecht's diary: 'It is better to await the enemy in the open, and then to counter-attack.' This procedure is described in practice in an autobiographical account given in the German official monograph *Flandern 1917* of the opening offensive: 'The bursts of the high-explosive shells rocked the pill-box about on its watery foundations like a small boat in a stormy sea, while the shrapnel bullets pattered on its concrete roof. The shelling died down, and the hissing, rustling song of the machine-gun bullets took its place. "Now they'll be coming!" All the men in the pill-box rushed out to a position among the shell-holes.'

This rush into the open applied to the whole garrison except for certain specified machine-gun nests in the forward battlezone, and more particularly to the divisional S.S. machine-gun nests at the back of it, which were all that remained of the defended localities, or *Widas*, of the Hindenburg Position. There were, however, a number of so-called permanent garrisons (*Sicherheits-besatzungen*), which, although out in the open, were to take no part in counter-attacks. The intention was that there should at all times be the framework of a defence in depth on which to reorganize the defence garrison; the reoccupation in depth of a position, immediately after a counter-attack, had in fact become a regular drill. The proportion of permanent garrisons in each zone of the Flandern Position is shown in Sketch 21; and in this way it was hoped to avoid that moment of weakness at the conclusion of a counter-attack, such as had become apparent on occasions during the Scarpe battles when a chaos of units had become crowded in the foremost line with no defence in depth behind, and therefore an easy prey to exploitation by a vigilant enemy.

The principal feature in the conduct of the defence within the Flandern Position was its counter-attack organization. This was anchored to the teaching of Clausewitz that the defensive battle should take the form not of a pure defence but of parry and thrust; the parry was to be the fire-power of artillery and machine guns and the thrust was the infantry counter-attack. Two developments since the construction of the Hindenburg Position had enabled this idea to be perfected by July 1917. The first was the completion by that time of the issue of the new German light machine gun (Mark 08-15) to most German regiments, thirty-six to a regiment; the second was the evolution of a new German doctrine for the attack, based, as mentioned in the chapter on the Hindenburg Line, on Captain Laffargue's tactics of 'infiltration' which had been ignored by the French but adopted by the Germans. These two developments require further elaboration.

5

While the British and the French General Staffs continued to worship at the shrine of the long bombardment preceding the infantry assault, and consequently a kitchen-maid aspect of the infantry arm and the absence of surprise, the Germans had throughout aimed at and achieved a doctrine which retained surprise as a first essential, and also permitted the infantry arm to remain queen of the battlefield. This doctrine was first tried out in the German counter-offensive at Tarnopol on the 19th July 1916. Surprise was gained by a new artillery procedure worked out by Colonel Bruchmüller, nicknamed *Durchbruch-* (breakthrough) *müller*, an artillery officer who had been re-employed from reserve on the outbreak of war. His procedure was founded on the principle that the first blow of an assault should be delivered by an overwhelming artillery action which must come as a surprise and consist of accurately aimed fire against, if possible, previously located targets. It was to last only a few hours, so as to give the reserves of the defence insufficient time to reinforce the battlezone, but was to be of such a hurricane character, against both the infantry and artillery of the defence, that the garrison would be either destroyed or demoralized to such an extent that the assaulting infantry would be able easily to overrun the position. For the purpose of this crushing artillery blow he had organized a special artillery battering-train, each gun of which had a chart of its idiosyncrasies, so that ranging shots were unnecessary, and each battery was expert in its pre-allotted task. At Tarnopol, after a surprise and devastating bombardment lasting a couple of hours, the German infantry assaulted on a twelve-mile front; there was no delay at red, brown, and green lines drawn indiscriminately across the map, no British leap-frogging of battalions, but a continuous forward movement through the Russian defence, exploiting wherever any weakness offered, to beyond the artillery positions. Within a few days the assaulting infantry had advanced to eighty miles behind the Russian front and had captured 42,000 prisoners.

⌜Captain Laffargue's infiltration tactics fitted the further development of this procedure like a glove. His '*groupes de tirailleurs*' or *Stosstrupps* equipped with flame-throwers, hand-and-rifle grenades, and light mortars, followed closely by larger detachments to exploit the weak spots, were to ease the way for still stronger forces advancing behind. The infantry attack-organization therefore became a succession of continually stronger assault detachments arrayed in great depth, which were to advance without delays through a position the garrison of which had been overtaken by all the disadvantages of surprise, and overwhelmed by a sudden, accurate, and terrific artillery bombardment.

The advent of the light machine gun had given the leading assault detachments (*Stosstrupps*) an additional and most valuable weapon, both to attack with and with which to defend themselves if counter-attacked. The realization of this double purpose of the light machine gun led to a reorganization of the smallest infantry battle-unit of the German army. Previously it had been the squad (*Trupp*) of seven men under a leader; it was now to be the group (*Gruppe*) containing a light machine-gun *Trupp* of four men (two with the gun and two ammunition carriers) and an assault (*Stoss*) *Trupp* of seven riflemen, each *Trupp* under a leader. The *Trupps* of a *Gruppe* might be separated or be grouped with those of other groups, as circumstances demanded, but the important point was that this smallest molecule of the German infantry arm contained within it the essential requirements both for defence, the parry by the light machine *Trupp*, and for offence, the thrust by the *Stosstrupp*.

In July 1917 this new attack organization was incorporated into the counter-attack organization of the Flandern Position. The array of *Stosstrupps* (60 per cent of the garrison of the foremost trench system), followed by *Stossgruppen* (40 per cent of the garrison of the intermediate part of the forward battlezone), followed by *Stoss-Kompagnien* (80 per cent of the Second [*Albrecht*] Line), followed by *Stoss-Battaillone* in divisional reserve (100 per cent of *Stoss* formations), followed by the regiments of the *Eingreif* division (100 per cent *Stoss* formations) in the Fredericus Rex and Triarii areas was very similar to the assault organization for the great German offensive on the 21st

March 1918. In this manner was brought up to date another of the dictums of Clausewitz; that 'an effective defensive is only the preparation for a successful offensive' (see Sketch 21).

On further examination, too, it will be seen that the idea of parry and thrust runs through the whole Flandern organization. Just as it was contained in each smallest component (*Gruppe*), so for example was the *Stützpunkt-linie* of machine-gun nests the parry for the thrust by the reserve battalions or divisional reserves, and so was the whole resistance of the front divisions, with their machine-gun fire and local counter-attacks, the parry for the thrust, or 'flashing sword of retaliation', by the *Eingreif* divisions.

6

This great defence organization, the materialization of the defence in depth, was applied by Colonel von Lossberg on the whole twenty-five-mile front of the three Groups (Corps) of the Fourth Army; Dixmude (XIV Corps) Ypres (III Bavarian Corps), and Wytschaete (IX Reserve Corps). By the end of July the Group Dixmude, holding a twelve-mile front where no serious attack was expected, had four front divisions supported by two *Eingreif* divisions; the Group Ypres, holding a six-mile front from about Pilckem to the Menin Road, had three front divisions and two *Eingreif* divisions; and the Group Wytschaete, holding an equal frontage south of the Menin Road, had three front divisions and three *Eingreif* divisions.

This first line of *Eingreif* divisions was immediately behind the Passchendaele and Menin Ridges. Five miles behind again, about the line Thorout–Roulers–Menin, was a second line of four *Eingreif* divisions, at the disposal of the Crown Prince Rupprecht, commanding the Northern Group of Armies, in readiness to be handed over to the Fourth Army if required; and seven miles farther back, about Iseghem, was a third line of two more divisions in

Sector of German Flandern Position [Sketch 2]
on 31 July 1917: Theoretical Diagram.

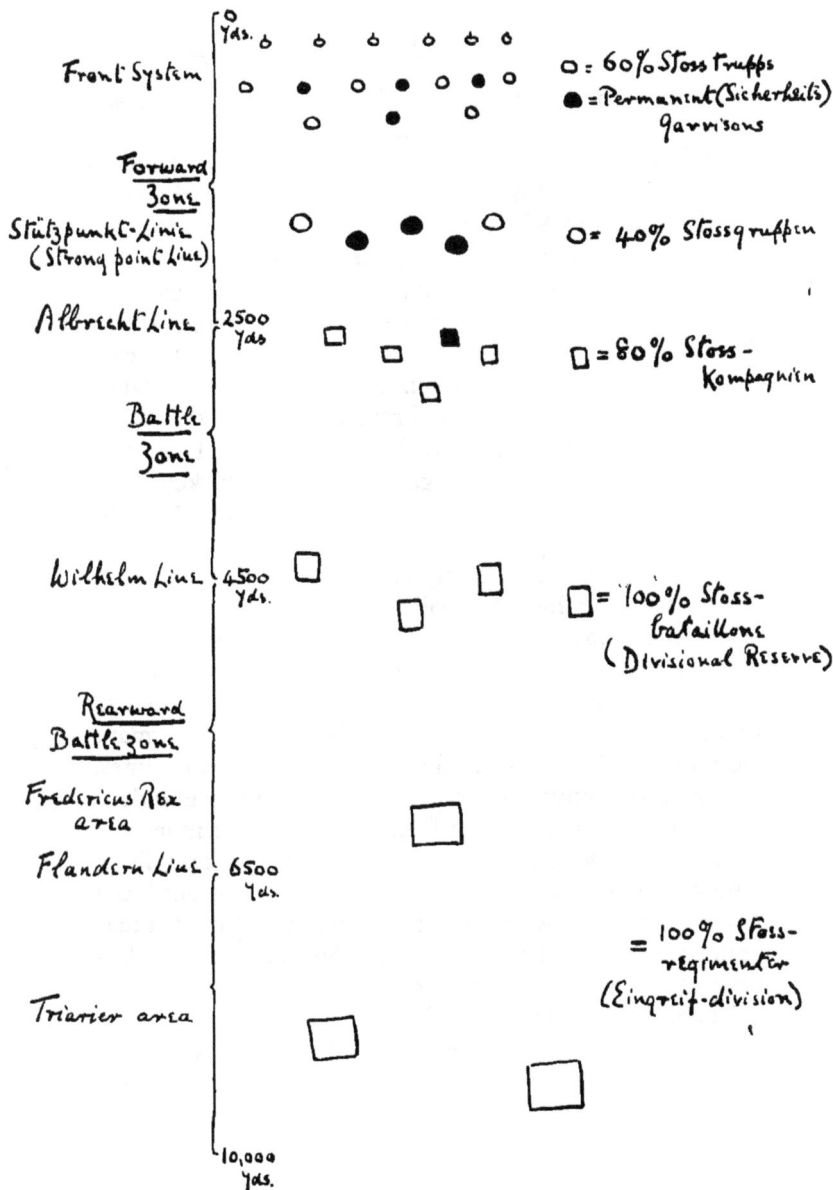

Front System

Forward
Zone

Stützpunkt-Linie
(Strong point Line)

Albrecht Line   2500
               Yds

Battle
Zone

Wilhelm Line   4500
             Yds.

Rearward
Battle Zone

Fredericus Rex
area

Flandern Line   6500
             Yds.

Triarier area

        10,000
        Yds.

0 = 60% Stoss trupps
● = Permanent (Sicherheits)
              garrisons

0 = 40% Stossgruppen

□ = 80% Stoss-
           Kompagnien

□ = 100% Stoss-
           bataillone
   (Divisional Reserve)

= 100% Stoss-
          regimenter
   (Eingreif-division)

O.H.L. reserve, ready to take the place of any of the second line which might be sent forward.

7

British G.H.Q. was kept fully informed of these German dispositions by a number of captured German documents, aeroplane photographs, and other means. If Sir Douglas Haig had allowed his Second Army to follow up its victory on the Messines Ridge by another offensive against the sector south of the Menin road, he might have had without great difficulty, according to the German evidence, the Passchendaele Ridge, or at least the flat-topped Menin Ridge, which was the key observation point to it. Instead, however, six weeks of dry summer weather passed while the British Fifth Army was brought up from the Bulle-court sector, and he staged with it a great frontal offensive north of the Menin road against the long Pilckem spur over which there was no observation. So, too, in April he had neglected the advantages north of the Scarpe given by the capture of the Vimy Ridge and had pressed his main attack against the foothills south of the river over which there was no observation (see Sketch 21a).

Once again red, brown, and green lines were drawn across the map as intermediate objectives regardless of ground conditions, and also of the fact that the Germans were disposed in zones in depth and not in trench lines. The final objective for the day was near to the Flandern Line on the Passchendaele Ridge, three to five miles distant, and Sir Douglas Haig considered that there might be fighting on the Ridge itself for several days until the *Eingreif* divisions were defeated there; but that a great opportunity would then occur in the plain of Flanders beyond for the employment of cavalry.

The stubborn retention of this plan had as a consequence that the Passchendaele campaign became a series of frontal assaults for the purpose of hammering through at its strongest part the greatest and deepest defence system ever organized in military history. The task of reaching even the Passchendaele Ridge by such a method was colossal; and it was only accomplished after four months of fighting in conditions unparalleled and with the loss of a quarter of a million (240,000) British casualties. It stands as an immortal example of the indomitable determination of the British man-in-the-street to accomplish what he has begun; but it seems a task he should never have been set.

8

The course of the opening battle on the 31st July 1917 is well known. The German forward battlezone had been turned into a puddled morass by a British artillery bombardment lasting two weeks at the rate of three million shells a week. Although it lay on a reverse slope the battle showed again, as the Crown Prince Rupprecht wrote in his diary after the Arras battle, that 'a sufficient supply of artillery ammunition can neutralize resistance in a zone as deep as the effective range of the field batteries, no matter how it is sited'.

The machine guns and local counter-attacks of the front divisions checked, broke up, and delayed the advance of the waves of attack through the forward battlezone. By midday, however, parties of British were passing on across the Second (*Albrecht*) Line and the Steenbeek, on either side of Saint-Julien towards the Wilhelm Line. It was here, in the centre of the assault frontage, that the offensive was being most successful. Colonel von Lossberg writes that it was at about this hour that he had gained a fairly clear idea of the situation. His intention was to use the *Eingreif* divisions as soon as the attack had reached any sector of the Second (*Albrecht*) Line, and 'I proposed to General

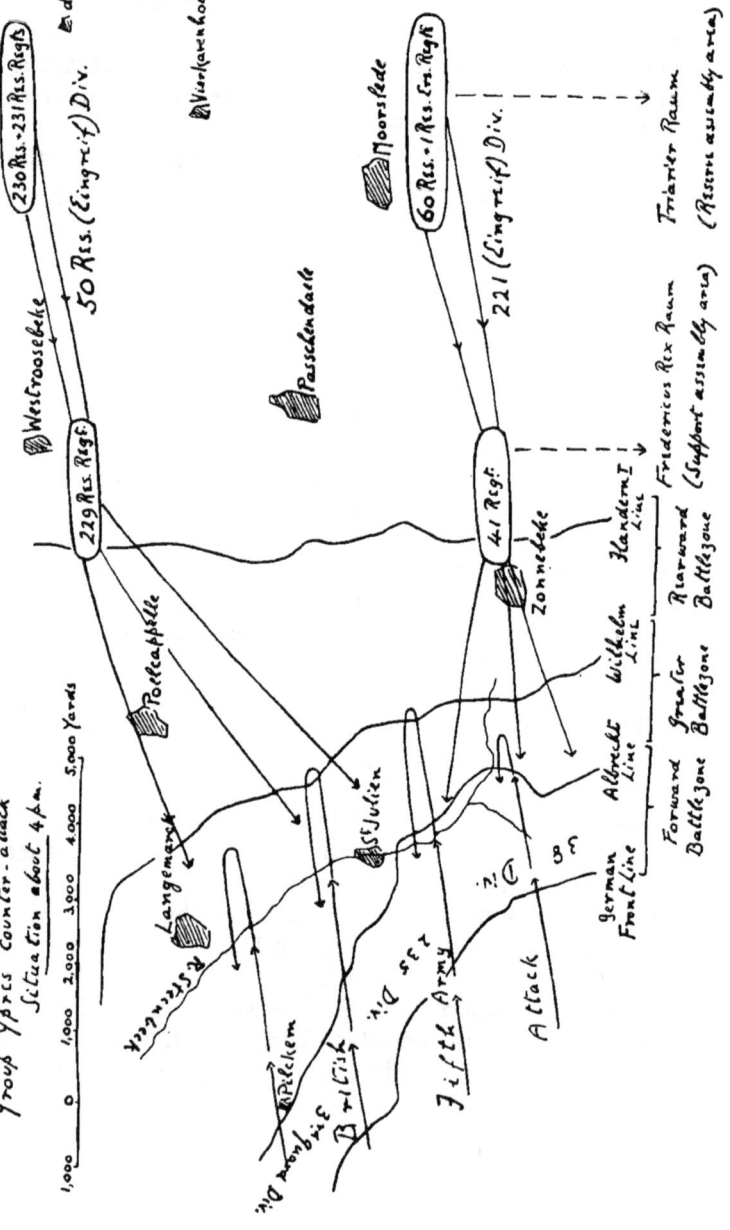

Sketch 21

Battle of Pilckem 31 July 1917
Group Ypres Counter-attack
Situation about 4 p.m.

1,000 0 1,000 2,000 3,000 4,000 5,000 Yards

Poelers

de Ruiter

Vierlavenhoek

Westroosebeke

230 Res. + 231 Res. Regts

50 Res. (Eingreif) Div.

Passchendaele

Moorslede

60 Res. + Res. Ers. Regt

221 (Eingreif) Div.

229 Res. Regt

Poelcappelle

41 Regt

Zonnebeke

Frederica Rex Raum
(Support assembly area)

Tranter Raum
(Reserve assembly area)

Flandern I Line

Wilhelm Line

Albrecht Line

German Front Line

Forward Battlezone

Gravlin Battlezone

Rearward Battlezone

Langemarck

St Julien

Boesinghe

Pilckem

R Pilckem

British

3rd Div.

39 Div.

38 Div.

Fifth Army

Attack

Sixt von Armin, the Army commander, that certain *Eingreif* divisions, which had moved forward to the assembly areas, should now be put in and deliver the counter-attack. He agreed, and a few minutes later I gave the order [*mit fester Stimme gab ich den Befehl*] by telephone for the counter-attack by the *Eingreif* divisions supported by all available artillery and aeroplanes.'

The main counter-attack was against the flanks of the break-in about Saint-Julien by the *Eingreif* divisions on either side; and it was delivered in a manner similar to the tactics of the defence in depth which Colonel von Lossberg had planned to meet the reported break-in at Flers during the Somme battles, but which never materialized; namely, to counter-attack from the flanks and, at worst, block them. The British centre beyond Saint-Julien was pushed back 1,000 to 2,000 yards across the Steenbeek, and the Germans recaptured some of the lost sectors of the Second (*Albrecht*) Line. About 2 p.m., while the counter-attack was in progress, the heavy clouds which had hung over the district all the morning broke, and rain came down in torrents. The ground, churned up by the bombardment and with all the natural drainage channels blocked, quickly became a morass and was a contributing factor to the check to the German counter-attack along the Albrecht Line and the Steenbeek. The Flanders rains had begun, and they continued.

The Crown Prince Rupprecht's comment in his diary on the evening of this battle-day is illuminating. He wrote that he was 'very satisfied with the results, all the more so as the *Eingreif* divisions of the Group Wytschaete have not had to be used at all'. In other words the British might hammer away at will in the Steenbeek valley so long as they left the Menin Ridge alone.

9

On further analysis it will be found that the Flandern

Position answered that vexed question which had so long perplexed the German General Staff as to whether the defensive battle should be fought *in* or *behind* the foremost line. The reply it had given was to fight it in both. The front divisions had fought it *in* and *for* the foremost line, and by doing so they had succeeded in breaking up and delaying the waves of the assault; the *Eingreif* divisions had fought it *behind* the foremost line, and their objective had been to recapture the whole position. So the heated discussions between Colonel von Lossberg and the junior members of his Operations Section at O.H.L. in Mézières in the summer of 1915 had ended in July 1917 in a combination of two apparently irreconcilable points of view Further, in this battle of the 31st July 1917 may be seen the partial materialization on a grand scale of the French Fifth Army instruction of the 30th April 1915, as interpreted by the junior members of the O.H.L. Operations Section in the summer of 1915. The assault had been disorganized and delayed by the front line units, and the defensive battle proper had been fought in the battlezone behind by the reserves.

On the following day Colonel von Lossberg was promoted major-general, and in none of the belligerent armies can any officer have better deserved that rank. The organization of the Flandern Position, and the conduct of the defensive battle within it on the 31st July 1917, is generally regarded as the masterpiece of this artist in war.

10

The fact that the forward battlezone had been more thinly held than at Arras on the 9th April explains why, although it was overrun in the same fashion, less than half the number of prisoners were captured (13,000 men and 200 guns at Arras compared with 6,000 men and 25 guns on the 31st July). In order to reduce still further the garrison of the forward battlezone, which had to suffer such a heavy sacrifice at each big onslaught until out of range of the mass of the British fixed artillery positions, regimental sectors were slightly increased, allowing more troops to be held back. The field artillery was also re-organized in two categories, one of which, copying the British system, was only to be used on big battle-days, and otherwise kept hidden from view.

With these exceptions the defence organization to meet the second big British offensive on an eight-mile front on the 16th August was unchanged. The original 'greater battlezone', between the Albrecht and Wilhelm Lines, was now the forward battlezone, and the foremost line was a line of shell-holes with the local supports in the Albrecht Line pill-boxes, or thereabouts. The British objective was, however, limited, owing to the puddled state of the ground and the difficulty of artillery movement. Instead of being three to four miles distant, as on the 31st July, the objective was 1,500 to 2,000 yards away. The assault was also timed to be much quicker, so that the final objective, the Wilhelm Line at the back of the forward battlezone, was to be reached by 8 a.m.

This alteration conformed to the precedent of the Somme battles in 1916, where the failure of the all-out offensive on the 1st July had also been followed by 'attrition' attacks with limited objectives; but it was a procedure which con-founded the German counter-attack divisions. After crossing two miles of mud they found the British already established along a new defence line. Consequently the forward battlezone and its weak garrison were lost beyond recapture. The result of this battle was a revision of the Flandern organization; but before any changes had been decided upon and put into effect, a British offensive south of the Menin Road, so long expected and feared by the Germans, had at last been delivered.

II

Continuance of wet weather prevented any but comparatively minor operations during the latter part of August and first half of September. The offensive by the British Second Army south of the Menin Road, combined with one by the Fifth Army in the Steenbeek valley, north of it, took place on the 20th September, and its effect on the Germans is expressed in the report of the chief of staff of the Second Army, General (now Sir C.) Harington, written six days later and reproduced in his biography of *Plumer of Messines*. He stated in it that 'the battle of the Menin Road on the 20th September disclosed the importance the enemy attached to the Tower Hamlets spur (one mile west of Gheluvelt) south of the Menin Road. The very heavy counter-attack which he launched against it was seen from the outset in the movements of infantry and artillery behind Tenbrielen (two miles due east of Houthem). This warning enabled annihilating fire to be brought against his troops as they assembled and deployed, and so disconcerted his counter-attack that but few elements of it reached even to close range.' This was a repetition of the Gavrelle affair; the weakness of the mobile defence in depth was again manifest. General Harington added in his report: 'It is not to be expected that the enemy will abandon his efforts to deny us observation about the Menin Road and Gheluvelt. The desperate manner in which he has since fought indicates the importance he attaches to observation from the heads of the valleys between Gheluvelt and Becelaere. The circumstances of his attack on our line here indicate how much he was willing to pay for denying us this ground.'

There lay, and had lain since the Messines victory in June, the key to the Passchendaele Ridge, and also the means of rapidly consuming the *Eingreif* divisions by artillery fire and with the minimum of loss to the British infantry. The British numerical superiority in guns and shells could be used to full advantage; offensives could be covered throughout by observed artillery fire, and the German counter-attacks could be neutralized almost before leaving the assembly areas.

In spite of this flagrant lesson, however, British G.H.Q. continued to order offensives on a wide front by the Fifth Army in the Steenbeek valley frontally against the Passchendaele Ridge, where they were overlooked in every detail by German observers on the Ridge, and where the counter-attack divisions were hidden away out of sight behind it.

12

General von Lossberg is silent on the subject of the alteration in the Flandern organization after the battle on the 16th August; in fact, he gives only the briefest account of the remainder of the Passchendaele battles. The battle-zone was now back behind the main lines of pill-boxes, and its garrison was mostly in the open. On the other hand, they were also out of effective range of the original British field battery positions, and so the bombardment would be of diminished severity.

Although the conditions of comparative open warfare now prevailed they were very different from those of the Wotan Position. The Scarpe district still had occasional woods, the undulating slopes gave cover, and the shell-holes were in the dry chalk soil. On the other hand, in the broad Steenbeek valley there were few undulations, the shell-holes were always filled with water, owing to the high water-level, and the woods and character of the Flanders landscape had vanished; as far as eye could see there was only a vast wilderness of water-filled shell-craters, with an occasional skeleton of a tree standing up out of it.

Such conditions were exceptional, and demanded different methods; as Crown Prince Rupprecht noted in his diary at the time, 'formulas are dangerous [*ein Schema ist schadlich*], and the defence must be conducted as the situation demands.' How General von Lossberg intended to act he does not say, but it is evident from all accounts that General Ludendorff from now on took an increasing interest in the Passchendaele campaign. The impression given by these accounts is that General Ludendorff's nerve was beginning to weaken under the strain of work and responsibility of the past year, and that he had become too fussy and interfering.

The Flandern organization probably required a strengthening of the front divisional reserves, the counter-attack force behind the forward battlezone, to meet limited objective offensives; but General Ludendorff demanded a more drastic overhaul. He states in his *War Memories* (p. 489) of this period that 'after each attack I discussed the tactical experiences with General von Kuhl (C.G.S. of the Army Group) and General von Lossberg (C.G.S. Fourth Army) sometimes at the front, sometimes on the telephone. This time I again went to Flanders in order to talk over the same question with officers who had taken part in the fighting.' The problem to be faced was, he adds, that the offensive with a limited objective gave immunity from counter-attacks and also enabled the counter-attack divisions to be broken up by massed artillery fire before they became engaged in the forward zone. It was decided to hold back the counter-attack divisions and to deliver with them methodical and carefully prepared counter-attacks (*Gegenangriffe*) instead, 'not earlier than the day following the enemy's offensive; this would give time to establish the exact position of the opposing front lines and enable more exact objectives to be given to the counter-attack divisions.' General von Kuhl in his *Weltkrieg* (p. 127) describes the new method as follows: 'In the conditions of the new British tactics (limited objective) our counter-attack divisions arrived too late. Their blow came up against a defensive position already organized in depth and protected by an artillery barrage. We had to try a fresh experiment. The front-line divisions were to maintain their position as much as possible with their own resources. The forward zone was to be more strongly garrisoned, and support and reserve battalions were to be brought up closer. If, in spite of these efforts of the front-line divisions, the enemy broke deep into the position, then it would be the business of the counter-attack divisions to push him back by a methodical counter-stroke on the next day or the day following.'

On this decision not only were the support and reserve battalions of the front-line regiments moved up nearer the front battalion, but the leading (*Stoss*) regiment of each counter-attack division was sent forward to occupy the artillery protective line, at the back of the forward battle-zone in its sector. To strengthen the defence all available machine guns, including those of the support and reserve battalions of the front-line regiments, were sent up into the front part of the forward zone, forming machine-gun batteries of four to eight guns at 250-yard intervals along the front.

The new defence tactics therefore aimed at checking the opening assault in the front part of the forward zone both by increased machine-gun fire and by immediate local counter-attacks, and the counter-attack by the *Eingreif* divisions was to be withheld until it could be methodically prepared. The system came into operation to meet the British offensive on the 4th October.

In the centre sector of the battlefield the defence arrangements were complicated by the presence of the German 4th Guard Division, which had come up overnight to make a methodical counter-attack to regain the Grote Molen spur, south of Zonnebeke, lost on the 26th September. Its regiments were lying out ready to assault in the forward zone, among the increased garrison, when the British bombardment opened. This mass of Germans was caught in the hurricane of shell-fire with consequent terrific losses, and half an hour later was overrun by the British assault battalions. Though this was the blackest patch of the battlefield, the creeping barrage demoralized the closely packed forward zone elsewhere, and the day closed as one of the worst of the Passchendaele campaign for the Germans. 'There can be no doubt', says the German official monograph (*Flandern 1917*, p. 124), 'that this new defeat was due first and foremost to the great superiority of the British artillery. The alterations that had been made did not take it sufficiently into account.' Many of the divisional commanders before the 4th October had expressed grave concern at the idea of massing the defence garrison in the forward zone.[1] The tremendous barrage of shell shattered the support and reserve battalions, closed up within the front zone, before they could come into action.

13

On the 7th October by a German Fourth Army order these new methods were to be abandoned. The front-line regiments were spread out again, with their reserve battalions back behind the artillery protective line, and the counter-attack divisions organized ready to come into the battle as soon as possible after the assault, despite the enemy's artillery barrage. Special efforts were to be made to neutralize the British batteries when the German counter-attack divisions advanced. General Ludendorff writes (p. 490): 'It was evident that the idea of holding the front line more densely, adopted at my last visit to the front in September was not the remedy. I now followed my own judgement without asking for further outside opinions and recommended the Fourth Army to form an advanced zone, that is to say a narrow strip between the enemy's front line and the line which our troops were to hold by mobile defence.'

[1] Nevertheless General Ludendorff writes in his *War Memories* (p. 490): 'I agreed to the tactical changes (for October 4th), although misgivings were expressed among my staff at this departure from the "Defensive Battle". I thought I ought to give way to the experience of officers at the front.'

General von Kuhl in his *Weltkrieg* (III, p. 127) elaborates General Ludendorff's description of this last stage of the defence in the Passchendaele battles. 'The foremost shell-crater area to a depth of 500 to 1,000 yards was to be considered merely as an advanced zone [*Vorfeld*] and only to be occupied by a thin line of sentries with a few machine guns. In the face of a big offensive these few troops were to retire on the main line of resistance [*Hauptwiderstandslinie*] at the back of this advanced zone, while the artillery were at once to lay down and maintain a dense barrage of shell in front of it. In the meantime the supports and reserves of the front-line divisions, and also the counter-attack divisions, would have been given time to move up towards this main line of resistance where the battle would be fought out, if the artillery had not already broken up the enemy's infantry in its movement across the advanced zone. There was, if possible, to be a counter-attack division behind each front-line division, but its counter-attack can only be successful if, with its units in good order, it reaches the enemy while he is still on the move or at least before he has had time to organize for defence the ground he has gained. Once this period, suitable for immediate counter-attack, has passed, the only course is to prepare for a methodical counter-attack, after ample artillery preparation, at some later time.'

The new proposals were, at the request of General Ludendorff, put into effect on the 13th October. They were based on an intensification of the idea of making the artillery the first and main line of defence; they carried a step further General von Lossberg's procedure of annihilating (*Vernichtung*) and barrage (*Sperr*) fire which he had used so successfully in the Champagne, Somme, and Scarpe defensive battles. It was hoped that the 'dense barrage of shell' in front of the main line of resistance would stop, or at least break up, an offensive before it had covered the varying depth of the *Vorfeld*. The 'thin line of sentries with a few machine guns' in the advanced zone consisted of one

or two groups (two N.C.O.s, eleven men, and a light
machine gun in each) in front of each company sector of
the main line of resistance; but, as a day and night procedure, this covering force was found to be unsatisfactory
and towards the end of the month a normal outpost system
replaced it; with a line of piquets, or outpost line of resistance, providing double sentry groups ahead. This organization is shown in Sketch 22, which gives a general idea
of the dispositions of a front-line regiment in the final stage
of the Passchendaele campaign. The companies were given
areas or zones, instead of lines, to hold, and they lay out in
shell-holes or shelters within it ready to occupy the main
line of resistance, which was some defined bank or track
across the regiment's sector.

14

From the middle of October onwards an *Eingreif* division
was provided behind each front-line division, and, according to an amendment of the 23rd October 1917 to General
Ludendorff's Defensive Battle text-book, it was to be
'brought up wholly or in part so close, i.e. within the
zone of the enemy's long-range fire, that it could if necessary intervene at once in the battle'.

In this final stage of the Flanders campaign there was
therefore a defence-unit of two divisions, one close behind
the other, on a frontage of 2,500 yards and with a depth of
8,000 yards. It has been estimated by German authorities
that under normal conditions, and with divisions at full
strength, two divisions assembled in depth in this manner
should be able to hold a frontage of 5,000 yards, while a
single division arrayed in depth back to 6,000 yards without its *Eingreif* division should hold a 3,000-yard frontage.[1]

[1] This was the actual frontage and depth held by single divisions,
for example, in sectors in Champagne early in 1918 where no *Eingreif*
divisions were present. The third (reserve) regiment was held back
behind the battlezone, about 6,000 yards from the front line, as an
Eingreif regiment.

Defence Organization of a German Regiment
on the Passchendaele Ridge : 10ᵗʰ November 1917. |Sketch 22

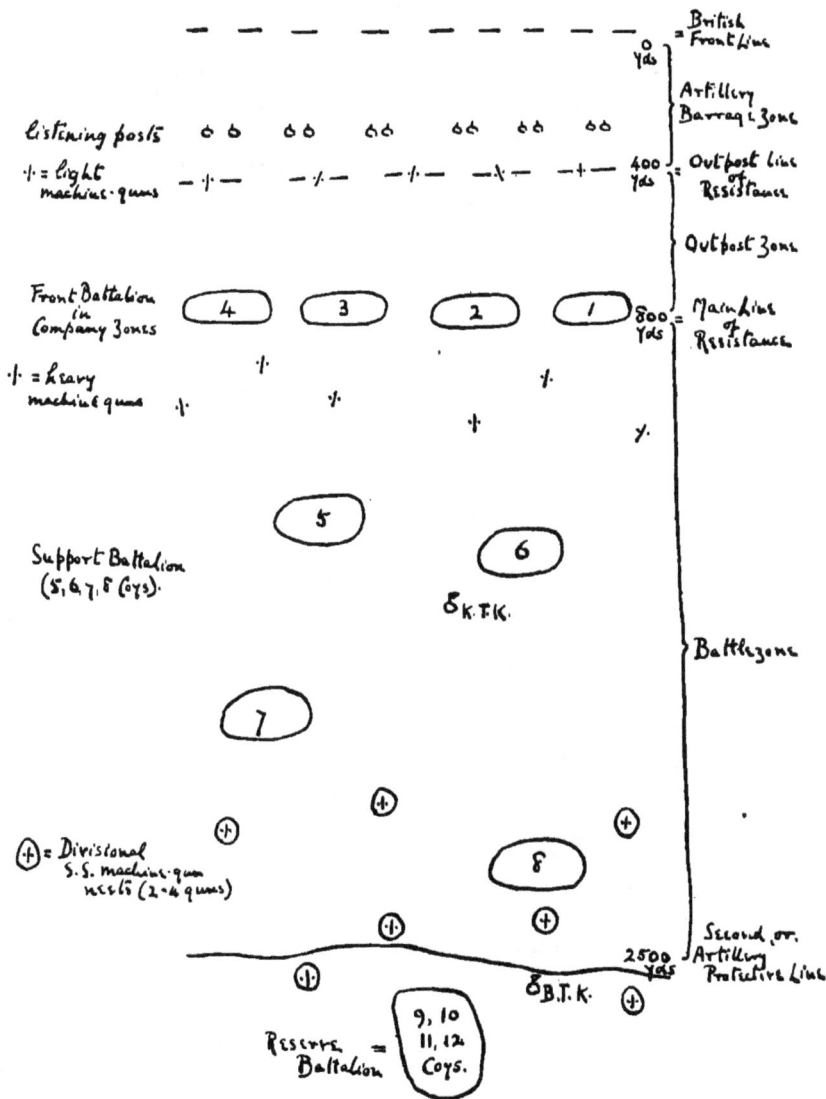

_ _ _ _ _ _ _ _ _ _ _   0 Yds = British Front Line

Artillery Barrage Zone

Listening posts   ϭ ϭ   ϭϭ   ϭϭ   ϭϭ   ϭϭ   ϭϭ

·|· = light machine-guns   —·|·—   —·/·—   —·/·—   —·\·—   —·+·—   400 Yds = Outpost Line of Resistance

Outpost Zone

Front Battalion in Company Zones   ④   ③   ②   ①   800 Yds = Main Line of Resistance

·|· = heavy machine guns   ·|·   ·|·
              ·|·   ·/·   ·/·
                          ·†·

Support Battalion (5, 6, 7, 8 Coys).   ⑤
                         ⑥
          δ K. T. K.

                                Battle Zone

          ⑦

          ⊕
⊕= Divisional S.S. machine-gun   ⊕   ⊕
   nests (2-4 guns)   ⑧

              ⊕   ⊕
                                   2500 Yds = Second or Artillery Protective Line

      ⊕   δ B.T.K.   ⊕

Reserve   =   9, 10
Battalion   11, 12
              Coys.

MATERIALIZATION OF THE DEFENCE IN DEPTH

The conditions of weather, the nerve-shattering superiority of the British artillery, and the falling quality and quantity of the German man-power had thus halved the hoped-for frontage the new two-divisional unit could hold.

The problem of concealing these two-divisional units along the shell-torn Passchendaele Ridge was solved by bringing to a fine art the idea of the 'invisible garrison' (*die Leere des Gefechtsfeldes*) already elaborated in the Wotan organization. For the front divisions 'there was no entrenched position or anything resembling a connected trench system which the enemy's artillery could have destroyed in a few hours; our lines were such that they were unrecognizable to the enemy's ground or air observers. There was no lack of accommodation, wet and filthy though it was; for every crater made by the heavy shells was a potential shelter for a machine-gun nest or a few men, with a tent or strip of corrugated iron as their only head-cover and a few planks as their only chairs and beds.'[1]

The regiments of the counter-attack divisions were able to shelter less uncomfortably in the cellars and ruined villages in the back areas. This system of the 'invisible garrison' was only rendered practicable in such conditions by inter-battalion reliefs within the front division every two days, and by inter-divisional reliefs every six days; so that each battalion of the two divisions was in the front line for only two days in twelve. Its success, however, is illustrated by the remark of the commander of the 44th Canadian Battalion before its assault on the 28th October in front of Passchendaele, that their 'objectives were garrisoned by only two men and a boy'; the reply given during the battle was that 'the boy must be working damn hard'.[2]

An important change in the organization of command

---

[1] Nausch, *Das Reserve Infanterie Regiment 10* (Oldenburg, Berlin, 1926), p. 146. This regiment was near Passchendaele village from the 1st to the 15th November.

[2] Russenholt, *History of the 44th Canadian Battalion* (De Montfort Press, Winnipeg, 1932).

was ordered in the same amendment (23rd October) to
the Defensive Battle text-book. It said that 'control of the
battle will be retained by the front divisional commander
in his sector regardless of seniority, and both the division
in the line and the counter-attack [*Eingreif*] division will
consequently be under his undivided command'. The
battle-powers of a front divisional commander in his sector
were thereby made as complete as those of a front battalion
commander (*Kampf-Truppen-Kommandeur*). 'All threads of
the battle passed through the three front battalion headquarters of each front division, who decided its course
[*Gepräge*]; in defence not only did they control their own
battalions and the other battalions of their regiment who
came up from support and reserve, but even when their
companies had been forced back to the rear part of the
defence zone it is still the front battalion commander
(K.T.K.) who, irrespective of rank or seniority, finally
directs and commands the troops of the counter-attack
divisions as they arrive up in his sector; for his responsibility
lies not only with his battalion but equally with his sector.'
The German official monograph (*Flandern 1917*), from
which that quotation is taken (p. 134), emphasizes that
the success of these defensive battles was due primarily to
the independence and responsibility given without reserve
to these two key points on a modern battlefield, front
battalion and front divisional headquarters, and that without it the organization would not have been practicable.

15

This amendment of the 23rd October 1917 therefore
marks the creation of a new battle-unit, a German legion
of two divisions under the front divisional commander. A
good example of it at work may be seen in the battles for
Passchendaele village on the 30th October. The British
offensive (Canadian Corps) had overrun the main line of
resistance of the 238th Division and was approaching the

western edge of Passchendaele village. By order of the
German front divisional (238th) commander the leading
regiment (172nd) of the *Eingreif* division (39th) moved up
from the Fredericus Rex area, about Vierkavenhoek, advanced through and north of the ruins of Passchendaele
and recaptured the main line of resistance. Simultaneously
the two remaining regiments of the *Eingreif* division had
moved forward from the Triarier area, about de Ruiter, to
the Fredericus Rex area, and thence to the artillery protective line east of the village 'ready to make an immediate
counter-attack should the high ground west of the village
be lost again'.[1] This affair offers an interesting parallel
with the action of the Roman Legion; the *principes* had
advanced up into the line of the *hastati*, and the *triarii* had
moved up into close support.

Success on this occasion was largely due to the fact that
the British line was now nearing the top of the Passchendaele Ridge, so that the *Eingreif* divisions had the advantage of being able to advance into the battlezone unseen
by the British artillery observers. The Canadian Corps,
which bore the brunt of these most difficult frontal assaults
for Passchendaele village on a sector of 3,000 yards, had
16,000 casualties in eleven days.

By the 20th November the British infantry, with unsur-
passed endurance and courage, had reached the Passchendaele Ridge and captured the Flanders I Line. Ahead was
now a Flanders II Position, and behind again a Flanders
III was well advanced in construction. But they remained
for the winter along the Passchendaele and Menin Ridges,
and along a line in front of the Oostaverne Line, which
they had reached after the Messines victory. The German
submarine base at Zeebrugge on the Belgian coast, which
was one of the original objectives of the Passchendaele
campaign, had not been reached; but the other principle
objective had been gained, namely to divert German attention from the French battlefront while the French army

[1] Steuer, *Das Infanterie Regiment 132* (Rolf, Berlin, 1931).

was recovering from the moral and physical blow it had received in the abrupt failure of the Nivelle (Rheims) offensive in April. It is not the British objectives of the Passchendaele campaign which have received condemnation, but the manner in which the battles to achieve them were directed.

16

The solution given by the Flanders organization in the Passchendaele battles as to how to dispose the front divisions to bear the weight of an asasult and how best to assist them with the *Eingreif* divisions so satisfied General Ludendorff that, at the end of November 1917, he ordered all the German Armies on the Western Front to adopt it in the event of being attacked, and to prepare defence schemes accordingly.[1]

Together, too, the Wotan and Flandern organizations have been accepted as the essence of German experience in the defensive battle during the last war, with the exception of certain minor changes during 1918 in the character of the advanced zone and of the *Eingreif* divisions, due to mechanization, which will be mentioned in the next chapter. And as the human imagination is so unreliable that the test by battle can alone be accepted for a doctrine, that experience may still be found almost intact in the German training regulations of to-day. If a comparison is made, it will be found that, of these two Lossberg creations, the Wotan has been accepted as a doctrine for defence in open warfare and the Flandern for position warfare. In both there is to be an advanced zone, to be explained later, ranging from five miles in depth in the former to fifteen

---

[1] General von Gallwitz, an army commander in the Centre Group of Armies (Crown Prince Wilhelm of Germany), states in his *Erleben im Westen 1916-1918* (p. 126): 'On the 28th November 1917 an instruction from the Group of Armies H.Q. ordered the strictest observation of the new advanced zone [*Vorfeld*] system in the defence; it was followed by *Vorfeld* instructions from O.H.L.'

miles in the latter as a protection against surprise by mechanized detachments. Behind that zone in open warfare is to be the Wotan elastic defence; for example, *German Infantry Training* (1936) states that 'the garrison of certain sectors of a defensive position will be detailed by regimental or divisional headquarters to be permitted to fall back elastically where the ground behind is suitable for counterattacks whether in or from behind the battlezone; elsewhere the main line of resistance is to be held.' For protracted or position warfare, however, behind the deep advanced zone, is recommended a defensive position organized on the same basis as was the Flandern Position to meet the British offensive on the 31st July 1917, apart from certain modifications to suit the fact that the *Eingreif* divisions will now be mechanized and motorized.

Part V

THE LEGACY

THE LEGACY

If I have succeeded in my intention there will have been
seen in the foregoing chapters a series of successive and
interdependent steps of development in the German defensive battle, from the elementary defence at the battle of
Neuve Chapelle in March 1915 to the elaborate Flandern
organization in July 1917. Before going further, it will be
as well to examine for a moment the intrinsic value of this
German experience.

To begin with, it may well be asked how did the German
General Staff manage to lose the war, when it had followed
so faithfully the teaching of its greatest military philoso-
phers and teachers, and had found, ready to hand, a master
of the art of tactical organization to apply that teaching.
Put in another way, the question becomes how did the
British and French armies manage to win the war despite
a succession of most expensive tactical setbacks. The best
critics of German methods are the Germans themselves
and the best answer I have found to those two questions is
given by the anonymous author of *Kritik des Weltkrieges*.[1]

While he praises the German General Staff for every
kind of excellence, he accuses it of one vital mistake; and
that mistake is the constantly recurring theme of his book.
He affirms that during the period from its victories over
the French in 1870 up to 1914 it had worshipped at a
shrine dedicated exclusively to 'bravery in battle' ('*so*

[1] Von einem Generalstäbler, *Kritik des Weltkrieges* (Leipzig, 1920).

319

war denn auch in der Tradition des Heeres der "Tapferkeit im Kriege" ein Tempel erstanden'); and that in its sacred devotions no other god (*nichts Fremdes*) was recognized. Another god should, he says, have been included; namely technical invention and mass-production (*Waffenwirkung und Technik*). He ascribes as a major cause of the final German defeat the underestimation by the German General Staff of the effect of fire-power, and a failure to perceive the need for a far-reaching alteration in its religion caused by the fact that a host of the stoutest hearts filled with the utmost will-to-victory could be neutralized in a few minutes by mass-produced shells and bullets accurately aimed. It was not until the late autumn of 1916 that the problem of organizing labour for the munition factories was properly taken in hand, under the 'Hindenburg programme'; but to the end of the war the German infantry continued to suffer untold waste of its substance owing to the unnecessary shortage of artillery, machine guns, and ammunition; in other words, owing to the failure of the German General Staff to realize that 'bravery in battle' must be supplemented by mass-production of munitions.

The author of *Kritik des Weltkrieges* admits that the British and French General Staffs, for all their clumsy tactical methods, had recognized the fundamentally important value of munitions and technical invention; and thanks to their Russian ally, who had kept half the German army engaged up to the end of 1917, had been able to make full use of it. Before a peace could be forced upon Russia and the full weight of the German army turned against the Western Front, the best of its officers and men had been already lost in the series of defensive *Material-schlachten*. This fatal weakness in the outlook of the German General Staff existed, says the author, even up to the end of the war; and he quotes as example the fact that when in the spring of 1918 experimental tanks were paraded for the opinion of O.H.L., and for a decision upon future construction, they were considered to be 'more suitable as

armoured ammunition carriers than as potential armoured and mobile field batteries or nests of machine guns, such as they had already been for two years in the British outlook'. And although he accuses both the British and French of having employed their invention most unskilfully, notably the French in the Nivelle (Reims) offensive in April 1917 and the British at Cambrai in November 1917, nevertheless it was the influence of large numbers of these machines in the later battles of 1918 which finally broke the back of the German infantry. The author points out that the deficiency of the German army in these fighting machines was not due to lack either of labour or metal, and he considers that with the steel used for the battleships *Bayern, Hindenburg, and Mackensen*, which were laid down in 1917 and went to the bottom of Scapa Flow on their first voyage, hundreds of tanks could have been built which might well have been decisive for victory in the German offensives in 1918.

In an assessment of the value of German experience in the defensive battle there is another matter which should not be lost to sight, namely that the German defensive battle was evolved to meet a particular doctrine of attack; a doctrine based upon an overwhelming superiority of artillery, ammunition, and generally of aeroplanes, and one in which the element of surprise was absent. The place of the attack was invariably known beforehand, so that time was given to make full preparations; and when the attack was launched it was primarily an attack by artillery, the infantry being used as a secondary arm to occupy what the guns had already conquered. It may well be doubted whether the Hindenburg organization, or its Wotan and Flandern variations, would ever have come into existence if the French and British armies had adopted a doctrine of attack such, for example, as that which Captain Laffargue advocated in the summer of 1915; with surprise as a first essential, with infantry as the queen of the battlefield, and with every other arm, such as artillery

and tanks, as her supporters to help her through and beyond the German defence zones as rapidly as possible. Again, even accepting the British and French attack-doctrine as it was, it may be doubted if the development would have followed the course it did if the weakness of the German mobile defence in depth had been exploited; if the attack had concentrated its efforts against sectors from which the infantry assault could be supported throughout by observed artillery fire and from which the *Eingreif* divisions could be seen from the outset.

To sum up these considerations it can be said that the legacy of the Passchendaele campaign, so far as it concerns the defensive battle, was not up to date in the matters of the mechanical and mass-production side of a battle; and that, owing to the British direction and method of attack, the apparent weakness of the German defence organization had not been severely tested. Nevertheless, with those reservations, it undoubtedly contains a number of principles of great value for the organization of a defence in depth to meet the changed conditions of modern warfare.

I

For the Germans, their constructive war-experience in the defensive battle ended with the Passchendaele campaign. The Battle of Cambrai shortly afterwards, at the end of November, although a classic example of the methodical counter-attack (*Gegenangriff*), was more a rehearsal for the 1918 offensives than a defensive experience. After the collapse of three great German offensives in March, April, and May 1918 the inner strength of the German infantry was broken, and the moral effect of the arrival from North America during that same period of the vanguard of the great army of the United States turned that weakening into demoralization.

The Germans continued to hold the big salients which

their offensives had made into the British and French battlefronts, and that extension of their line required an additional sixteen divisions to garrison it. It is true that the British and French front was equally extended, but the presence of twenty American divisions on French soil enabled this to be held without weakening any sector. The failure of the final German effort on both sides of Reims on the 15th July, betrayed beforehand by German deserters and forestalled by a French withdrawal to an intermediate line, was the last straw which broke the back of the German army; and the counter-offensives delivered by Marshal Foch from the forests of Villers Cotterêts completed its defeat.

General von Lossberg writes that he begged General Ludendorff, who by this time (19th July) seems to have lost his nerve and also his grip on the situation, to withdraw immediately from the big salients, where the infantry were lying out in open positions with no facilities for defence, back to the shelters of the Siegfried Position. But General Ludendorff declined this advice 'for political reasons', and said he would rather resign than give such an order. General von Lossberg adds that he regretted later that he did not encourage this idea of resignation; for, in their existing positions the German divisions had no hope of resisting the onslaught which was clearly imminent.[1] In the battles which followed from August to the Armistice on the 11th November, the Germans were astonished at the slow progress made by the French and British armies. In the circumstances, an overwhelming disaster was expected; but the German armies, though defeated, demoralized, ravaged by an epidemic of a most virulent type of influenza, and holding a frontage far beyond their capacity, were able to escape in comparatively good order.

There is, however, one change of importance which occurred in the defensive battle during this period. On the

---

[1] A note on the later career of General von Lossberg is given at the end of this book, in Appendix II.

20th July General von Lossberg was sent by General Ludendorff to report on the situation in the Marne salient after the French counter-offensive, and while investigating the battle-conditions in the front line there he found that the German divisions were using the new system of outpost zone and main line of resistance. 'This method', he writes, 'worked all right in the flat and devastated Flanders battle-fields, but it was quite unsuited for use against the French tanks pressing forward through the woods and fields of standing corn in the unspoilt valleys of the Vesle and Aisne. With so much cover available the scattered groups of the outpost garrisons were taken by surprise from flank and rear by these tanks, and few escaped death or capture. I at once demanded that the O.H.L. instruction in this matter be revised.' From that time there was a return to the idea, as outlined by General von Kuhl in the previous chapter, of a line of observation groups in an advanced zone in front of the main line of resistance, but these groups were rein-forced by fire-power to make an enemy deploy earlier. A form of delaying action in one or more lines of observation was evolved; and from that beginning has developed the *hinhaltendes Gefecht*, which has so prominent a place in the present German training manuals both for open and posi-tion warfare.

The German army of to-day has accepted the legacy of war experience of its predecessors unreservedly, and modernized it. The German General Staff has placed the god of mass-production and technical invention alongside that of 'bravery-in-battle' in its Temple. The result may be seen in the Siegfried Position of 1939 (or West Wall) along Germany's western frontier. Published photographs show the concrete shelters and concealed machine-gun nests with hot and cold water laid on, but behind these modern comforts still lives the spirit of the Flandern Position in a modern dress. The principle alteration appears to be that its depth has been increased from six to about thirty miles, the greater part of this extra depth being given up to the advanced zone. If the construction of the Position has followed the principles of the German training manuals, the front half or more of its depth, according to the lie of the selected main position, will consist of a series of lines of resistance (*Sicherungs-Widerstandslinie*) in which delaying actions (*hinhaltendes Gefecht*) will be fought to cover the main position from surprise and give time for the garrison to occupy it. Behind this advanced system (*vorgeschobene Stellung*) will begin the main position with its forward (*Kampffeld*), battle (*Grosskampffeld*) and rearward battle zones (*rückwärtige Kampffeld*), and these defended areas will contain strong-points and machine-gun nests distributed in a similar manner to those of the Flandern organization of 1917. Behind this main position will be, and according to German Press reports during the September 1938 crisis there were, the mechanized and motorized *Eingreif* divisions and formations; the fire-power and mobility of these modernized shock-troops, organized on the Flandern model, may enable General Ludendorff's ideal to materialize more fully than he ever expected, and their *Gegenstoss aus der Tiefe* become in truth the decisive factor in the defensive battle of the future.

There is a special anti-aircraft zone within the main position; there is a line of anti-tank guns, and various tank-traps and minefields, and there will be groups of mobile anti-tank guns (*Panzerjäger*) behind the battlezone, which together are expected to play a similar and as annihilating a part against attacking armoured tanks as the machine guns against infantry. But there can be no doubt that all the concrete defences are of secondary importance, and that the Siegfried Position of 1939 is based on the same offensive foundation as its predecessor of 1917, that 'an effective defensive is only the preparation for a successful offensive'. The new weapons, the tank and the aeroplane, are primarily weapons of offence; and the new German Army is being trained essentially in the spirit of mobility, striking power, and fire power. The great strength of the new Siegfried Position, therefore, most certainly lies in its mobile or counter-attack organization, in its mechanized 'flashing sword of retaliation'.

Neither can there be any doubt that the present Siegfried Position is only a beginning, that is to say it is a Siegfried I Position, and that, should any sector of it be penetrated a Siegfried II and then a Siegfried III Position will be found organized behind it, and so on. The preparation of a new position on the German model is not a lengthy process of digging and concrete so much as the proper concealment and distribution in depth of the defence force, the actual construction work being carried out as time allows; for example, the Wotan I Position was organized in three days, between the 10th and 13th April, 1917, on a frontage of eighteen miles mostly on fresh ground and with a defence force of fifteen fresh divisions in a position of readiness to a depth of ten miles; and it withstood successfully three powerful British offensives within the next three weeks. With modern mechanized and motorized units that period of three days could be very considerably shortened.

In this manner the Siegfried Position probably has as unlimited a capacity for expansion in depth as had the Hindenburg, Wotan, and Flandern Positions in 1917.

Since the war the various weapons of defence have improved relatively to those of the attack and there is no reason to believe that progress through the successive zones of the new Siegfried Position will be much quicker or less costly than through those of similar German Positions in 1917. The series of German Positions on the Western Front in France was not broken through in 1918 until the German Army and also the German nation, hungered by blockade and demoralized by propaganda, were defeated; and there seems no reason to believe that the Siegfried Position of 1939, capable of almost unlimited expansion, can be broken through until the will-to-victory of the German nation has been similarly exhausted.

2

Since the last war the French nation has made but one demand on its army, namely to defend her frontiers; and the energies of the French General Staff for the past twenty-one years have been directed to that sole end. To achieve it they have relied almost exclusively on mass-production of munitions and technical invention. During the last war, especially in 1915 and 1916, the ammunition supply was inadequate to justify the doctrine of 'l'artillerie conquiert, l'infanterie occupe'; but they now regard Weight of Metal as all-dominant both for attack and defence.

This outlook is expressed in the organization of the smallest French infantry unit, the *groupe*. It consists of eleven men, five to serve and carry ammunition for a light machine gun (automatic rifle), five riflemen and a grenadier, with a leader. In numbers it is one less than the German *Gruppe*, but whereas the German equivalent is divisible into a *Stoss* (thrust) *Trupp* and a light machine gun *Trupp*, the French *groupe* is indivisible. The riflemen are tied to the light machine gun to protect it, whereas in the German *Gruppe* the light machine gun is the fire-power to enable the riflemen to thrust forward.

This difference in the organization of the smallest component of the French and German infantry reflects the difference between the doctrines of the two armies. Whereas the German doctrine is based on fire-power combined with movement or manœuvre, the French is still based on fire-power preceding movement. In the French view the attack is fire-power advancing, the infantry occupying what fire-power has already conquered, and the defence is the establishment of a barrage of fire-power by every possible weapon, from the air, from the ground, and from beneath the ground, through which an aggressor cannot pass. On the other hand, the German doctrine for the attack is a combination of thrust and parry, each unit containing within itself the means for both attack and defence, and their doctrine for the defence is a combination of parry and thrust, as exemplified in the Flandern organization; it might be said that their attack organization is the Flandern defence organization advancing.

The outward visible sign of this French doctrine is the Maginot Line. Begun soon after the war in order to protect the important Briey and Lorraine minefields near the frontier from a surprise attack, it was later extended along the remainder of the French northern and eastern frontier at a cost of some hundreds of millions of pounds in order to cover the French mobilization areas. It is a line of massive underground fortresses, connected by electric-lighted tunnels and with all the paraphernalia of modern scientific invention, and lies at a distance varying from six to sixteen miles inside the frontier. Whatever the strength of each individual fortress, the doctrine on which it was built was essentially that of a rigid line of defence. The next phase of its construction, about 1934, was to build smaller forts in the area between the main line and the frontier, so that it was given depth, and it then became a rigid defence in depth.

Looked at from the point of view of the experience of the war, these forts and fortresses are similar to the defended localities which both in German and British experience in 1917 and 1918, proved to be man-traps; that was against an assault by infantry on foot. Against a modern mechanized assault, supported by massed aeroplanes, the forts and fortresses of the Maginot Line might in comparison appear to be the biggest potential man-traps in history. As a defence organization they have no resilience, they can contain few surprises for a vigilant enemy, they offer definite and finite targets for aeroplanes, artillery, and every sort of modern missile and means of destruction, and for the machinations of spies and wreckers.

And yet the French General Staff may be right to flout this war-experience, and to gamble all on the impregnability of the Maginot Line, even though it has meant immobilizing over half the French active army in its forts and fortresses. These super defended localitites are the labour of years to make them proof against every form of projectile and gas, whereas those of the Flandern organization, or of the British Third and Fifth Armies on the 21st March 1918, were the labour only of a few weeks. Further, the only method of laying such a barrage as the French doctrine demands is by having a stationary garrison in shell-proof shelters supplied with an ample and secure ammunition supply.

There is a limit to the 'bravery-in-battle', the self-sacrifice, and the power of endurance of human beings, and it is both possible and probable that mass-production of munitions has reached such a pitch to-day that a barrage so laid can set that limit, and make impracticable the complicated procedure of supply involved in an assault upon such a position. It may well be that the barrage of lead which it is now in the power of the Maginot Line, and of the Mareth Line in North Africa, to lay down will cause such a holocaust of men and machines as will revolt the ranks of any aggressor, whatever gods his General Staff may worship. Weight of Metal may be the correct answer to the French problem.

It was not until about 1935 that the provision of a certain number of mechanized and motorized formations behind the main fortress-line was taken in hand, and arrangements made to send forward detachments to fight a mobile defence in front of it. But from all the evidence available, this additional and most important insurance has not received the attention it deserves. To take the Flandern organization as a model, the main line of Maginot fortresses can be regarded as the Flandern Line and there should be, about and behind its most threatened sectors, support and assembly areas for a line of mechanized and motorized counter-attack formations sufficiently near to be able to fight elements of an assault which may break through any part of the barrage while they are still disorganized. That will be the moment when, to quote General Ludendorff's text-book, 'the immediate counter-attack acquires decisive importance; it is the most effective and economical method, both of human lives and of ammunition, of restoring the situation quickly and decisively.' As there can be no Maginot II Line with anything approaching the barrage capacity of the Maginot I, it will be the more essential to recapture any lost sectors of the foremost belt of forts, and to maintain the position intact. Such a counter-attack organization will give some elasticity to the rigid character of the Line, even though the elastic band must be a fixed one.

The action of these counter-attack formations will call for speed and manœuvre, and it is in this respect that the French training, with its dominating doctrine of fire-effect, appears to be too sticky. And yet in the hour of test by battle, should it ever unhappily occur, it may be found that the strength of the Maginot Line will lie as much in the presence and training of its mechanized and motorized counter-attack formations as in its concrete forts and fortresses. General Ludendorff shortly before his death a few years ago prophesied that the principle battles of the next European conflict would be fought in the countries bordering the Mediterranean and in North Africa. Should that happen it might tend to disperse or eliminate the mechanized and motorized counter-attack formations behind the Maginot Line. But it is probable that the final decisive battle of such a conflict will have to be fought about the Maginot Line, and if historical evidence is of any value those counter-attack formations should be regarded as essentially a part of its organization as its fortress-troops.

Postscript

Since this chapter was written last July the British and

French empires have again been forced to the crude expedient of war. Armed masses are facing each other across the Franco–German frontier, and a mighty blow by Germany's armed strength next spring (1940), with a consequent clash of the doctrines which have been discussed in these pages, seems to be as inevitable as it is inconceivable. It is to be hoped that by that time the essentials of a defence in depth will have been established, and that an array of suitably trained counter-attack formations will be ready as an échelon of reserves behind the Maginot barrage If the blow should be struck, and no other idea, such as 'the sleeping army' of Loos fame, supplant Weight of Metal, it may then be said with confidence that none shall pass.

APPENDIX I

(See page 288)

German Fourth Army Order of 27th June 1917

1. *Strength of the Defensive Position.* The strength of the
defence lies in concealment from enemy observation. It is
not possible to hold trenches, shelters, fixed machine-gun
nests, and battery positions during a preliminary bombardment prior to a big offensive. To attempt it exhausts
the troops, causes heavy losses, and is only work in vain.
Other methods must be employed and previously prepared. Trenches, dug-outs, and shelters are only man-
traps. Experience has shown that troops who cling to them
either lose their lives or are taken prisoner. Troops are only
fully ready to give battle if in the open, and the evacuation
of dug-outs and shelters must be strictly enforced. The
movement from these into the open should, if possible, be
in a forward direction. It should be practised beforehand
and carried out by order immediately the enemy's heavy
bombardment begins. This applies also to units in support
and reserve. In quiet periods a fairly strong garrison is
essential; therefore if divisional sectors are too wide defence
in depth is sacrificed, which is a mistake; divisional sectors
should be narrow, about 2,500 to 3,000 yards.

2. *Disposition of the Infantry for the Battle.* Each regiment
to have its three battalions in échelon—front, support,
and reserve battalions.

Front battalion to have an area from the foremost shell-
crater line back to a depth of 500 to 1,000 yards according
to the ground and the width of its sector.

Support battalion to be in the area in front of, in and behind the artillery protective line. Both front and support battalions must always be disposed in readiness in depth.

Reserve battalion, at first back for rest and training and then for relief of front battalion. On alarm it will move up to a previously arranged assembly area.

For the defence in depth of front and support battalions there is no fixed formula (*kein Schema*). It should conform to the ground. But, as a rough guide, for the companies of the front battalion, a half-platoon should be in the foremost shell-hole line, one platoon behind it (in 1*a* breastwork), a half-platoon behind again (in 1*b* breastwork), and one platoon at the back (1*c* breastwork). The support battalions should be in similar formation, but their platoons should not be split up.

Permanent garrisons under responsible leaders must be organized throughout the entire defence organization in depth; and they should not be too weak.

3. *Machine guns.* The light machine guns will be partly in front, not usually more than four to six in a regiment's sector, to form a barrage in front of the foremost line in the shell-craters (*Postengraben*). Remainder at disposal of company commanders to assist in the immediate counter-attacks. Heavy (·08) machine guns écheloned in depth towards the back of battlezone, in such a way that not one inch of ground within the battlezone can remain unswept by fire. Employ always in pairs, and, if possible, with permanent protection by a few riflemen. They should not be in fixed positions as a rule, but able to suit their position to the situation and the enemy's fire. Arrangements for an ample ammunition supply must be made. Headquarters of front, support, and reserve battalions to be provided with at least one machine gun each.

Of the divisional S.S. machine-gun brigades, two companies only to be in the position, and the third held back for relief purposes. They should not be employed farther forward than the artillery protective line, and should be given limited and definite tasks.

4. *Trench mortars (Minenwerfer)*. Light trench mortars écheloned in the forward part of the battlezone, for barrage fire and gas shells.

Medium trench mortars are dependent on munitions supply, which is difficult to arrange far forward; therefore they should be disposed mostly about the artillery protective line, and open fire after the enemy assault has broken in. Heavy trench mortars seldom to be used, except for special purposes, such as clearing enemy machine-gun nests.

5. *Communications*. Organization of a good method of communicating information and reports during the battle is a factor of decisive importance. There should be at least one wireless connection between the K.T.K. (front battalion commander) and the divisional battle or observation headquarters. Whole organization to be so arranged that telephone cables forward from brigade headquarters are not taken into account. Therefore signalling, messengers, special back observers, carrier pigeons, dogs, etc.

6. *Artillery*. There should be sufficient field batteries for a barrage sector each of 200 to 250 yards, and sufficient heavy batteries to have four to every 1,000 yards sector (two heavy field howitzers, one mortar, and one heavy gun battery).

Artillery to be also disposed in depth. Forward boundary about 2,000 yards and back to 5,000 to 6,000 yards from foremost line. Heavy batteries to be organized into long-distance and in-fighting groups; former most of the heavy gun and howitzer batteries, latter chiefly for disturbing (*Zerstörungs*) and annihilating (*Vernichtungs*) fire. Former therefore well forward, latter écheloned in depth farther back so that deep areas in the enemy's forward lines can be affected.

Ground observation to be striven for everywhere, and assisted by all other methods, aeroplane, captive balloon and survey.

Artillery commanders to be in closest possible touch with the divisional headquarters; if possible under the same roof, and door to door. Subordinate artillery commanders at headquarters of infantry brigades and regiments; shelters alongside. Liaison officers during a battle are not sufficiently reliable. These headquarters should be away from villages and cross-roads, etc. Advanced observation groups must have good position and exceptionally good means of communication.

Regulation of artillery fire before and during a battle is of the utmost importance. Therefore written artillery orders, after previous discussion with artillery commanders: especially targets, batteries to be engaged and expenditure of ammunition. In battle conditions such written orders to be issued morning, afternoon, and evening.

Mobility of artillery necessary to maintain its fighting strength for a big battle. Skilful use of ground and quick change of position if fired upon. Smoke screens valuable during enemy counter-battery fire.

7. *Artillery during the battle*. Especially important to fight enemy's artillery before the battle. Spare no ammunition to this end.

A careful regulation of the annihilating (*Vernichtungs*) fire on the enemy's assault infantry very important. Not rigid, but flexible, corresponding to the enemy's assembly trenches and deep into his position. His probable assembly areas to be marked on maps. British troops frequently assemble for attack in front of their front line.

Special groups for barrage (*Sperr*) fire for regimental sectors; field and light howitzer batteries mixed. Barrage fire along the foremost line of shell-holes, but avoid waste of ammunition.

Gas-shelling of enemy battery positions and sectors of his infantry position to be carefully prepared, especially immediately before an enemy infantry assault, if recognized in time. Advanced night battery positions to fire

335

from, under cover of darkness; batteries withdrawing before daylight.

Especially important is the organization of artillery fire against an enemy who has broken in to our position. Arrange if possible for direct observed fire from the battery positions. Cross-fire by batteries often feasible. Special observation posts generally necessary to watch areas within the position, as the main observation posts for watching the ground in front of front line will be captured by an enemy who has broken in. These observation posts to be as near as possible to the batteries. Fire-control officer must follow through his field-glass enemy and own infantry movements, and his direct battery fire, controlled by his voice, on the enemy. Shelling of own infantry in to-and-fro-battle in the battlezone almost inevitable if fire is directed by map. If fighting cannot be overlooked by own batteries, some must be limbered up, and batteries from the mobile artillery reserve sent, to go quickly to suitable positions.

Behind the artillery in position should be ready a second artillery wave (*Artilleriewelle*) of field and heavy batteries, whose chief task is to fight an enemy who has broken in. These batteries should remain hidden, and therefore not participate beforehand in the battle, unless urgently required. Guns of these batteries should under no circumstances be sent up to replace casualties in the forward batteries.

8. *Air.* In spite of the numerical superiority of the enemy in the air the available air-force must be organized for offensive action both against enemy aeroplanes and against his captive balloons, munition dumps, detraining stations, battery positions, etc. But aeroplanes must not be used normally more than necessary, and saved to participate in big battles. One chaser-squadron must be kept at the disposal of the army commander to strengthen the air-force available in a decisive sector.

9. *Battle reserves.* Reserve divisions will be disposed behind

threatened sectors of the army front, and placed under Groups (Corps) for shelter, training, and preparation for intervention in the battle. Before the battle they will be billeted beyond range of enemy's fire. One-third of division will be nearer, two-thirds held back; close up on word 'Ready for battle' (*Erhöhte Gefechtsbereitschaft*) from Group headquarters after sanction by Army headquarters.

Tactical intervention of reserve divisions will only be allowed with sanction of Army commander. Forward movement to battle assembly areas by rail, road, and motor-lorry must be prepared and practised beforehand. The advanced échelon will consist of one infantry regiment and one artillery brigade. An additional artillery brigade will be at the disposal of Groups (Corps) as a mobile artillery reserve. Each reserve division will detail 400 men to work on the shelter accommodation in the battle-assembly areas.

Detailed instructions must be given for the intervention of reserve divisions in the battle, generally providing for intervention in several directions. Careful reconnaissance of probable battleground according to these instructions by all leaders concerned, down to company and battery commanders. Knowledge of sites of batteries in position, command headquarters, infantry dispositions, etc. The reserve divisions (*Stossdivisionen*) must have copies of the position-maps of the front divisions (*Stellungsdivisionen*), and officers of the *Stossdivisionen* should be sent to the headquarters of the *Stellungsdivisionen* for this purpose.

The purpose of the battle-reserve divisions is mainly that all the local reserves of the front divisions may be sent forthwith into the battle, as the forward movement of the reserve divisions will at once give for the Group (Corps) a new and sufficient background of reserves. The speed and strength of the immediate counter-attacks will thereby be ensured.

A second line of battle-reserve divisions will be arranged behind specially threatened sectors. These divisions will be retained as *Stossdivisionen* for a possible second big battle-day. Therefore these, too, will prepare for a rapid forward movement towards the battlefield, which may have to be carried out on the first battle-day.

10. *Course of the battle.* To be forewarned of the enemy's assembly for an attack is of the utmost importance. This assembly is necessarily generally by night, so that an attack must as a rule start at daybreak. For this reason reports from listening posts in the foremost shell-holes are most valuable if confirmed by a sufficient number. Air patrols should fly low over the enemy's front line at daybreak, and give the signal for annihilating artillery fire if assembled infantry are seen there.

An assault will probably enter the front defence system, nevertheless the garrison, even of the foremost line of shell-holes, must fight in their positions till the last man, and even though surrounded. The assault will be checked mainly by machine-gun fire.

Experience has shown that the entry of the assault into the position will be to very varying depths in different sectors, and that the enemy therefore has great difficulty in discovering the situation of his own units. Artillery support for his further advance is not possible until he has gained communication with his foremost units of attack. For a while therefore the enemy infantry who have broken in will be fighting without effective artillery support, and this period must be exploited by the artillery organization of the defence described above. It is a period during which the enemy's infantry is in unknown ground and without artillery support, whereas our infantry will be fighting in known ground and with artillery support. This period is the one which gives the main advantage for the offensive defence; in other words for the immediate counter-attack (*den sofortigen Gegenstoss*).

The quicker the counter-attack is delivered, the greater the advantage given. Once the enemy has established a defence, particularly if with machine-guns, and has regained communication with his artillery, the principle advantage of the immediate counter-attack will have passed. Therefore every infantry and artillery subordinate commander must be trained in the idea that counter-attacks delivered independently, and without awaiting orders, are of fundamental importance for the offensive defence.

When the enemy is driven out of the position, the units must be at once reorganized in depth. In an offensive defence there arises naturally a massing of reserves in the forward part of the battle area, which offers a mass-target to the enemy's artillery, with consequent heavy losses. For this reason, speed in the reorganization of the garrison in depth after the counter-attack must be practised beforehand as carefully as for the delivery of the counter-attack itself; even though it may not be possible till under cover of darkness.

The British very often attack in a succession of waves, sometimes even with two divisions one behind the other; an artillery barrage (*Abriegelungsfeuer*) must therefore be placed in front of our original foremost line after a break-in to make the advance of the waves in rear more difficult. It will be fired by those batteries which have not been previously detailed to take part in the battle within the position.

The enemy's infantry attack is often supported by tanks. It is important to fight these at once, even at long range. One gun of a battery can be specially detailed for the task, while the other three continue their pre-allotted fire. Special guns for fighting tanks are also to be detailed, such as infantry-gun batteries, a few mobile sections of field artillery, and also light trench mortars and machine guns with K-ammunition. The terror of tanks has now been practically overcome, but careful watch for them is still necessary.

11. *Behind the front.* The strictest discipline must be maintained in the back areas. Movement of vehicles organized on one-way traffic principle to avoid blocks; both in

quiet periods as well as on battle-days to accustom vehicles to the roads. Villages near the front must be by-passed. Alter road organization if shelled at night.

Good organization of artillery ammunition supply very important; new guns must be ready to replace at once those needing repair. Also special attention to be given to clearing battery positions of all used material, particularly after big battle-days.

APPENDIX II

(See page 323)

Note on General von Lossberg

When, on the 26th October 1918, General Ludendorff resigned, the German and British Press announced that General von Lossberg had been appointed in his place as Chief of Staff at O.H.L.; but that thankless task, which included ordering the defeated German armies back to their home garrison, was taken over by General Groener.

After the war General von Lossberg held high appointments in the Reichswehr, the nucleus of the German army of to-day, and retired in 1926 with richly deserved honours. He now lives at Lübeck, in north Germany, from where a few months ago, at the age of seventy-two, he has given to the world an account of his remarkable career, the book which has been so freely quoted in these chapters.

INDEX OF PERSONS PRINCIPALLY CONCERNED

INDEX TO PRINCIPAL PLACES

SUBJECT INDEX